北京一零一中生态智慧教育丛书——课堂教学系列

丛书主编　陆云泉　熊永昌

北京一零一中

农村校学生
初中英语听说能力
培养理论与实践

NONGCUN XIAO XUESHENG
CHUZHONG YINGYU TINGSHUO NENGLI
PEIYANG LILUN YU SHIJIAN

李岩　李文　著

北京理工大学出版社
BEIJING INSTITUTE OF TECHNOLOGY PRESS

图书在版编目（ＣＩＰ）数据

农村校学生初中英语听说能力培养理论与实践／李
岩,李文著 . －－北京:北京理工大学出版社,2023. 11
　ISBN 978 - 7 - 5763 - 3104 - 2

　Ⅰ.①农… Ⅱ.①李…②李… Ⅲ.①英语－听说教
学－教学研究－初中　Ⅳ.①G633. 412

　中国国家版本馆 CIP 数据核字(2023)第 219741 号

责任编辑：武丽娟　　　文案编辑：武丽娟
责任校对：刘亚男　　　责任印制：李志强

出版发行／北京理工大学出版社有限责任公司
社　　　址／北京市丰台区四合庄路 6 号
邮　　　编／100070
电　　　话／（010）68944439（学术售后服务热线）
网　　　址／http：//www.bitpress.com.cn

版 印 次／2023 年 11 月第 1 版第 1 次印刷
印　　　刷／三河市华骏印务包装有限公司
开　　　本／710 mm×1000 mm　1/16
印　　　张／13. 75
字　　　数／234 千字
定　　　价／75. 00 元

丛书序

教育事关国计民生，是国之大计，党之大计。

北京一零一中是北京基础教育名校，备受社会的关注和青睐。自 1946 年建校以来，取得了丰硕的办学业绩，学校始终以培养"卓越担当人才"为己任，在党的"教育必须为社会主义现代化建设服务，为人民服务，必须与生产劳动和社会实践相结合，培养德智体美劳全面发展的社会主义建设者和接班人"的教育方针指引下，立德树人，踔厉奋发，为党和国家培养了一大批卓越担当的优秀人才。

教育事业的发展离不开教育理论的指导。时代是思想之母，实践是理论之源。新时代的教育需要教育理论创新。北京一零一中在传承历史办学思想的基础上，依据时代教育发展的需要，守正出新，走过了自己的"教育理论"扬弃、创新过程。

学校先是借鉴了前苏联教育家苏霍姆林斯基的"自我教育"思想，引导师生在认识自我、要求自我、调控自我、评价自我、发展自我的道路上学习、成长。

进入 21 世纪以来，随着教育事业的飞速发展，学校在继续践行"自我教育"思想的前提下，开始探索"生态·智慧"课堂，建设"治学态度严谨、教学风格朴实、课堂氛围民主、课堂追求高远"的课堂文化，赋予课堂以"生态""智慧"属性，倡导课堂教学的"生态、生活、生长、生命"观和"情感、思想、和谐、创造"性，课堂教学设计力求情景化、问题化、结构化、主题化、活动化，以实现"涵养学生生命，启迪学生智慧"的课堂教学宗旨。

2017 年党的十九大召开，教育事业进入了"新时代"，北京一零一中的教育指导思想由"生态·智慧"课堂发展为"生态·智慧"教育。北京一零一人在思考，在新的历史条件下发展什么样的基础教育，怎样发展中国特色、国际一流的基础教育这个重大课题。北京一零一人在探索中进一步认识到，"生态"意味着绿色、开放、多元、差异、个性与各种关系的融洽，所以"生态教育"的本质即尊重规律、包容差异、发展个性、合和共生；"智慧"意味着点拨、唤醒、激励、启迪，所以"智慧教育"的特点是启智明慧，使人理性求真、至善求美、务实求行，获得机智、明智、理智、德智的成长。

2019年5月，随着北京一零一中教育集团成立，学校办学规模不断扩大，学校进入集团化办学阶段，对"生态·智慧"教育的思考和认识进一步升华为"生态智慧"教育。因为大家认识到，"生态"与"智慧"二者的关系不是互相割裂的，而是相互融通的，"生态智慧"意味着从科学向智慧的跃升。"生态智慧"强调从整体论立场出发，以多元和包容的态度，欣赏并接纳世间一切存在物之间的差异性、多样性和丰富性；把整个宇宙生物圈看成一个相互联系、相互依赖、相互存在、相互作用的一个生态系统，主张人与植物、动物、自然、地球、宇宙之间的整体统一；人与世界中的其他一切存在物之间不再是认识和被认识、改造和被改造、征服和被征服的实践关系，而是平等的对话、沟通、交流、审美的共生关系。"生态智慧"教育是基于生态学和生态观的智慧教育，是依托物联网、云计算、大数据、泛在网络等信息技术所打造的物联化、智能化、泛在化的教育生态智慧系统；实现生态与智慧的深度融合，实现信息技术与教育教学的深度融合，致力于教育环境、教与学、教育教学管理、教育科研、教育服务、教育评价等的生态智慧化。

学校自2019年7月第一届集团教育教学年会以来，将"生态智慧"教育赋予"面向未来"的特质，提出了"面向未来的生态智慧教育"思想。强调教育要"面向未来"培养人，要为党和国家培养"面向未来"的合格建设者和可靠接班人，要教会学生面向未来的生存技能，包括学习与创新技能、数字素养技能和职业生活技能，要将学生培养成拥有创新意识和创新能力的拔尖创新人才。

目前，"面向未来的生态智慧教育"思想已逐步贯穿了办学的各领域、各环节，基本实现了"尊重规律与因材施教的智慧统一""学生自我成长与学校智慧育人的和谐统一""关注学生共性发展与培养拔尖创新人才的科学统一""关注学生学业发展与促进教师职业成长的相长统一"。在"面向未来的生态智慧教育"思想的指导下，北京一零一中教育集团将"中国特色国际一流的基础教育名校"确定为学校的发展目标，将"面向未来的卓越担当的拔尖创新人才"作为学校的学生发展目标，将"面向未来的卓越担当的高素质专业化创新型的生态智慧型教师"明确为教师教育目标。

学校为此完善了教育集团治理的"六大中心"的矩阵式、扁平化的集团治理组织；研究制定了"五育并举"、"三全育人"、"家庭—学校—社会"协同育人、"线上线下—课上课后—校内校外"融合育人、"应试教育—素质教育—英才教育"融合发展的育人体系；构建了"金字塔式"的"生态智慧"教育课程体系；完善了"学院—书院制"的课程内容建设及实施策略建构；在教育集团内部实施"六个一体化"的"生态智慧"管理，各校区在"面向未来的生态智慧教育"思想指引下，传承自身文化，着力打造自身的办学特色，实现各美其美、美美与共。

北京一零一中教育集团着力建设了英才学院、翔宇学院、鸿儒学院和 GITD 学院（Global Innovation and Talent Development），在学习借鉴生态学与坚持可持续生态发展观的基础上，追求育人方式改革，开展智慧教育、智慧教学、智慧管理、智慧评价、智慧服务等实验，着力打造了智慧教研、智慧科研和智慧学研，尤其借助国家自然科学基金项目《面向大中学智慧衔接的动态学生画像和智能学业规划》和国家社会科学基金项目《基础教育集团化办学中学校内部治理体系和治理能力建设研究》的研究，加快学校的"生态智慧"校园建设，借助 2019 年和 2021 年两次的教育集团教育教学年会的召开，加深了全体教职员工对于"面向未来的生态智慧教育"思想的理解、认同、深化和践行。

目前，"面向未来的生态智慧教育"思想已深入人心，成为教育集团教职员工的共识和工作指导纲领。在教育教学管理中，自觉坚持"道法自然，各美其美"的管理理念，坚持尊重个性、尊重自然、尊重生命、尊重成长的生态、生活、生命、生长的"四生"观；在教师队伍建设中，积极践行"启智明慧，破惑证真"的治学施教原则，培养教师求知求识、求真求是、求善求美、求仁求德、求实求行的知性、理性、价值、德性、实践的"智慧"观；在拔尖创新人才培养中，立足"面向未来"，培养师生能够面向未来的信息素养、核心素养、创新素养等"必备素养"和学习与创新、数字与 AI 运用、职业与生活等"关键能力"。

北京一零一中教育集团注重"生态智慧"校园建设，着力打造面向未来的"生态智慧"教育文化。在"面向未来的生态智慧教育"思想的引领下，各项事业蓬勃发展，育人方式深度创新，国家级新课程新教材实施示范校建设卓有成效；"双减"政策抓铁有痕，在借助"生态智慧"教育手段充分减轻师生过重"负担"的基础上，在提升课堂教学质量、高质量作业设计与管理、供给优质的课后服务等方面，充分提质增效；尊重规律、发展个性、成长思维、厚植品质、和合共生、富有卓越担当意识的"生态智慧"型人才的培养成果显著；面向未来的卓越担当型的高素质专业化创新型的"生态智慧"型教师队伍建设成绩斐然；教育集团各校区各中心的内部治理体系和治理能力建设成绩突出；学校的智慧教学，智慧作业，智慧科研，智慧评价，智慧服务意识、能力、效率空前提高。北京一零一中教育集团在"面向未来的生态智慧教育思想"的引领下正朝着"生态智慧"型学校迈进。

　　为了更好地总结经验、反思教训、创新发展，我们启动了"面向未来的生态智慧教育"丛书编写。丛书分为理论与实践两大部分，分别由导论、理论、实践、案例、建议五篇章构成，各部分由学校发展中心、教师发展中心、学生发展中心、课程教学中心、国际教育中心、后勤管理中心及教育集团下辖的十二个校区的相关研究理论与实践成果构成。

　　本套丛书的编写得益于教育集团各个校区、各个学科组、广大干部教师的共同努力，在此对各位教师的辛勤付出深表感谢。希望这套丛书所蕴含的教育教学成果能够对海淀区乃至全国的基础教育有所贡献，实现教育成果资源的共享，为中国基础教育的发展提供有益的借鉴和帮助。

中国教育学会副会长
北京一零一中教育集团总校长
中国科学院大学基础教育研究院院长

为落实教育"立德树人"的根本任务，北京一零一中持续开展基于核心素养的生态智慧教育的实践研究。生态智慧教育倡导以学生的素养发展和生命成长为目标，最大限度地开发和启迪智慧，让教育焕发出生命的光彩。

英语作为当今世界广泛使用的国际通用语，是国际交流与合作的重要沟通工具，也是思想与文化的重要载体。义务教育英语课程作为一门学习及运用英语语言的课程，既有其工具性，也有其人文性的特点。不仅为学生学习其他学科知识、汲取世界文化精华、传播中华文化创造良好条件，也为他们未来继续学习英语或选择就业提供更多机会，帮助他们更好地适应世界多极化、经济全球化和社会信息化，参与知识和科技的创新。

《义务教育英语课程标准（2022年版）》的颁布，凸显了新时代下课程目标、课程内容、教学实施和评价方式等方面的新理念和新要求。所倡导的以学生为主体、以素养发展为目标、知行合一、学以致用的英语学习活动观，与我们所探索的走向核心素养的生态智慧教学的理念和要求是一致的。如何将活动观和生态智慧理念落地，关键在于教师。

本书作者李岩老师，深耕英语教学二十载。长期以来刻苦钻研业务，多次承担国家级、市级、区级示范课和研究课，在国家级、市级刊物中发表文章和教学设计，参与多项国家级、市级课题研究，成果丰硕。2019年，他主动支援山后地区教育，面对薄弱的学生学情迎难而上，探索出了行之有效的听说教学方法。在刚刚结束的2022年中考听说考试中，满分人次32人。

我是听过李岩老师的课的。在他的课上，我看到老师有激情，我听到学生有声音，我感到课堂有温度、教学有活力，我知道学习一定是有成效的。他带的徒弟李文老师也很出色，在北京市启航杯教学风采展示大赛中获得了一等奖。

读者朋友们翻开这本书，不仅能看到新课标下一线英语教师对学生听说能力培养的思考，能了解中外英语听说教学理论和方法，还能看到李岩老师带领的教学团队基于农村校学情、深入开展课堂教学实践的成果和智慧，包括如何从听说技能训练走向能力培养的主要路径、方法和策略，以及丰富的教学案例。

英语教育发展的趋势以及英语课程和考试改革都对英语教育教学产生了很大的影响。期待本书能为更多英语教师提供可借鉴的途径和方法，也期待更多英语教师将教学经验转化为个人实践理论，从自己的生命体验中领悟终身学习的意义和价值，引领学生一起体验探索未知带给内心的快乐，实现共同成长。

北京一零一中书记、校长　熊永昌

前　言

2019 年，我初到海淀北部某农村校任教。此时正是北京中考英语听说改革方案实施的第二年，英语听说测试成绩计入中考总分，比重占到英语科目总分值的 40%。执教不久，我就意识到英语听说机考对山后农村校习惯了"哑巴英语"教学的学生带来的挑战。有鉴于此，也出于对教学研究的热爱，我申报了"聚焦核心素养的生态智慧课堂实践研究"课题下的"基于海淀北部农村校学生的听说能力培养"子课题。

然而研究的难度超出我的想象。一方面，此前我们从没有对听说教学领域进行过系统的研究，初中阶段，尤其是针对农村校的研究几乎是空白。2022 年，教育部颁布了《义务教育英语课程标准（2022 年版）》，提出了新的课程目标，重构了英语课程内容。这又一次促使我们改变教学方式，变革教学路径。

另一方面，写作的过程充满煎熬——从研读相关理论成果到教学实践，从听说教学实践再到经验沉淀，我不断反思：农村校英语听说教学的难点是什么？如何将听说技能的训练转化成对听说能力的培养？学生听说能力的培养又如何指向核心素养的发展？

在反复的学习、思考、写作过程中，我们将一些心得汇成此书。这本书的第 1 章立足最新课标，从听说的能力要求、"六要素"整合的内容标准、学业质量水平表现等，梳理听说教学中需要培养的关键技能，明确教学目标和评价依据。在第 2 章中，通过介绍听说教学理论（包括输入理论、建构理论、多元智能理论、支架理论和生态智慧课堂理念）以及听说教学法（包括直接法、听说法、情景法、交际法），分别指出了它们对于农村校听说教学的启发。第 3 章针对农村校英语听说教学的现状，首先探索了培养学生听说能力的教学原则与策略，然后用案例剖析的方式呈现了听说前、中、后的活动设计和教学评价与反馈的可行路径，最后加入了我们在研究过程中对特色教学和听说资源开发的探索与思考。

可以说，本章对教师设计听说教学、学校建设听说课程和资源最具借鉴意义和参考价值。第 4 章回归中考，以样题例析如何在听说机考中走向成功。在第 5 章中，我们呈现了团队教师多次实践并打磨的听说教学设计案例，以供教师参考选用。

写到这里，也是本书完成之际，我心中充满喜悦，也满是感激。我要感谢北京一零一中学教育集团陆云泉校长、熊永昌书记为我们搭建了生态智慧课堂这一平台，让我有了研究的契机和指导理念。诚挚的感谢还要送给北京一零一中温泉校区英语组正高级教师毛筠校长，以及所有北京一零一中温泉校区英语组的老师们。你们的帮助和支持让这本书的写作过程顺利而美好。最后，我还要感谢我2019 届的学生。我在书中引用的大量案例都来自我的亲学生。如果没有他们，我的写作就是无源之水、无本之木。

真心希望本书能够带给农村校一线教师和学校一些启发，切实帮助农村校学生提高英语听说能力和语言综合运用能力。书中难免存在不足之处，恳请读者朋友们批评指正。这些宝贵的建议将指引我不断探索，继续完善，将研究变成一种自觉。

目 录

第 1 章
认识新课标

《义务教育英语课程标准（2022年版）》（以下简称《课标（2022年版）》）的颁布，预示着义务教育英语课程的目标从"综合语言运用能力"全面转向"核心素养导向"。全面进入核心素养时代，义务教育英语课程更关注工具性与人文性的有机融合，具有基础性、实践性和综合性特征。

在工具性方面，义务教育英语课程旨在培养学生学习和运用英语知识和技能，发展跨文化交流与合作能力；汲取文化精华，形成传播中华文化和跨文化沟通与交流能力；用英语学习其他学科知识，为终身学习、适应未来社会发展奠定基础。在人文性方面，义务教育英语课程旨在涵养学生的家国情怀，坚定文化自信，树立正确的历史观、民族观、国家观、文化观；树立国际视野和人类命运共同体意识，学会客观理性看待世界；形成开放包容态度、健康审美情趣和良好人文修养。

此外，《课标（2022年版）》倡导以主题为引领、以语篇为依托、以单元形式呈现的教学理念，秉持在体验中学习、在实践中运用、在迁移中创新的学习理念，注重将评价贯穿英语课程教与学的全过程，鼓励技术赋能和精准施教。

明确以上两点，有助于我们进一步思考，如何针对山后地区农村校的学生学情，组织有意义、有内涵、有成效的英语教学活动，让英语的工具性和人文性得到实质上的融合统一，从而落实立德树人的根本任务，培养能适应21世纪挑战的有理想、有本领、有担当的高质量人才。

■ 1.1 核心素养与听说能力发展

核心素养概念由 OECD 于 1997 年首次提出，旨在聚焦深化课程改革，优化教学评价，提升教师专业水平。我国于 2014 年首次提出"核心素养体系"的概念。核心素养是学生在接受相应学段的教育过程中适应个人终生发展和社会发展所需要的正确的价值观、关键能力和必备品格（林崇德，2016）。核心素养框架回答了为谁培养人，培养什么人，以及怎样培养人的问题。

发展学生的核心素养，一方面是让学生学会做人，培养学生独立思考、对事物做出正确的价值判断的能力、良好的品德修养和健康向上的人生态度；另一方面是让学生学会做事，具备解决问题所需要的观念、知识和方法，并有效运用交际能力和信息技术等工具在新的情境中创造性地解决问题的能力。

那么，英语学科应该培养学生的哪些素养呢？《课标（2022年版）》提出，英语课程要培养学生的核心素养包括语言能力、文化意识、思维品质和学习能力等方面。语言能力是核心素养的基础要素，文化意识体现核心素养的价值取向，思维品质反映核心素养的心智特征，学习能力是核心素养发展的关键要素。

《课标（2022年版）》明确了义务教育英语课程的总目标，即发展语言能力、培育文化意识、提升思维品质、提高学习能力。具体到7～9年级学段，基于核心素养四个方面的英语课程学段目标中，听说相关的目标如下（表1.1）：

表1.1 《课标（2022年版）》7～9年级学段听说相关课程目标

语言能力学段目标	
感知与积累	能识别不同语调与节奏等语音特征所表达的意义；能听懂发音清晰、语速较慢的简短口头表达，获取关键信息；积累日常生活中常用的习惯用语和交流信息的基本表达方式；……在收听、观看主题相关、语速较慢的广播影视节目时，能识别其主题，归纳主要信息
习得与建构	能在听、读、看的过程中，围绕语篇内容记录重点信息，整体理解和简要概括主要内容；能根据听到或读到的关键词对人物、地点、事件等进行推断，能根据读音规则和音标拼读单词
表达与交流	能围绕相关主题，运用所学语言，与他人进行日常交流，语音、语调、用词基本正确，表达比较连贯
文化意识学段目标	
比较与判断	能用所学语言描述文化现象与文化差异，表达自己的价值取向，认同中华文化
调适与沟通	能认识到有效开展跨文化沟通与交流的重要性；能初步了解英语的语用特征，选择恰当的交际策略；初步具备用所学英语进行跨文化沟通与交流的能力

思维品质学段目标	
观察与辨析	能发现语篇中事件的发展和变化，辨识信息之间的相关性，把握语篇的整体意义
归纳与推断	能根据语篇推断人物的心理、行为动机等，推断信息之间简单的逻辑关系
批判与创新	能针对语篇的内容或观点进行合理质疑；能依据不同信息进行独立思考，评价语篇的内容和作者的观点，说明理由
学习能力学段目标	
乐学与善学	对英语学习有持续的兴趣和较为明确的学习需求与目标；能主动参与课内外各种英语实践活动，注意倾听，积极使用英语进行交流
选择与调整	能借助不同的数字资源或平台学习英语
合作与探究	能在学习活动中积极与他人合作，共同完成学习任务

通过研读学段目标可以看到，听说作为语言能力培养的重要内容，不能孤立发展。一方面，英语语言能力的提高有助于学生提升文化意识、思维品质和学习能力，发展跨文化沟通与交际的能力。另一方面，语言能力的提高离不开文化意识、思维品质和学习能力的培养。核心素养的四个方面相互渗透，融合互动，协同发展。

■ 1.2 "六要素"整合的内容标准

《课标（2022 年版）》在课程内容方面也作出了调整，提出英语课程内容由主题、语篇、语言知识、文化知识、语言技能和学习策略等要素构成。这"六要素"是一个相互关联的有机整体，通过学习理解、应用实践、迁移创新等活动，共同推动核心素养的持续发展。

基于以上内容，《课标（2022 年版）》对学习范围和要求进行了分级描述。我们选取了语言知识、语言技能三个方面与听说相关的三级、三级 + 内容摘录如下（表 1.2）：

表 1.2 《课标（2022 年版）》听说相关三级、三级 + 分级描述

语言知识	
语音知识	1. 了解语音在语言学习中的意义和在语境中的表意功能； 2. 辨识口语表达中的意群，并在口头交流中按照意群表达； 3. 根据重音、意群、语调与节奏等语音方面的变化，表达不同的意义、意图和态度； 4. 根据读音规则和音标拼读单词； 5. 查词典时，运用音标知识学习单词的发音

语言知识	
语法知识	在口语和书面语篇中理解、体会所学语法的形式和表意功能
语用知识	1. 在社会情境中，使用得体的语言和非语言形式进行日常生活交流，如请求和提供帮助等； 2. 具有一定的语用意识，尝试选择正式或非正式、直接或委婉的语言，进行社会交往，表达情感、态度等，保持良好的人际关系； 3. 在交际情境中，正确理解他人的情感、态度和观点，运用恰当的语言形式表达自己的情感、态度和观点
语言技能（三级——9 年级，三级＋）	
理解性技能	1. 理解和推断日常生活中说话者的意图，如请求、计划、建议、邀请、道歉、拒绝、询问、告知等； 2. 借助语境克服生词障碍，理解口语语篇的信息和意义； 3. 获取和梳理口语语篇中一系列事件的主题和因果关系，预测故事情节的发展和可能的结局； 4. 在听、读、看的过程中，针对语篇的内容有选择地记录信息和要点； 5. 课外视听活动每周不少于 30 分钟
表达性技能	1. 沟通信息，参与讨论，恰当运用一般社交场合的礼貌用语； 2. 口头概括所读故事或短文的大意，转述他人简单的谈话； 3. 围绕相关主题口头表达个人的观点和态度，并说明理由； 4. 就口语或书面语篇的内容、观点和态度作出简单的口头评价，并说明理由； 5. 借助语调和重音突出需要强调的意义； 6. 根据所读语篇内容和所给条件，进行简单的口头或书面改编、创编； 7. 在口头和书面表达中使用常见的连接词表示顺序和逻辑关系，连接信息，做到意义连贯； 8. 在口头和书面表达中进行适当的自我修正，用语得当，沟通与交流得体、有效

在听说教学中，教师要认识到学生是学习的主体，只有经过学习者个人的主动选择、知识和经验的加工，才能转化为个人的认知、形成新的情感和价值观。在组织听说教学时，不能仅仅围绕语言这一符号体系展开，要关注语言背后所承载的主题和跨文化知识，以主题为引领，以语篇为依托，以意义探究为目的的展开。通过精心设计，体现语言、文化、思维和学习能力融合发展的学习活动与内容六要素的有机互动和融合，实现培养学生核心素养的目标（王蔷，2022）。

以语言知识中的语法知识为例，我们用人教版《英语》七年级英语上册 Unit 2 This is my sister. Grammar Focus 部分（图 1.1），分析内容标准给我们听说教学设计的启示。

This is my friend Jane.	That's my grandfather.
These are my brothers.	Those are my parents.

图 1.1 人教版《英语》七年级上册 Unit 2 Grammar Focus

首先，我们根据内容标准确定教学目标（表 1.3）。

表 1.3 教学目标

语法知识	在口语和书面语篇中理解、体会所学语法的形式和表意功能
教学目标	1. Identify the differences of *this*, *that*, *these*, and *those* in use; 2. Use *this*, *that*, *these*, and *those* accurately to identify people in a family photo.

明确教学目标后，我们结合补充视频设计系列活动来达成教学目标（表 1.4）。

表 1.4 人教版《英语》七年级上册 Unit 2 Grammar Focus 教学设计

听说活动	设计意图
学生观看歌曲视频 "This, That, These, Those" Song，体会指示代词在不同语境下的用法 学生总结 this, that, these, those 的用法，全班讨论 教师板书指示代词的区别 师生跟唱视频里的歌曲，深化语法知识	在听、看、唱的活动中体会语法知识，实现教学目标 1
教师请学生运用 this, that, these, those 来介绍自己的全家福	运用所学语法知识，实现教学目标 2

在以上案例中，学生通过听唱歌曲，体会指示代词 this, that, these, those 的区别和用法，再通过介绍自己的全家福，运用所学语法知识。该设计将语法学习和听说活动融合，将语言知识与基于意义的实践结合，有效达成了教学目标。可见只有全面和准确地把握课程内容，才能在教学中确定合理的、适切的教学目标，将听说教学与语法知识的学习有机结合，设计情境真实的教学活动，确保教学目标的有效达成。

■ 1.3 学业质量与听说教学评价

《课标（2022 年版）》还要求教师树立"教—学—评"的整体育人观念，以评促学，以评促教，并对不同学段提出了英语学业质量水平的具体要求。

学业质量是指学生在完成课程阶段性学习后的学业成就表现，反映的是核心素养的要求。学业质量标准以核心素养为主要维度，结合课程内容，对学生学业成就具体表现特征进行整体刻画。具体来说，英语学业质量标准以学生在语言能力、文化意识、思维品质和学习能力等方面的核心素养及其学段目标为基础，从学习结果的角度描述了各学段学业成就的典型表现。

初中阶段，即三级（7~9 年级）的概括性要求是：

学生能够在本学段要求的主题范围内，围绕相关主题群和子主题，根据规定的语言知识和文化知识等内容要求，有效运用听、说、读、看、写等语言技能和学习策略，依托三级内容要求规定的语篇类型，归纳并分析不同的语言和文化现象，使用较为规范的语言进行口头和书面表达，定期反思学习情况，调整学习计划，学会自主探究，主动与他人合作，共同完成学习任务。

具体要求中，涉及听说方面的内容如下（表 1.5）：

表 1.5 《课标（2022 年版）》听说方面的学业质量描述

序号	学业质量描述
3 – 1	能听懂相关主题的语篇，借助关键词句、图片等复述语篇内容
3 – 2	能利用语篇所给提示预测内容的发展，判断说话者的身份和关系，推断说话者的情感、态度和观点
3 – 3	能理解多模态语篇（如广播、电视节目等）的主要内容，获取关键信息
3 – 4	能通过图书、影视作品等材料获取与中外文化有关的基本信息，比较文化异同
3 – 8	朗读相关主题的简短语篇时，连读、停顿自然，语音、语调基本正确
3 – 9	能根据口头交际的具体情境，初步运用得体的语言形式，表达自己的情感、态度和观点
3 – 10	能选用正确的词语、句式和时态，通过口语或书面语篇描述、介绍人和事物，表达个人看法，表意清晰，话语基本通顺
3 – 11	能用所学英语，通过口语或书面语篇简单介绍中外主要文化现象（如风景名胜、历史故事、文化传统等），语义基本连贯

续表

序号	学业质量描述
3 – 12	能讲述具有代表性的中外杰出人物的故事，如科学家等为社会和世界作出贡献的人物，表达基本清楚
3 – 17	积极参与课堂活动，与同伴一起就相关主题进行讨论，合作完成学习任务

学业质量标准一方面为教师提供了学生学习指标，明确了学生要学到什么程度，从而根据学生语言能力，来确定教学目标、设计教学活动、把握教学成效。另一方面，学生作为学习的主体，也应积极参与到学习过程和评价活动中。不仅从一开始明确要学什么，学到什么程度，更可以通过自评或者互评的方式，检测自己是否达到了课堂学习目标。这样一来，学生能够反思自己的学习计划，进行自我规划和调控，更主动地参与到学习过程中来。教与学以终为始，形成一个良性互动过程。

具体到教学中，教师应该如何细化质量描述，制定可操作、可达成、可检测的教学结果描述呢？崔允漷（2013）基于布鲁姆及其追随者的教育目标分类学，提出了指向学生习得结果的三类目标、指向意义形成的三阶目标以及指向教学实践的三维目标；并指出，目标陈述的四个基本要素包括：行为主体、行为表现、行为条件和表现程度。其中，行为主体必须是学生；行为表现可以是动词，也可以是动词＋名词；行为条件可以是评价情境，也可以是过程与方法目标；表现程度是指一个群体的学习结果的最低表现。具体陈述时，并不是每个要素都需要包涵，但任何目标都必须清晰、可操作、可检测。

以人教版《英语》七年级上册 Unit 1 My name's Gina. 为例。作为中小衔接的起始单元，学生已经学过问候他人的相关表达，也可以说出数字 1 ～ 10 的英文。因此，参照《课标（2022 年版）》的相关要求，这个单元的听说教学目标可以这样叙写（表 1.6）：

表 1.6　人教版《英语》七年级上册 Unit 1 My name's Gina. 单元听说教学目标

序号	质量描述
1 – 1	能听懂"介绍自己和问候他人"的语篇，准确记录说话人的姓和名、电话号码
1 – 2	能根据人物的对话内容，判断说话者的身份和关系
1 – 3	能根据不同的人物关系和交际语境，选择合适的用语打招呼和自我介绍，询问电话号码

有了以上的质量目标，教师可以知道一节课后学生是否达到了标准的要求，

学生也能判断自己已经掌握了什么，还有哪些需要巩固的。因此，细化并贯彻学业质量标准能帮助教师更好地把握教学方向和进度，促进学生有效学习，完善过程性评价，从而落实"教—学—评"一体化，提高课程育人质量。

　　《课标（2022 年版）》的颁布，为山后地区农村校的英语教学指明了新的方向。教师应认真研读《课标（2022 年版）》内容，将理论知识转化为实际行动。听说课作为重要课型之一，应该在实施中通过学习理解、应用实践和迁移创新活动，将听说能力的培养渗透在主题意义引领下的探究活动中，将《课标（2022年版）》对听说方面的分级描述和学业质量的描述具体到每节课的教学目标和教学评价中，发展语言能力，落实学科核心素养。

第 2 章

听说教学的理论基础和教学法

■ 2.1　听说教学理论基础

"听"是人们日常交际中最基本的形式，也是沟通成功的关键因素之一。Morely（2001）指出，听力在日常生活中比其他任何单一语言技能的使用都要多。平均下来，听是说的两倍、阅读的五倍、写作的六倍。Murcia（2001）也提到，听力理解是一项基本技能，它让说、读和写得以发展。由此可见，听力的重要性在语言学习中很难被高估。

相比之下，口语也先于书面语问世。儿童首先学会听说，然后才学习读和写。钱乃荣（2005）提出，"在语言中，或在人们口中的口语是第一性的，是紧跟着社会发展不断变化的"。

因此，不管从语言发展视角，还是从语言学习规律来看，听和说都是开启语言学习大门的钥匙，听说能力的高低也是衡量英语交际能力的重要标杆（范文芳，庞建荣 2018）。

现实考试也决定了听说能力的培养在初中英语教学中的重要地位。根据《九年义务教育全日制初级中学英语教学大纲（试用修订版）》的要求，听力测试在学期考试、学年考试、中考、会考中所占比例应不少于 20%；要积极创造条件，将口试列入学期、学年考试项目。北京自 2018 年以来，开始进行中考英语听说机考，分值 40 分，一年两考，取最高成绩与笔试成绩一同组成英语科目成绩计入总分。

如何在山后农村校开展有效的英语听说教学？输入理论、建构理论、多元智能理论、支架理论及生态智慧课堂理念都从不同视域给我们带来了启示。

2.1.1 输入理论及其启示

美国语言学家克拉申基于母语教学研究，提出了著名的二语习得理论。该理论包含五个假说，即语言习得与学得假说、监控假说、自然顺序假说、输入假说和情感过滤假说。其中，"输入假说"是其核心内容。克拉申认为，一个人的语言能力主要是通过习得途径而获得的，而第二语言习得则是在自然语言环境下，学习者大量地接触略高于自己现有水平的可理解性语言输入（Comprehensible Input）自然而然地习得语言。换句话说，有效的语言输入要满足"i+1"关系式。其中，i 代表学习者目前的语言能力，而学习者接受的语言输入要略高于已有水平，即 i+1。

克拉申还提出了理想输入（Optimal Input）的条件：

（1）输入的语言是可理解的。

（2）输入的内容是有趣的或者有关联的。

（3）输入不按语法顺序进行。

（4）输入量要足够、充分。

该理论还强调，语言使用能力是伴随着大量可理解性输入自然形成的。因此，可理解性输入是语言学习的关键，是输入假说的核心。

输入假说理论对听说教学设计的启示首先体现在输入材料的选择上。一方面，英语课堂是学生习得语言、提升听力能力和口语表达力的主阵地，而教师的语言对于学生就是最直接的学习范本。教师的语言应当是基于学生理解的一种表达，并根据学生的反馈进行适时调整和动态生成。因此，教师语言的输入应该在真实性、准确性和复杂性方面有质量的保证，才能满足学生习得语言的要求（李赟，2011）。另一方面，教师要准确把握学生的学情，确保学生在听力课堂上听到的材料难度略高于他们当前的英语水平。要增加对学生可理解性的输入，课堂就要立足于学生的真实生活。教师选用的听力材料应该是真实的、学生熟悉的、与生活相关联的、感兴趣的话题。只有这样，才能激发学生的学习兴趣，让他们主动参与到学习过程中来。此外，大量输入是习得语言的重要条件，有了丰富的语言输入，学生才能有大量的语言输出，才能提升学生口语表达的丰富性；教学内容不能完全局限于教材，要为学生提供多元化的题材，如对话、独白、新闻广播、故事、讲座、歌曲、电影等；要考虑到真实交际场景中不同地区语音的差别，尤其是英、美、澳等，从而帮助学生适应生活中多样化交际的需要。

其次，在教学过程中，教师还需要思考如何输入、何时输出、输出反馈的问题。克拉申认为，只要有足够的可理解输入，必要的语法就会被自然而然地习得。因此，在听前活动的设计上，教师不能只关注语言的形式、单词和语法等，而缺失了内容图式的输入。只有创设了真实的语言环境和交际需求，激活了学生的背景知识，才能更好地帮助学生理解输入的新信息。此外，教师还需要保持足够的耐心和持续的输入。克拉申指出，学习者在沉默期（Silent Period）虽然没有第二语言产出，但始终在潜移默化累计足够的语料来支持后期的产出。因此，教师要关注学生学习的表现，把握输出的时机。在鼓励学生输出时，还应该思考谁来纠错、何时纠错、纠什么错，以及以何种方式纠错等问题，从而减少或消除学习者的"情感障碍"，保持学生的自信心。

最后，输入假说理论还启示我们在听说教学中应该重视不同途径、不同环境下的语言输入。语言学习应该从课堂内延伸到课堂外，从校内延伸到校外。借助信息技术的普及，跨越时空限制，让学生随时随地接触到所学语言。要做到这一点，教师需要积极引导学生在课内外主动接触目标语言，广泛参与各种形式的语言交流活动，从而在实践中提高语言综合运用能力。

2.1.2　建构理论及其启示

建构主义（Constructivism）又称作结构主义，是认知理论的一个分支，是学习理论中行为主义发展到认知主义以后的进一步发展，是与素质教育相吻合的、西方教育心理学的最新教学理论。最早由认知发展领域最有影响的瑞士著名心理学家皮亚杰（J. Piaget）于 20 世纪 60 年代提出。

从建构主义学习观来看，学习是一个积极主动的、与情境联系紧密的建构内部心理表征的过程。在这个过程中，学习者不是被动地接受外部信息，而是以已有的知识结构为基础，有选择性地知觉外部信息，构建当前事物的意义。即，语言的习得是学习者积极主动建构的结果。

在建构主义的关照下，初中英语听说教学要考虑以下因素：

首先是输入材料的选择。建构主义理论认为，二语习得中的语言输入是一个非常复杂的认知过程。学习者面对许多语言输入，常常会根据自己的需要、先前的认知结构和知识水平，主动地选择自己所需要的一些信息，构建当前事物的意义。因此，输入的材料要得到主题的选择性注意。也就是说，教师应该充分把握学生学情，确保所选的听说教学材料能够创设有利于学生发现和探索的学习情境，从而激发学生的学习兴趣。

其次，引导学生建构图式。语言学习并不是外部输入的简单累加，它同时包含着新旧经验的冲突而引发的观念转变和知识重组。学习过程是新旧知识经验双向作用的过程。外部输入只有通过认知主体的积极建构，才能使学习者原有的陈述性知识变为程序性知识（李炯英，2005）。一方面，合适的输入材料能激发学生已有的图式，帮助他们对输入信息进行预测和分析，从而深化对学习内容的理解；另一方面，建构主义强调学生的内在潜能，认为教师在教学时要把学生现在拥有的知识经验作为新知识的生长点，引导他们从原来拥有的知识经验中"生长"出新的知识经验。教师要引导学生对新材料进行内化，利用角色扮演、复述等活动，帮助学生建构新的图式，在相关情境中运用新知。

最后，在协作对话中输出。学习是一个意义构建的过程，这个过程是学生在特定的社会文化背景下，通过人际协作活动来实现的。学习者之间的合作使理解问题更加丰富和全面；教学应该提倡师徒式传授及学生间的相互交流、讨论和学习；提倡学生和教师进行对话与协商，这样对学生疑难问题的解决很有帮助（么海燕，2019）。例如，在听后活动的设计上，教师可以安排以情景对话操练为主的口语输出任务。通过创造真实的交际需求，使学生身临其境，在师生之间、生生之间、学生与教学内容和多媒体的交互作用中，提升表达能力。

2.1.3　多元智能理论及其启示

1983 年，美国哈佛大学心理学家加德纳首次提出多元智能理论（The Theory of Multiple Intelligence）。这一理论的提出打破了传统智能研究中单一智能的观点。加德纳将智力定义为在单元或多元文化环境中解决问题并创造一定价值的能力，是一整套使人们能够在生活中解决问题的能力，也是人们在发现难题或寻求解决难题的方法时不断积累新知识的能力（黄远振，2003）。

加德纳先后提出了八种智能要素，包括①言语—语言智能（Verbal-Linguistic Intelligence），即创造性地使用口头和书面语言表达观点并理解他人的能力。②逻辑—数理智能（Logical-Mathematical Intelligence），即使用数字和推理、抽象思维分析与归纳问题的能力。③视觉—空间智能（Visual-Spatial Intelligence），即空间和图像思维的能力，体现在对色彩、空间等方面的敏感度上。④身体运动智能（Bodily-Kinesthetic Intelligence），即使用自己的身体来表达思想和感情以解决问题的能力。⑤音乐智能（Musical Intelligence），即辨认节奏、音乐和旋律的能力。⑥人际交往智能（Intrapersonal Intelligence），指交往和与他人沟通、协调、合作的能力。⑦自知智能（Intrapersonal Intelligence），了解自己、约束自己以及评价自己的能力。⑧自然观察智能（Naturalist Intelligence），体现在一个人感知并分辨自然界不同事物的能力上。

同时，加德纳还提出了多元智能理论的四个重要特征：整体性、差异性、实践性和发展性。认为以上八种智能同等重要，教师要对其给予相同注意力。但每个人的智能又各具特点，因此教师要充分关注。智能应该是个体解决现实问题的能力、发现新知的能力，是可以通过后天的教育和学习得到开发和加强的。

结合多元智能理论，英语听说教学可以有以下发展：

首先，在进行英语听说教学时，教师要相信每个学生都有可发展的潜能，并要创造各种条件开发学生的创造力和潜能。在教学前充分了解学情，把握学生多元智能发展情况及英语能力水平。在听说素材的选择上，话题要广泛；在课堂活动的组织上，形式要多元，从而提高学生的参与感和学习的主动性。

在单元整体教学中，教师应围绕主题情境，本着语言智能优先的原则，系统设计与多元智能理论整合的所说教学活动（李志颖、闫寒冰，2002），具体见表 2.1。

表 2.1　多元智能整合的听说教学活动

英语能力	与多元智能理论整合的英语教学活动	可开发的智能
听	听英语故事、新闻、歌曲 听演讲 英语游戏 借助实物、图像或配以动作表情教学 用英语进行交流讨论 学习英文歌曲 要求学生配以动作、表情来朗读、讲故事 要求学生用英语表达画面、图片或漫画等的含义 借助实物、图像配以动作、表情回答问题	语言智能 视觉空间智能 音乐智能 人际智能 自知智能 语言智能 数理逻辑智能
说	配乐诗朗诵、趣配音 要求学生表达自己的思想感情 英语小组交流 英语演讲 英语访谈 英语游戏 学习英语歌曲	语言智能 身体运动智能 视觉空间智能 音乐智能 人际智能 自然观察智能

需要注意的是，活动的组织必须在主题语境下开展，并服务于单元教学目标。在教学过程中以及教学活动后，应建立对学生的多元评价体系和多种评价工具，以全面评估学生的表现、客观反映学生的实际学习成果，从而促进学生综合运用多种智能，使每个学生都能自信地学习。

以音乐智能为例。音乐智能主要指的是对旋律、音调和节奏的感受力，以及用音乐来表达自己思想和感情的能力。初中学生正处于青春期，听觉敏锐，擅长模仿，对音乐具有很强的感知力。在进行英语听说教学时，可以将音乐（如歌曲、戏剧等）与教学内容有机融合，具体方式有：唱与单元话题相关的英文歌曲、用朗朗上口的英文歌来学习发音、用听歌填词的方式巩固词汇、通过戏剧表演锻炼表达能力等。研究表明，听歌是有效促进输入、内化和习得外语的方法之一。这是因为唱歌既可以开发学生对音乐的理解力，还可以增强学生对目的语的感知能力，提升语感。同时，上课时引入歌曲还能将课堂气氛变得轻松，减轻学生记忆的负担，激发学生对英语的学习兴趣和学习动机。

2.1.4　支架理论及其启示

支架（Scaffolding），最早是由美国著名的心理学家和教育学家布鲁纳从建筑行业借用的一个术语，用来说明在教育活动中，学生可以凭借由父母、教师、同伴以及他人提供的辅助物完成原本自己无法独立完成的任务。一旦学生能独立完成某种任务，这种辅助物就像建筑竣工后的支架，会被逐渐撤离。这些由社会、学校和家庭提供给学生，用来促进学生心理发展的各种辅助物，就被称为支架。

支架理论的核心是：一方面通过教师的指导和有效的师生互动，帮助学生完成其自己无法独立完成的任务；另一方面通过学生之间的生生互动，取长补短，共同提高。提供支架的过程，是教师和学生、学生与同伴之间交互作用的社会过程，也是培养学生自主学习能力的过程。

在教学活动中，支架式教学的优点是"化繁为简"，使复杂的知识体系通过支架辅助"易于理解和掌握"（鲍勤，2007）。支架最重要的作用就是帮助学生穿越"最近发展区"（the Zone of Proximal Development）。维果斯基的"最近发展区"理论，是支架理论的基础。维果斯基（Vygotsky，1978）认为：至少要确定个体的两种发展水平。第一种水平是现有发展水平——这是由一定的已经完成的发展系统的结果而形成的心理机能的发展水平。第二种水平是指学生在其发展的现阶段还不能独立解决问题，却能借助成年人和同伴的指导与合作或其他相关知识以达到解决问题的水平。这两种水平的差异，决定了学生心理发展的最近发展区。

基于支架理论，英语听说教学可以得到以下启示：

首先，教师搭建的支架，应符合学习者的认知规律，做到由易到难，由浅入深，使学生自然掌握目标策略。搭建支架是决定支架式教学是否成功的关键。确定学生的最近发展区是实施支架式教学的前提，教师必须深入分析学生的学习现状和学习需求（钱萌，2016），包括已有的语言知识和经验、个人兴趣、思维发展的特点和水平等；然后，根据教学目的要求，选择适当的话题和题材，设置不同类型的支架，将学生引入问题情境中，直到学生能独立完成任务，达到新的发展水平。

具体的教学实施步骤如下：

1. 创设教学情境

根据所学内容确定单元主题，结合学生的学习兴趣和特点，创设真实的听力和口语情境，从而激发学生的探究兴趣和学习动机。

2. 搭建"脚手架"

在充分了解学生学情的基础上，针对学生在学习中可能遇到的学习障碍（如词汇、背景知识等），通过主题意义引领下的活动，建立概念框架，降低学生的听说焦虑。"脚手架"的难度应该契合学生现有的发展水平，并衔接后续的探究活动。

3. 独立探索

教师引导学生就主题内容进行独立学习和思考，在概念框架中向上攀爬。

4. 协作学习

协作学习是独立思考的渐进过程。通过小组和团队合作的形式共享集体的成果，从而加深对框架概念的理解。需要注意的是，在此之前，教师要有意引导学生进行安静思考，将想法自己说出来或者写下来，为接下来的口语活动做好充分准备，从而提高活动的参与性和积极性。

5. 效果评价

借助多元反馈来帮助学生增强学习信心。例如将形成与终结评价、师生评价、学习成效与教学评价有机结合起来，从不同角度帮助学生认识到自己的进步，从而逐步达到新的发展水平。

随着学生学习能力的提高，教师还应逐步撤回支架，让学生独立探索，实现意义的自我建构。

在教学过程中，教师可以为学生提供多种类型的支架。一种是交互式支架，具体包括：教师讲解与解释、模拟或示范、为降低学习材料难度向学生提问、提示和暗示、游戏活动、头脑风暴、小组讨论、合作学习反馈与评价等。在这个过程中，教师要对自身角色进行重新定位，教师起着组织者、管理者、鼓励者、合作者和指导者的作用。另一种是工具型支架，也就是科技辅助支持。随着技术的不断进步，将声音、图像、动画融为一体的多媒体课件以及其他的电子和媒体工具，为学生的听说活动提供了崭新的学习环境。特别值得一提的是，网络极大地扩展了教学的时空，让学生可以随时随地学英语。

2.1.5　生态智慧的听说课

20 世纪 90 年代以来，生态课堂在国外得到重视。研究者们认为人类就像自然界的动物，需要学习了解环境、利用资源，才能更好地生存。对于生态课堂主体（教师和学生）的研究表明，教师的教学行为对于学生同伴关系的形成举足轻重。Wilkins 注意到教师行为可使课堂师生关系和谐的几大因素，分别是：在学业和生活方面帮助学生；真诚地关心、同情学生；关注他们的兴趣；理解、尊重并鼓励学生；与学生相处融洽等。可见，国外研究者们对于生态课堂的定义随时代而发展，不仅考虑教学方法、课堂组织，而且对于师生关系、学生的心理特点等越来越关注。

国内对于生态课堂的研究可以追溯到 2001 年汪霞的《一种后现代课堂观：关注生态课堂》。随后，对生态课堂的研究相继展开。李顺英（2007）认为课堂生态环境由物理（色彩、温度等）、社会（师生生态位、男女比例等）和价值环境组成。董晓燕（2015）则认为课堂生态由课堂生态主体（教师、学生）和课堂生态客体（物理环境、心理环境）组成。

《国家中长期教育改革和发展规划纲要（2010—2020）》提出运用"启发式、探究式、讨论式、参与式教学"以"激发学生的好奇心，培养学生的兴趣爱好，营造独立思考、自由探索、勇于创新的良好环境"。"生态智慧"课堂理念的提出，正是指向这一目标。

"生态智慧"课堂理念认为人是教育的根本目的，生活是教育的唯一主题，校园的主人就是学生和老师。"生态智慧"课堂从人本身出发，关注的是学生的生命、生活和生长。课堂本身就是一个生态系统。和传统的"一言堂"课堂不同，"生态智慧"课堂关注的是每一个鲜活的学生个体，教中有学、学中有教，教学相长，彼此依存，动态转化。在"生态智慧"课堂理念的指导下，"生态智慧"听说课应具有以下特征：

第一，教师要创造宽松、自由、开放的课堂空间，通过启发式、互动式、探究式的教学，提升山后学生的学习兴趣，逐步建立学生的学习信心，让学生爱上学英语，敢于开口说英语，即情感场。

第二，教师要在创设主题情境时，联系学生的生活实际，也就是生活场；在设计活动时，要提出真实的问题，引导学生分析和解决，提升学生的思维能力，即思维场；通过对主题意义的自主探究、同伴探讨，实现新的知识建构，提升学科核心素养，即生命场。

第三，教师要夯实基本功，深入研读课标，提升自己的文本分析和解读能力，从而保障教学活动的有效性，确保学生最终有所收获，在英语学习和生命成长方面有获得感。

通过对听说教学相关理论的梳理，我们可以看到理论之间有相通之处。如输入理论和支架理论，都启示我们在进行听说教学时应深入分析学情；建构理论和多元智能理论，都要求教师帮助学生形成新的知识结构或者开发不同的智能。而理论之间又有不同之处，如"生态智慧"课堂理念就更注重协和共生的生态课堂的营造。教师只有掌握这些理论，才能在实施听说教学时有法可依。

■ 2.2　听说教学法

18 世纪以来，聚焦听说教学的方法或者以听说教学优先的教学方法，可以概括为直接法（包括连续法）、听说法（包括情景法）和交际法（包括自然法和任务型教学）。

2.2.1　直接法

直接法是作为语法翻译法的对立面出现的。其最根本的特征是认为语言的本质是一整套说话的习惯，主张在外语教学过程中使用目标语作为教学媒介，禁止使用母语解释和交流，禁止使用翻译作为教学和练习的手段。连续法的创建者Gouin 是倡导和实践外语口语教学的先驱。他使用目标语组织教学，以动词为中心描述事件的发生过程，使学习者通过描述事件发生的一系列连续的动词和句子理解并学习语言。这种方法易于使学习者积极参与到教学活动中，教师也容易创设互动的情境，引导学生根据现实生活生成有意义的话语。

但并不是所有的学习内容都适合用连续法来呈现。19 世纪末，以儿童习得母语为模板的直接法诞生。同样，采用直接法的课堂教学完全使用目标语进行。通过师生之间的互动和话轮转换培养学生的日常口语交际能力。这有利于学习者理解所学语言的意义，帮助学生形成目标语的语感。但如果任课教师的母语不是目标语，或者任课教师不能达到熟练使用目标语的程度，课堂教学效果是不能保证的。换言之，此时教师的个人教学技能和魅力决定了直接法教学是否成功。

2.2.2　听说法

听说法是以行为主义心理学的学习理论和结构主义语言学为理论支柱的教学方法。听说法把教学的重心放在口语教学上，主张听先于说、读先于写。通过学生反复模仿、机械记忆所学语言来形成语言习惯，使得学习者最终能够自动操控所学句型结构，能够像本族语者那样自如地表达自己的想法。但这样的方法也很快遭到批评，主要原因就在于它忽略了学习者的主观能动性，没有充分体现学习的过程以及语言的本质，因此不可能真正培养出学习者的语言交际能力。即便学习者能够记住所学的对话材料，在课堂上表现出色，也无法在现实中使用目标语进行交际。

2.2.3　情景法

情景法（即情景语言教学，Situational Language Teaching），也提倡把口语教学放在第一位。和听说法不同的是，情景法的理论基础是 John R. Firth 提出的"情景语境"概念。情景法认为，语言学习要基于情景。通过语境呈现教学内容——往往是播放电影片段——能够让学习者印象更深刻，同时也使得图像和语言联系起来，从而形成一个有意义的整体。然后教师指导学生重复、改变对话，从而达到在相同或相似情景中使用目标语言进行交际的目的。这种教学方法得益于技术的发展，也开拓了多媒体教学的领域。但是，情景法教学依然无法摆脱对句型的模仿和机械操练，也无法为学生提供真实的互动交际机会。

2.2.4　交际法

交际法（Communicative Methodology）是以培养学生语言交际能力为目标的外语教学法。它以互动的观点来看待语言教学，主张学习者通过使用语言来习得语言。在学习过程中，难免出现试错和犯错，这是一个创造性的建造过程。交际法理论框架下又有不同的教学法分支，包括自然法、合作语言学习和任务型教学法等。其中，自然法和任务型教学法对中国的英语口语教学影响较大。自然法，顾名思义，倡导在轻松的课堂环境中，通过师生之间愉快的交流，各种有趣的、能够激发学生学习动力的课堂活动，使得学生轻松地学习语言，让口语自动地"涌现"出来。这种教学方法固然理想，却对师资力量、班级大小等有要求。任务型教学法是目前课堂中常用的教学方法。虽然不同学者对"任务"的定义不尽相同，其基本原理却是一致的——学习者需要参与真实的互动活动，才能实现语言学习的最佳效果。在具体的课堂教学中，强调通过组织活动学习语言，将真实的课文引入学习情景中，试图让学习者通过课堂内的语言学习来完成在课堂外需要从事的交际任务。自此，培养语言交际能力成为新的教学目标。但任务型教学法也存在一个严重的问题，那就是在学生没有掌握足够的语言时，完成交际任务就变得困难，甚至有时成了"表演"。

综上所述，三大教学法各有所长，也都有其适用性。在实际教学中，由于教学内容、教学环境、教师和学生情况以及语言学习目的等的不同，很难将一种教学方法一以贯之地落实，也没有哪一种方法能放之四海而皆准。因此，在具体的教学情景中，教师需要根据各方面因素，决定使用哪一种方法或哪几种方法来实现提高学生听说能力的教学目标。这不仅要求教师熟悉各种教学法，更要求教师对不同的教学法有足够的课堂实践，以根据具体的教学环境灵活应变。

第 3 章
农村校学生英语听说能力的培养

3.1 教学原则与策略

3.1.1 单元整体教学

在对山后学校的课堂观察中，我们发现教师在教学中缺乏单元整体教学的概念，对于课本内容的教学呈现出碎片化的特点。教师对单元内容没有整合，看不到单元主题的概貌，把握不住语篇的深层内涵，无法真正从对学生听和说的技能训练走向听说能力的发展。

1. 单元整体教学的内涵、意义、组织方式、特点

单元整体教学是指教师基于课程标准，围绕特定主题，对教材等教学资源进行深入解读、分析、整合和重组后，结合学习主体的需求，搭建起的一个由单元大主题统领、各语篇次主题相互关联、逻辑清晰的完整教学单元，使教学能够围绕一个完整的主题设定单元目标，引导学生基于对各单独语篇小观念的学习和提炼，逐步建构基于该单元主题的大观念。

之所以开展单元整体教学，首先是因为单个语篇难以实现学科育人的目标或促进学生大观念的形成。学科育人需要依托与单元主题相关的不同视角的语篇，帮助学生形成对主题的完整理解，构成单元大观念。其次，单元整体教学的作用要大于单一语篇的教学。它强调教学的整体与部分之间的联系，凸显以单元整体目标来组织单元的教学过程，通过有序的教学环节，判断学生的学习效果并及时进行反馈和调整。同时，单元整体教学有利于解决教师备课缺乏大局意识和单元内各课时缺乏关联的问题，引导教师将凌乱的知识点串成线、连成片、织成网，纳入知识结构，从而形成一个系统、完整的单元知识体系，使教师的教学能够理清主次，突出重点，前后衔接，简约有序。最后，单元整体教学可以引导教师从大观念的视角整合课程内容，优化教学方式，推动教学方式变革，落实立德树人和学科育人的课程目标。

这里提及的"大观念"对学生的发展具有重要意义。通过单元整体教学，依托大主题下的多个语篇的协同，可以帮助学生从多角度分析问题和解决问题，建构起围绕特定主题相对稳定的认知结构、情感态度和价值判断力——形成大观念。在教学过程中，通过为学生提供深入理解主题背后的大观念的基础，教师能引导学生建构更加全面和相对完整的对某一主题的认知。这一过程给予学生以主体地位，推动他们参与主题意义探究的活动。从而帮助学生更有层次、更系统地围绕意义建构开展学习，潜移默化地发展学生的逻辑思维和自主探究能力。

在实际教学中，一个单元的教学可以通过多语篇、多课时组成。不同的课时可以从不同的角度或深度，采用不同的教学方式围绕同一大主题进行解析。当然，单元整体教学不是几节课放到一起拼凑出来的，或者由知识间的逻辑关联起来的。而是以学生的认知发展为基础，由几个相互关联的子主题构成单元整体教学可达成的目标，强调整合性与整体性。在进行单元整体教学时，应基于明确的单元教学目标，设计统整单元的教学活动和评价活动，力求将单元中内容的各主题进行最佳组合。一来避免对内容的肢解，二来可以使教师站在整体的高度规划教与学的方式，让学生体会多样化的教学方式和学习方式，使得教学在规定的时间内尽可能以较少时间和精力达到最佳的效果，实现重点突出，安排合理，逻辑严谨，生成自然。

单元整体教学具有以下特点。首先，教学目标紧紧围绕单元大主题的建构展开，具有关联性和建构性特征。单元目标的实现必须基于各个课时目标的实现，因为每一课时都会承担单元目标的一部分或者一个阶段，每课时也都不再孤立存在。同时，课时与课时之间也有更紧密的关联，这节课承接上节课的部分内容，同时为下节课奠定基础。在教学内容上，单元整体教学设计具有整合性特点，对于教学内容的组织和安排是在深入研读教材基础上进行的内容整合与优化调整。在教学活动的设计上，围绕单元主题展开，具有连续性、层次性和完整性的特点。教学活动的设计充分考虑学生的认知特点和学习规律，通过单元内不同语篇的深度学习，使学生对主题的认知由初级到高级、由简单到复杂逐步建构，体现出学习过程的连续性、层次性和相对的完整性。最后，单元整体教学强调目标设计、方法设计和评价设计的三位一体，追求目标、活动和评价的统一。在具体语篇中，更是如此，只有这样，才能实现单元整体教学目标、活动和评价的统一。

2. 单元整体教学案例

以人教版《英语》八年级下册 Unit 10 I've had this bike for three years. 为例。

通过教师对课本内容和学生学情的深入分析，将单元主题确定为"hard to say goodbye"，并具体分为"say goodbye to old things"和"say goodbye to home-town"两个小观念。该主题属于"人与自我"和"人与社会"范畴，涉及"身边的事物与环境"和"社区环境与设施"。

1）单元内容分析

本单元内容围绕 Living Environment 这一话题展开，涉及 6 个语篇，包括 4 组对话、2 篇短文。

Section A 1a－1c 的听说任务链通过庭院售卖（Yard Sale）的场景展现话题语境。图片中的 Amy 看到 Jeff 在庭院售卖，好奇地问他自行车用了多久。交谈中，Jeff 说到"it's hard to say goodbye to certain things"，正和单元话题对告别旧物、告别家乡契合，可以借用为单元的主题"it's hard to say goodbye"。

Section A 2a－2d 的听说任务链也是对话形式。Amy 和 Jeff 聊完，回家也准备整理旧物。在 2a－2c 中，母亲和女儿 Amy 讨论捐赠什么物品给儿童之家。

Section A 2d 中，Amy 和儿童之家的 Linda 对话，呈现了 Amy 到儿童之家捐赠物品的情景。

Section A 3a－3c 是阅读语篇，以父亲的口吻介绍了一家人如何不舍地告别自己的旧物件，并将庭院售卖所得捐献给儿童之家的故事。

Section B 1a－1d 的听说活动转到了周围环境的变化这一话题，Martin 到 Jenny 的故乡参观，二人讨论了 Jenny 家乡建筑物的变迁。

Section B 2a－2d 是阅读语篇，图文并茂地讲述了农村到城市工作的 Zhong Wei 对家乡的依恋，包括家乡的变化和特色等。

本单元的 6 个语篇从不同人物的视角谈到了旧物和家乡。在对旧物和家乡的讨论中，引导学生学会使用现在完成时询问并表达持续性的动作或状态。最重要的是，一方面通过将旧物进行庭院售卖，将所得捐给儿童之家，或直接将旧物捐赠给儿童之家，启发学生让自己不用的东西变得更有价值；另一方面从 Jenny 和 Zhong Wei 的视角，帮助学生积极对待身边环境的变化。

2）学情分析

在学习本单元之前，学生在七年级上册 U3 和 U4 谈论过身边的事物，在七年级下册 U8 谈论过社区，在八年级上册 U4 谈论过自己的小镇。因此，在话题内容上有一定储备。在语言方面，本单元承接 U8 和 U9 现在完成时描述过去经验的语法功能，也是整本书最后一个单元。

从学生层面分析，学生已经学习过现在完成时，但不能熟练运用 since 和 for。他们在学校参与过类似庭院售卖的义卖活动，积极有爱心，但不太了解美国的庭院售卖文化和国内捐赠的渠道。此外，学生正处于初二下学期，对过去的初中生活有些不舍，对未来又有些迷茫。

3）单元主题框架和教学目标

基于对单元内容和学情的分析，可以将主题结构化知识设计如下（图 3.1）：

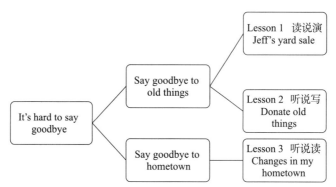

图 3.1　Hard to Say Goodbye 单元主题内容框架图

从中可以提炼以下主题意义：As we grow, things get old and places get changed. But memories don't. It's hard to say goodbye. But let's make useless things useful and make old places change for the better. 即师生通过谈论旧事物，学会让无用之物变得有用，让老地方变得更好，进而学会断舍离。

单元教学目标和课时教学目标如下（表 3.1）：

表 3.1　Hard to Say Goodbye 单元教学目标

单元教学目标	课时教学目标
本单元学习后，学生能够： 1. 口头谈论自己从小到大保留的物品； 2. 笔头描述自己从小到大保留的物品及其特殊意义； 3. 用现在完成时口头谈论自己家乡的变化和积极的感受； 4. 了解国外的庭院售卖文化，学会处理无用的物品、和过去告别	第 1 课时：Section A 1a－1b＋3a－3c 获取 Jeff 一家庭院售卖的物品信息； 分析 Jeff 如何将无用的物品变得有用； 角色扮演 Jeff 庭院售卖的场景
	第 2 课时：Section A 2a－2d＋Section B 3a－3b 口头谈论自己从小到大保留的物品； 获取、梳理、评价 Amy 捐物的过程和表现； 捐赠物品，并写一个便条描述它
	第 3 课时：Section B 1a－2d 听并获取 Jenny 家乡变化的细节； 阅读获取 Zhong Wei 家乡变化的细节和感受； 口头描述自己家乡的变化和积极的感受

4）案例分析

在上面的案例中，教师深入研读课本语篇，基于学情，挖掘出语篇背后的育人价值。在单元主题 hard to say goodbye 和各语篇子主题之间建立关联，从而整合单元内各版块的学习内容，搭建出基于主题意义的整体性和结构化的内容框架。

所设计的单元教学目标符合这一阶段学生的认知水平、思维特点和生活经验，体现出了学生对"旧物"认识的不断进步，引导学生将无用的物品变得有用，积极面对家乡的变化。如第 1 课时，学生先通过听力语篇了解 Jeff 庭院售卖的相关信息，然后分析语篇内容中 Jeff 是如何将自己不需要的物品变得有用的，最后通过角色扮演内化语言和语篇价值。在单元活动的组织上，将听说和读写看有机融合起来。学生在对单元主题不断深化理解的过程中，形成了对待旧事物的积极价值观，实现了语言学习和育人价值的双重目标，发展了核心素养。

5）案例语篇

语篇一 Section A，1b

Amy：You have some great things at this yard sale，Jeff.

Jeff：Thanks，Amy. Our family has collected so many things over the years，but we don't use them anymore.

Amy：But isn't it hard to sell some of your things? There are many things I've had since I was a child. I don't think I could sell them.

Jeff：Yes，it's hard to say goodbye to certain things.

Amy：By the way，how long have you had that bike over there?

Jeff：I've had it for three years！I learned how to ride a bike on it.

Amy：Old things really bring back sweet memories. But it's true that we may never use some of these things again.

Jeff：Yes，like old toys or books you've already read. You can sell those，or you can also give them away to kids or people who need them.

Amy：Oh！How much is this book？

Jeff：You can have it for 75 cents.

语篇二 Section A，2a，2b

Mom：Let's look through this box of old things and decide what to give away.

Amy：I think I want to keep this book. I've had it for three years. Even though I've already read it twice，it's still my favorite book. But we can give away the magazine.

Mom：What about these soft toys？

Amy：I want to keep the bear because I've had it since I was a baby. It has special meaning to me because grandma gave it to me. I'll give away the lion and tiger.

Mom: OK. And this old bread maker of mine can go, too. I've had it for more than 10 years. Aunt Taylor bought a new one for me last week.

Amy: That's great. We can still have homemade bread. And I can give away this sweater and dress, too. They don't fit me anymore. But I want to keep the hat and scarf for ice skating.

Mom: Great. You can take these things to the children's home tomorrow then.

语篇三 Section A, 2d

Linda: Welcome to the Sunshine Home for Children. I'm Linda.

Amy: Hi, I'm Amy. I have some things for the kids. I've had this magazine for a couple of months. The stories inside may be a bit old, but they're still interesting.

Linda: Great! Many children here love reading.

Amy: And check out these soft toys and board games for younger kids. I've had them since I was a child. There's also a sweater and a dress.

Linda: Perfect! We always need toys and clothes.

Amy: One last thing is a bread maker. My mom's had it for a long time but it still works.

Linda: Thanks so much!

语篇四 Section A, 3a

My children are growing up fast. My daughter is 16 and my boy is already in junior high school. As they get bigger our house seems to get smaller. So we want to sell some of our things in a yard sale and give the money to a children's home.

We have already cleared out a lot of things from our bedrooms. We have decided to each sell five things that we no longer use. My son was quite sad at first. Although he has not played with his old toys for a long time, he still wanted to keep them. For example, he has owned a train and railway set since his fourth birthday, and he played with it almost every week until he was about seven. And he did not want to lose his toy monkey, either. He slept next to the monkey every night when he was a child. My daughter was more understanding, although she also felt sad to part with certain toys.

As for me, I did not want to give up my football shirts, but, to be honest, I have not played for a while now. I am getting older, too!

语篇五 Section B, 1b, 1c

Martin: Hey, Jenny, your hometown is really beautiful.

Jenny: Yes, I've been away for the past few years, but I still love this town. Even though it's old, it's full of interesting places to see and things to do.

Martin: Wow, look at that building! I've never seen anything like it!

Jenny: Yes, that's one of the oldest buildings in this town. It's been around for hundreds of years. It's now the town library.

Martin: What about the building next to it?

Jenny: Oh, that's the new science museum. It's only been here since last August. There's a really big park behind the museum. Many families go there on weekends to let the kids run around and climb the hills.

Martin: Nice. Can we check it out?

Jenny: Sure. But first, let's have lunch at this restaurant down the street. It's been around for as long as I can remember. It serves the best food in town.

语篇六 Section B, 2b

Hometown Feelings

Some people still live in their hometown. However, others may only see it once or twice a year. Nowadays, millions of Chinese leave the countryside to search for work in the cities. Among these is Zhong Wei, a 46 - year-old husband and father. He has lived in Wenzhou for the last 13 years. With a hard job in a crayon factory, he doesn't find much time to visit his hometown. "I used to return home at least once a year, but I haven't been back for almost three years now. It's a shame, but I just don't have the time," he says.

Many people like Zhong Wei regard with great interest how their hometowns have changed. Perhaps large hospitals and new roads have appeared. In many places, the government has also built new schools and sent teachers from the cities to help.

"I noticed that's true of my hometown," adds Zhong Wei. "Children have learned to read and count at my old primary school since the mid - 20th century. But now the buildings are really old. I hear they're going to build a new school there." Zhong Wei thinks such developments are good, and he also knows that his hometown cannot always stay the same.

According to Zhong Wei, however, some things will never change. "In my hometown, there was a big old tree opposite the school. It is still there and has become quite a symbol of the place. Most of the children in my time liked to play together under that big tree, especially during the summer holidays. It was such a happy childhood. Our hometown has left many soft and sweet memories in our hearts."

3.1.2 英语学习活动观

1. 英语学习活动观的内涵

英语学习活动观——基础外语教育的中国主张与实践方案，是《普通高中英语课程标准（2017年版）》（以下简称《课标（2017年版）》）首次提出的。《课标（2017年版）》提出，教师要努力实践英语学习活动观（以下简称活动观），实施深度教学，落实培养学生英语学科核心素养的目标。同时，《课标（2017年版）》还指出，"活动观为整合课程内容、落实课程总目标提供了有力保障，也为变革学生的学习方式、提升英语教与学的效果提供了可操作的途径"。

英语学习活动观的核心是以培养核心素养为目标，以学生为主体，由教师和学生共同参与的一系列相互关联又循环递进的活动构成，为教师组织和实施课堂教学提供指导。具体而言，英语学习活动观是一种组织和实施英语教学的理念和方式。从理念来说，它提倡以学生为参与的主体，促进学生在语言、文化、思维和学习能力方面的融合发展，重视在体验中学习、在实践中运用、在迁移中创新。英语学习活动的前提是学生在教师的指导下，以主题为引领、以语篇为依托。基于已有的知识，围绕问题的解决，展开意义的探究。学生在这一过程中学习语言和文化知识，发展语言技能和学习策略。具体而言，学生通过学习理解类活动，获取和梳理语言和文化知识，形成基于主题的知识间的关联，建立结构化知识；通过应用实践类活动，如描述阐释、分析判断和内化运用等活动，内化所学语言和文化知识，加深对主题的理解，并能初步应用所学语言和知识；通过迁移创新类活动，围绕主题和内容开展推理论证和批判评价等活动，形成个人的认知和观点，继而联系实际，尝试在新的情境中运用所学语言、知识、思想和方法，解决真实生活中的问题，用英语表达对所学主题的新的认知态度和价值判断。

实施英语学习活动观能给英语教学带来积极的变化。从对学生的角度来看，活动观有助于开设以学生为中心的课堂，使学生重新成为课堂的主体；提高了学生的课堂参与度和积极性，发展了自主学习能力；让学生有更多机会参与英语口语的输出；应用实践类活动促进了学生在体验中理解和运用所学的内容；促进了学生运用所学的知识进行创新活动，推动学生核心素养及思维品质的培养。对于教师来说，活动观能够帮助教师更快地梳理教学目标，更有层次地设计教学活动；使教师在备课中有更多的思考，更注重以学生为本，注重语篇教学，同时迁移到生活中的场景，让教学和生活贴近，最终实现高阶思维的培养。

对山后地区农村校的英语教学而言，实施英语学习活动观更是一个迫切的任务。教师要积极学习理论，加深对活动观的理解。

2. 活动观指导下的听说课案例

以人教版《英语》八年级下册 Unit 10 I've had this bike for three years. Section A 2a – 2d 对话语篇教学为例。

1）语篇研读

What：本课时包括两个对话语篇。2b 的对话内容围绕 Amy 和妈妈讨论捐赠哪些物品给儿童之家展开。最后妈妈告诉 Amy 明天可以去儿童之家捐赠了。2d 的对话内容则是 Amy 带着旧物到儿童之家捐赠，她和管理员 Linda 描述所捐赠的物品。

Why：通过 Amy 和妈妈的讨论，明确了哪些东西舍去、哪些东西保留，以及物品背后的意义；通过 Amy 和儿童之家 Linda 的对话，使学生发现对自己没有用处的东西可能他人正需要，从而体会捐赠的价值。

How：两段对话分别发生在母女之间和捐赠场合，涉及现在完成时态 since 和 for 的表达，如"I've had it for three years. ""I've had it since I was a baby"等。学生已经在前面的单元学习过现在完成时的用法，对话的情节简单，容易理解，具有现实意义和教育意义。

2）教学目标

通过本课时的学习，学生能够：

（1）口头谈论自己从小到大保留的物品。

（2）获取、梳理、评价 Amy 捐物的过程和表现。

（3）捐赠物品，并写一个便条描述它。

3）教学过程（表3.2）

表3.2　人教版《英语》八年级下册 Unit 10 教学设计

教学目标	学习活动	效果评价
1. 口头谈论自己从小到大保留的一件物品	上一节课后，教师请学生回家整理旧物，本节课带一件有意义的物品来上课； 教师请学生分享自己童年旧物，谈论 What is it? How long have you had it? Why do you like it? 学生先 4 人一组进行交流，然后请 2 位同学全班分享； 教师追问： Do you use it now? If not, how are you going to make it useful again?	教师观察学生能否主动参与互动和交流，分享自己所带的童年旧物。 教师观察学生小组分享的情况，根据学生表现给予指导和反馈。 教师对上台分享的学生给予指导和鼓励

续表

教学目标	学习活动	效果评价
设计意图：本阶段学习活动是对上一节课的学习进行回顾和评价。学生通过联系自己的生活实际，用现在完成时描述旧物。教师及时追问，引出本节课的问题，即 how to make useless things useful again？		
2. 获取、梳理、评价 Amy 捐物的过程和表现	听说活动 1 听前导入： 教师引入情境，Amy 从 Jeff 家回来以后，也想把自己的旧物变废为宝。教师呈现相关旧物图片，请学生预测： How did she do it? What are the things the family are keeping? 听中： 学生听第一遍录音，检验自己的推测是否正确； 学生听第二遍录音，回答细节问题 How long did Amy had these things? Why did Amy want to keep them? What are the things Amy's family decided to give away? 听后复述： 教师请学生根据笔记内容，以 "Back from Jeff's yard sale, Amy decided to make her good old things useful again…" 开头，首先跟自己复述对话内容，然后在全班复述； 教师追问学生，引出下一个听力活动：What will Amy do next? 听说活动 2 教师请学生听录音，并验证自己对上一个问题的猜测，归纳对话大意； 教师请学生再听录音，回答细节问题： What are the things Amy gave away? How long has she or her family had them? Why are they useful? 教师请学生跟读对话，然后评价 Amy 的行为，并说明理由	教师观察学生是否能根据话题情境和图片提示，预测听力内容。根据学生的表现给予必要的提示和指导。 教师观察学生能否听出对话的大意，并获取细节信息。根据学生表现及时提供帮助或鼓励。 教师根据不同能力水平学生复述对话的情况，给予指导或鼓励。 教师观察学生能否听出对话的大意，并获取细节信息。根据学生表现及时提供帮助或鼓励。 教师根据学生对问题的回应与反馈，引导学生讨论和正确评价
设计意图：本阶段学习活动引导学生在根据图片和情境预测听力内容的基础上，通过获取对话的大意和细节理解文本的意义，通过复述和跟读对话内化语言，再通过对人物的评价发展学生的思维品质，从学习理解过渡到应用实践，为后面的语言输出做准备		

续表

教学目标	学习活动	效果评价
3. 捐赠物品，并写一个便条描述它	教师呈现捐物箱的图片，创设情境：班级将要通过小区内的捐赠箱捐赠物品，请学生谈论： What do you want to give away? How long have you had it? Why is it special? Can you say anything more about it? 教师请学生写下自己的想法，并给出对便条的评价标准（包括内容、语言和结构等）	教师观察学生运用所学语言交流自己想捐赠的物品的情况，给予鼓励或帮助。 教师观察学生便条的完成情况，引导学生借助评价标准完善自己的写作
设计意图：本阶段学习活动旨在帮助学生在迁移的语境中，创造性地运用所学语言描述自己的旧物，并说明物品对于自己的意义。学生从课本走向现实生活，在口头描述和写作便条的过程中，发展语用能力，加深对变废为宝和捐赠价值的认识和理解		

4）案例评析

本课时是单元学习的第二课时。学生在本节课经历了三个学习阶段。第一阶段，学生回顾上节课的学习内容，和同伴描述分享自己带来的旧物，巩固上节课所学语言。这些是应用实践类活动。接着，教师追问如何让旧物变得有用，课程进入第二个学习阶段。这一阶段，学生通过听前预测、听中获取大意和细节、听后复述、听后讨论并评价人物品质等，在学习理解和应用实践类活动中探究将旧物变废为宝的意义，并内化目标语言、发展思维品质。第三阶段，学生在真实的情境中，运用所学语言谈论自己想要捐赠的旧物及其特殊意义。在评价量表的指引下，完成便条写作。这些迁移创新类的活动，是学习活动的最高层次。可以看到，学生通过这一系列螺旋上升的学习过程，逐渐从基于语篇的学习走向真实的生活世界；从理解、内化语言到运用所学语言，表达自己的想法，认识旧物的价值和捐赠的意义。在教学中，教师始终关照学生的学习表现和成效，并及时给予指导和鼓励，推动了"教—学—评"一体化的实施。

3.1.3　从技能训练到能力培养

1. 语言是形式和意义的统一体

在进行英语听说教学时，我们观察到山后地区教师在学生听和说的技能训练方面下的功夫更多。这一方面和学生的基础比较薄弱有关，另一方面也与新形势下对听说能力的考试要求有关。然而只重视技能训练或者说一味进行技能训练，往往容易导致语言形式和意义的分割，学生只会考试、不懂交际。

语言符号是形式和意义的统一体。"形式和意义是不可分离的，二者的结合才构成符号，没有无意义的符号形式。"（叶蜚声，徐通锵 2010）一方面，语言的意义是由语言的形式，即语音、词汇和语法体现出来的；另一方面，离开了交际意义，即使表述完全正确的语言形式也不能算作语言。然而实际教学中却不乏脱离语言意义进行听说教学的案例。

以人教版《英语》七年级上册 Unit 5 Do you have a soccer ball？某节听说课为例，教师给学生播放录音，请学生听独白，补充下面的文本，每空一词：

I don't _____ a soccer ball, but my brother Alan _____ . We _____ to the _____ school and we _____ soccer. We play it _____ school with our _____ . It's _____ .

听力播放结束，教师提问学生来核对答案：

T：I don't what？

S：Have.

T：Good. I don't have a soccer ball，but my brother Alan what？

S：Does.

T：Yes. But my brother Alan does...

在这个教学片段中，学生虽然通过听录音补充出了文本，但只停留在听到什么单词就写什么单词的程度上。教师在随后的教学中也只是核对了学生单词是否听到、拼写形式是否正确。而如果把文本盖上，让学生回忆自己听了些什么，学生多半是回想不起来的。也就是说，学生只是听到了，却没有听进去，更没有理解这段独白。这很明显是忽略了语言的意义。

除了独白语篇以外，只重视技能训练的教学还容易忽视对话语篇中语言的交际意义。以人教版《英语》七年级上册 Unit 7 How much are these socks？Section B 1b 活动为例。案例语篇如下：

Mom：Oh, look！I like that blue sweater. How much is it？

Kate：Fifteen dollars. Oh，I like these socks.

Mom：Oh，no. I don't like red.

Kate：Do you like this T－shirt？

Mom：Mmm，yes，I do，but it's eleven dollars.

Kate：Oh. How much is the green sweater？

Mom：It's twenty dollars. But you have a green sweater.

Kate：Mmm.

Mom：Oh，do you like these trousers？

Kate：Oh，yes. How much are they？

Mom：Only sixteen dollars.

Kate：OK，I'll take them.

某教师请学生听录音，并完成练习（表 3.3）。

表 3.3 人教版《英语》七上 Unit 7 Section B 1b 听力活动

Clothes	Price
Blue _____	_____
_____ socks	
T – shirt	
_____ _____	20 dollars
_____	

在上面的活动中，教师希望学生听出对话中提及的衣服及其价格。然而对话中更具有价值的是其交际意义。比如，教师可以提问学生：

（1）Why don't they buy those socks？

（2）Why don't they buy that T – shirt？

（3）Why don't they buy the green sweater？

（4）What did they buy in the end？

此时，学生不仅要听出对话的表面含义，还要听出其言外之意。如问题（2），之所以没买 T 恤衫，不是因为妈妈不喜欢，实际上妈妈说"Yes，I do"喜欢这件衣服，"but it's eleven dollars"但这件衣服要卖 11 美元，也就是说没买的真正原因是价格太高了。这就是语言背后的交际意义。如果此时仍然用填表练习让学生获取信息，无疑降低了任务的难度，也贬低了听力材料的价值。

另外，建构主义启示我们，学习是一个积极主动的建构过程。学习者并不是被动地接收信息，而是结合自己已有的知识结构，有选择性地构建当前事物的意义。不同的英语学习者在听到同一段对话或者独白时，会因为个人经历和知识结构的不同而产生差异化的理解。例如，"What nice weather！"这句感叹在不同的人听来可能是完全不一样的理解。如果外面是艳阳天，A 心情也很好，对这句话的理解就是字面意义的。但刚刚淋过大雨回来的 B 听到这句话，可能就会认为是一句反讽。换句话说，语言理解具有主观性。

口语教学时也存在语言的形式和意义分离以及语言的意义和情境分离的现象。以人教版《英语》七年级上册 Unit 5 Do you have a soccer ball？为例，在教授学生表达自己拥有多少运动器材时，教师希望学生使用目标语言"How many…do you have？""I have…"，请学生互问互答，有以下生生对话：

A：How many basketballs do you have？

B：I have 3,000 basketballs. How many ping-pong balls do you have？

A：I have 9,000 ping-pong balls.

这是发生在课堂上的真实片段。从对话可见，学生掌握了语言表达的形式，但传递的内容却是无任何交际意义的。甚至可以说，学生对这个任务不感兴趣，迫于无奈，只能打趣完成。

另外，忽略交际情境的口语教学也不少见。例如：

T：Now repeat after me. How are you？

S：How are you？

T：I'm fine. Thank you.

S：I'm fine. Thank you.

接下来教师请两位同学进行对话练习：

A：How are you？

B：I'm fine. Thank you.

T：Great job！

在以上的教学片段中，教师先带领学生诵读目标句型，接下来就让学生进行操练。然而模仿和背诵不是说本身，学生操练后的句型也无法在真正的交际中用上，反而容易形成刻板印象，让学生在未来的真实交际中遭遇文化冲击。

通过以上分析，我们更明确听说教学的目标。听力教学不仅是训练学生听的技能，让学生学会听（Learn to Listen），而且要培养学生听的能力，让学生学会为了理解而听（Listen to Learn）；口语教学不仅是让学生用清晰可理解的语音语调说出正确的词汇和句子（Learn to Talk），而且要让学生具备用得体的交际方式与他人交际或表达自己想法的能力（Learn to Communicate）。

2. 培养听说能力的前提

如何才能实现从听说技能训练到听说能力的培养？首先要明确的是，这二者是不可分割的。学生只有经过充分的听说训练，掌握一定的听说技能之后，才能在交际中将这种技能转变为能力。而这一转变的实质，就是帮助学生从学会如何听到为理解而听，从学会如何说到能交际和表达的过程。要实现这个过渡，需要有以下两个前提。

第一，创设课堂英语语言环境，坚持使用英语教学。就像学习游泳必须下水一样，学习一门语言也必须置身于该目标语的语言环境中。培养听力理解能力首先必须置身于水中，而培养口语交际能力还得在水里游起来才行。山后地区的学生在英语学习方面得到的家庭支持是非常有限的。换句话说，学生学英语主要依赖学校的课堂教学。因此，在每天有限的上课时间里，教师需要为学生创造尽量充分的语言环境。

从课前的寒暄开始，教师就可以用英文和学生闲谈，鼓励学生用英语和老师交流。例如，教师可以问学生："How do you feel today?"学生可以用单词也可以用完整的句子来交流，如 A 学生说："Happy."，而 B 学生说："I'm really tired."此时教师可以继续追问："Why do you feel tired?"这样真实的交际不仅能够锻炼学生的听力理解能力，逐步帮助学生建立说英语的信心，养成说英语的习惯，还能够拉近师生关系，提高学生对学习英语的兴趣。

在我们的访谈调查中，也有教师担心学生听不懂，或者认为用中文组织教学易于学生理解，能够提高课堂教学的容量，加快教学进程，从而保证较高的教学效率。为此，有老师甚至将单词和课文翻译成中文给学生讲解。但事实证明，这是不利于学生听说能力培养的。根据 Krashen 的可理解性语言输入假设理论，只要教师充分把握学情，在课堂教学中为学生提供比目前已有的语言能力高出一步，即 i + 1 的输入，就能够发生语言习得。此外，外语习得还要经历一个沉默期，即外语学习者在首次接触目标语和能说出该目标语之间那段相当长的时间。此时，学习者虽然不具备说的能力，却在潜移默化中习得目标语的语音、词汇和句法，内化目标语的语言规则，为理解和使用目标语做准备（刘东楼、周海平，2013）。这就好像婴儿在学习母语时，也需要经过长时间的语言沉浸，沉默到一岁左右才开始说话。因此，教师在教学中不必急于让学习者开口说话，而是给予充分的可理解语言输入，就像父母教导婴儿咿呀学语一样，等待学习者自然而然开口说英语。

第二，教师在教学中应使用简单、清晰的教学指令。在对山后地区教师的访谈和调查中，我们发现一小部分教师对自己的英语口语并不自信，在课堂用语上会出现错误或者"卡壳"的现象。这主要是因为教师走上教学岗位后，基本上很少有机会参与英语口语培训。在平时的备课中，也没有准备课堂教学用语的意识。通过课堂观察，我们也发现，即使具备一定口语能力的教师在课堂教学时也难免使用冗长的教学用语，比如：

（1）Now, I would like for you to take out a piece of paper and put it on your desk.

（2）Could you please write down five sentences beginning with the sentence pattern "there is/are…"?

（3）Now that you have written five sentences, I would like for you to fold the paper in half.

（4）Now, when I turn on the music, please pass the paper to the person on your back, and I would like for you to continue passing your papers until the music stops.

以上教学片段中的用语完全可以替换为：

（1）Take out a piece of paper.

（2）Write down five questions starting with "there is…"

（3）Fold your paper in half.

（4）When the music starts, pass your papers to the back. Continue passing your papers until the music stops.

而且在给到指令（3）时，如果学生理解 fold 有困难，教师可以拿起一张纸进行示范，由此学生便知道"Fold your paper in half."是将纸对折的意思。

要解决以上问题，教师不仅要注重提升自己的英语口语水平，还要锻炼给出简单、清晰教学指令的本事。首先，教师在备课时就应当将教学指令写在教案上。教师可以从写下这个句子开始，如果太长，则在保持原义的前提下能删则删，确保教学指令又短又方便理解。其次，教师应该积极练习教学用语，并思考如何借用肢体语言或其他材料示范，来帮助学生理解新的指令。最后，教师可以将常用的教学用语固定下来，帮助师生建立习惯，从而提升课堂教学效率。常见的课堂教学用语如下（表3.4）：

表3.4 常见课堂教学用语

1）It's time for class.

2）Please listen to me carefully.

3）Let's learn some new words.

4）Take out a pen or a pencil.

5）Take out a piece of paper.

6）Open your books.

7）Turn to page ____ .

8）Read page ____ .

9）Close your books.

10）Put your books away.

11）Stand up please.

12）Sit down please.

13）Find a partner.

14）You are going to work in a group of ____ .

15）Look at the board.

16）Look at the teacher.

17）Repeat after me.

18）If anyone knows the answer, please raise your hand.

19）Put your hand down.

20）Pass your paper to the front.

21）Be quiet please. /Silence, please.

22）It is a test. You have ____ minutes to complete it.

23）Have you all finished?

24）There's the bell. It's time to stop.

25）That's all for today. You can go now.

26）Don't forget to bring your ＿＿＿ tomorrow.

3. 从学会听到为理解而听

要培养学生从学会听（Learn to Listen）到为理解而听（Listen to Learn），教师在教学中应该遵循以下两个原则。

1）坚持精听与泛听相结合

就像一个硬币有正反两面一样，听力理解是由"自下而上"（Bottom-up）和"自上而下"（Top-down）两种模式相结合组成的。所谓自下而上理解模式，指的是用线性的方式解码语言输入的过程。此时，语言是一个线性单位，从音位、音节、单词、语块到句子，再到语篇，通过听力逐级理解语言输入的意义。而自上而下模式，则认为语言的理解涉及多方面的知识。听者不是被动接收，而是运用自己的有关背景知识和认知策略，积极地进行预测、推理、总结和概括等活动，对语言输入做理解。

（1）精听。

精听就是从自下而上理解模式出发，通过教师的教学，培养学生以线性的方式接收和解码语言单位，即语音、语调、单词、语块、句子和语篇。只有通过精听练习，正确地接收和理解语言本身，才能以自下而上的方式理解所听内容。

在精听教学中，教师要注意选择合适的材料。如在音标教学时，教师可以通过示范最小对立体（Minimal Pairs）的发音，来帮助学生辨识音素。

如图 3.2 所示，教师呈现出音标中仅有一个音素不同，而其他音素完全相同的两个单词 mouse 和 mouth，帮助学生区分/s/和/θ/；ship 和 sheep 来区分/i/和/iː/，以及 fan 和 van 来区分/f/和/v/。

此外，教师还可以选择意义相对完整的段落，创设不同的基于意义探究的听力任务，来提高学生对单词、语块、句子和语篇的听力理解能力。例如人教版《英语》七年级上册 Unit 9 My favorite subject is science. Section B 的课文：

Dear Jenny,

I am very busy on Friday. At 8：00 I have math. It's not fun. The teacher says it is useful，but I think it is difficult. Then at 9：00 I have science. It is difficult but interesting. At 10：00 I have history. After that，I have P. E. at 11：00. It is easy and fun. Lunch is

图 3.2　最小对立体示例

from 12:00 to 1:00, and after that we have Chinese. It is my favorite subject. Our Chinese teacher, Mrs. Wang, is great fun. My classes finish at 1:50, but after that I have an art lesson for two hours. It is really relaxing!

How about you? When are your classes? What is your favorite subject?

Your friend,

Yu Mei

该语篇为书信，结构完整，开头便是主题句"I am very busy on Friday"，接下来开始对这一天的活动按时间顺序进行介绍。教师可以设计不同的听力任务来进行精听教学。如首先让学生完成以下任务，巩固单元目标词汇（表3.5）。

表 3.5　人教版《英语》七上 Unit 9 精听活动 1

Yu Mei's Friday	
Time	Subject
8:00	
9:00	Science
10:00	
11:00	
12:00—1:00	Lunch
1:00	
1:50	

Yu Mei writes a letter to her friend Jenny about her classes at school. Listen to the letter and fill in the missing information.

　　教师可以在听前引导学生根据表头内容 Yu Mei's Friday，time，subject 对所填内容进行预测。学生要听出科目，就必须将时间和课程对应起来，还要具备本单元单词的听辨和书写能力。如此一来，学生不仅锻炼了听说技能，还能将知识结构化，考察了思维能力。

　　此外，教师还可以设计以下问题，检验学生对所听内容的理解是否正确，如表 3.6 所示。

表 3.6　人教版《英语》七上 Unit 9 精听活动 2

1. What does Yu Mei think of math? _____
2. What does Yu Mei think of science? _____
3. What does Yu Mei think of P. E. ? _____
4. What is Yu Mei's favorite subject? _____

　　这个练习相比听辨单词增加了难度，学生需要听出人物对某一个科目的看法，也就是听句子，还要用完整的句子或者语块写出 Yu Mei 的观点。比如问题2，学生可以回答 She thinks it's difficult but interesting. 或者 Difficult but interesting。由此锻炼学生听说话人态度的能力和语言组织能力。

　　如果要发展学生的语篇能力，则可以让学生再听一遍信件，将两个任务的内容结合起来，连接成一个有意义的段落，请学生复述：

　　Yu Mei has a busy Friday. At 8:00, she has _____ . She thinks it's _____ . Then at 9:00, she has _____ . She thinks it's _____ . After that, she has _____ at 10:00. At 11:00, she has _____ . She thinks it's _____ . Lunch is from 12:00 to 1:00. Her favorite subject is _____ , because she _____ . Her classes finish at 1:50. Then she has _____ for two hours.

　　完成以上精听任务后，教师可以请学生打开课本，听录音，对课文进行逐句跟读，大声朗读，以锻炼学生的语音语调和语感。

　　在上述案例中，学生通过三个任务分别发展了获取信息的能力、归纳信息的能力，并内化了目标语言。每一个任务都基于一定的情境和主题意义，要完成任务需要具备一定的思维能力。这样的任务学生完成具有挑战性，也是学生喜欢的、能真正培养听力能力的。

　　(2) 泛听。

　　泛听则是自上而下，将语篇作为一个整体来听，从宏观层面对语篇进行理解，如主要内容、中心思想、作者观点等，而不去关注语言上的细节问题。

要从宏观层面上理解所听内容，是具有一定难度的。首先，宏观问题的理解要建立在微观细节的把握上。如果学生连单词都听不出来，对语言本身不理解的话，就不谈把握语篇的中心思想或者推测作者的态度了。其次，学生还需要对接收的语言信息进行一定的整合，并运用概括、推理等能力来回答这些问题。对于外语学习者，尤其是初学者来说，这并不容易。教师要做好背景知识的铺垫、生词障碍的处理等。我们再以上面的语篇为例，教师在教学时可以设计如下（表3.7和表3.8）泛听活动。

表 3.7　人教版《英语》七上 Unit 9 泛听活动 1

music _____	art _____	English _____
history _____	science _____	Chinese _____
P. E. _____	math _____	geography _____

Ⅰ. What do you think of these subjects? Write a description for each one. What's your favorite subject? Why do you like it?

Ⅱ. What classes do you have on Friday?

表 3.8　人教版《英语》七上 Unit 9 泛听活动 2

Time	Subject
8:00	
...	...

Ⅲ. Listen to a letter written by Yu Mei. Then answer the questions.

1）What is this letter mainly about?

2）What are the subjects Yu Mei like?

3）What are the subjects Yu Mei doesn't like?

4）What's the relationship between Yu Mei and Jenny?

5）If you are Jenny, what will you do when you receive this letter?

Ⅳ. Now suppose you are Jenny. Write back to Yu Mei and talk about your Friday.

在上面的教学设计中，活动Ⅰ调动了学生的相关词汇，并对话题进行了引入。这就扫除了生词障碍，同时为听力活动做了准备。活动Ⅱ通过询问学生周五一天的课程安排，联系生活实际，进一步对所听内容进行了铺垫，也为最后回信提前预热。活动Ⅲ考查了学生对信件主要内容的理解（如问题1））、归纳信息的能力（如问题2）和3））、推断人物关系和情节发展的能力（如问题4）和问题5））。通过假定学生自己是 Jenny，询问收到信会做什么，调动了学生的已知图式，培养学生的推断能力，并引出了最后一个任务，即回信给 Yu Mei，谈论自己周五一天的安排。

如上所述，教师可以使用同一个语篇设计精听和泛听的活动，培养学生自上而下和自下而上的听力理解能力。当然，教师也可以对不同语篇进行精听和泛听的处理，也可以在不同的课时分别进行精听和泛听的活动。

2）坚持课上控制听与课后自主听相结合

如果说教师指导下的精听和泛听活动是控制听，那么学生还应该充分发挥自己的主观能动性，进行自主听。自主听是指学生根据自己的听力水平、兴趣爱好和所拥有的资源等，选择自己可以理解的、喜欢的听力材料，不以回答问题的目的自由地听。这是因为教材提供的影音材料往往数量上有限，内容上不具有时效性。无论是难易程度，还是题材丰富性上，都不能满足所有学生的需求。另外，课堂教学的时间有限，语言输入不够充分。因此，只有将控制听和自主听相结合，才能从根本上培养学生的听力理解能力。如何激发学生自主听的学习动机呢？

首先，教师应该为学生提供丰富多样的语料资源。除了利用课本上的听力资源进行教学，教师还可以选取一些时效性强、适合学生语言水平和兴趣爱好的影音材料用于课堂教学。例如，在指导学生听连读时，教师可以将流行歌曲作为素材。在圣诞节、感恩节时，教师可以引入一些简单的广告。如果订阅了报纸，如21 世纪英文报，教师还可以将报纸所带的听力作为资源进行听、读结合的教学。到了高年级，简单的新闻、名人的演讲、英语电影、纪录片等，都可能受到学生的欢迎。但只有教师在课堂上引入了这些形式，学生才会受到引导而进行课外的听力活动。

其次，教师可以通过各类课前活动给学生提供展示的机会。例如，课前请学生推荐自己喜欢的英文歌曲、故事、电影等。初中生正处于建立自己身份的关键时期，重视自己在同伴心中的形象，这种同伴效应甚至比老师的作用更大。通过分享和推荐，学生具备了在课余时间听英文歌、看英文电影等的动机。而我们观察发现，学生在听同伴分享的材料时，往往更为认真。

最后，教师还要为学生提供技术支持和选材指导。虽然学生想听，但未必能够找到相关材料。尤其是山后地区的学生，更需要教师为他们扫除获取材料的障碍。比如，教师可以下载好歌曲，通过家长分享给学生。还可以给学生推荐电影，比如万圣节电影《寻梦环游记》（*Coco*）、《鬼妈妈》（*Coraline*）、《僵尸新娘》（*Tim Burton's Corpse Bride*）等。如果学生不具备上网的条件（通常是有手机但是家长无法监督），我们可以给学生推荐英语绘本或故事读物，如《典范英语》《书虫·牛津英汉双语读物》等。学生购买后就可以听读。有了听的材料，另一个关键的问题就是材料的难易度把握。从某种程度上来说，听力材料的难易度决定了学生能否坚持自主听的习惯。材料中新信息的含量、是否符合学生的认知水平、是否是学生感兴趣的内容、材料的长度、生词量以及口音和语速等，都要考虑到。因此，教师不仅要引导学生自主听，还要关注学生自主听的效果。如果学生在选材上遇到困难，要和学生一起分析原因，及时给予帮助。

总的来说，听力理解是一个听者与说话者互动的过程。听者自下而上理解语言输入的意义，又自上而下根据所听材料，动态地建构意义。教师要让学生学会听（Learn to Listen），培养学生的听力理解能力（Listen to Learn），就要坚持精听与泛听相结合、课上控制听和课后自主听相结合的原则。

4. 从学会说到学会交流

要培养学生从学会说（Learn to Talk）到学会交流（Learn to Communicate），教师在教学中也应该遵循以下三个原则。

1）充分利用课堂的多重互动交际

课堂是一个特殊的交际场地。这里不仅有教学所需要的课堂交际，有角色扮演的模拟交际，还有师生之间、生生之间的真实交际。这些交际形式各有其特点。如课堂交际往往是教师为了呈现目标教学内容而与学生之间产生的"明知故问"式的交际。以人教版《英语》七年级上册 Unit 2 This is my sister. 学生辨识人物的教学片段为例：

（教师通过 PPT 呈现图片，提问学生）

T：Look at this picture. It's Peter's family photo. Now，who is the woman in pink？

S：She is his grandma.

T：Who is the girl holding a flower？

S：She is Peter's sister.

T：Who is the man with yellow hair？

S：He is Peter's father.

在以上对话中，教师明明知道图片中的人物和 Peter 的关系，仍然要问学生他们是谁。而学生也明确地知道教师知道图片中的人物关系，仍然配合回答。这个过程显然是"明知故问"，也是"明知故答"。但这是在课堂这种特定的场景中产生的交际行为，服务于教学目的。这也是一种真实的交际。

角色扮演的模拟交际则更为常见。在英语教学中，包括课本里，都有大量通过创设模拟情景，学生扮演不同角色进行模拟交际的活动，如问路、就餐、购物等。我们仍然以人教版《英语》七年级上册 Unit 2 This is my sister 为例，课本内容中 Section A 的 2d 就是一个模拟交际任务。

Role-play the conversation. 分角色表演对话

Sally：Good morning，Jane.

Jane：Good morning，Sally.

Sally：Oh，Jane，this is my sister Kate. Kate，this is my friend Jane.

Kate：Nice to meet you，Jane.

Jane：Nice to meet you，too. Are those your parents?

Kate：Yes，they are.

Jane：And who's he?

Sally：He's my brother，Paul.

Jane：Oh，I see. Well，have a good day!

Sally/Kate：Thanks! You，too. Bye!

上面的教学活动提供了语言脚本，比较适合语言能力比较薄弱的学生或者初学者。更多的时候，教师在组织学生操练完课本对话后，可以在此基础上鼓励学生自编对话完成交际。以下教学片段来自人教版《英语》七年级上册 Unit 7 How much are these socks?。教师请学生进行结对练习（Pair Work），A 学生扮演导购员，B 学生扮演顾客，完成购物的模拟交际。课堂教学片段如下：

A：Can I help you?

B：Yes，please. I want to buy a dress.

A：OK. What color do you want?

B：Blue.

A：How about this one?

B：It looks nice. How much is it?

A：20 dollars.

B：I'll take it.

A：Here you are.

B：Thank you.

A：You're welcome.

以上两种教学活动的对话框架基本上是已经规定好的，学生自我表达和发挥的空间有限。这属于控制性的练习。这样的控制性口语输出活动能够培养学生口语表达的流利度和准确性（张献臣，2014）。

课堂教学中还存在很多真实的交际任务，即非控制性的口语输出活动。除了师生之间的寒暄和对话以外，小组讨论、采访、演讲、问卷调查、口头汇报等形式，都可以锻炼学生的口语表达能力。其中，小组讨论、采访、问卷调查等，属于短话轮的交际任务。学生可以用较短的语句来互动，如：

A：What's your favorite sport?

B：Basketball.

A：Why do you like it?

B：It's great fun.

而演讲、口头汇报等，则属于长话轮的交际任务。学生可以通过这些活动表达自己的观点看法和思想。以人教版《英语》八年级上册 Unit 6 I'm going to study computer science. 为例。本单元的主题是 life goals（生活目标），教师请学生就"梦想"这一话题开展演讲，发表自己的观点和看法。下面是某同学的演讲稿：

Future Dream

When we are young, our parents, teachers, or friends always ask us a question：what do you want to be in the future? And our answers were different. And I found that people at different ages have different dream jobs.

When I was little, I want to be a pilot or a car racer. And I dreamed that I could fly a big plane one day. When I grow older, I want to be a doctor because doctors can save lives. Now I want to be an engineer like my dad, because I found myself fascinated by math. So why would people change their minds as they grow up? I think there are two reasons.

First, I think as we get older, we know better of ourselves and gain more life experiences. When I was ten, I know that not everyone could easily be a pilot, especially those who are nearsighted, like me. Then when I grow older, I found that I'm afraid of blood and organ in my biology class, so maybe I'm not cut out to be a doctor. But now I think I'm interested in math and my dad gives me a good example, so I want to be an engineer in the future. So you see, as our knowledge and experiences broadened, we change our mind.

Second, another reason is social influence. When we are young, we often think we can be a scientist, an artist, or an astronaut. But when we truly step into the society, we will find that it's difficult to be a "tist", or an expert. Most of us are reduced to average workers and our dreams become "cheaper" but more realistic.

But is the second reason well-founded? I think not. Although it's true that it's difficult to reach our dreams, we still need to believe and try. In the 13th century, no one believed that the earth is round, until Magellan made his great sail. In the 17th century, people thought that the letter was the only way to contact with others, until Bell invented the telephone. Before the 20th century，scientists were confident that human would never fly in the sky. But Wright Brothers invented the plane. So history tells us，there are many "crazy" things that break people's common sense. As Bill Gates said："The most terrible enemy is no strong belief." On the way to your dream，never be afraid and try your best to reach it!

上面这篇演讲稿虽然语言还略显稚嫩，小作者却是在用英语表达自己的所感所想。在表述中，小作者以自己为例，从自身和社会角度分析人们改变梦想的原因，展现出了一定的思维能力。但最后又笔锋一转，呼吁大家无论何时都不要放弃那些看似"疯狂"的想法。从学生的表达中，我们可以看到一个少年对人生的思索，对梦想的追求。

从上面的例子可以看出，这些拓展类的口语交际活动不仅发展了学生的思维能力，更帮助教师关注到了除语言的流利度和准确性以外的复杂度和得体度。复杂度指的是能够使用较为丰富的语言词汇和结构表达思想，而不是总是使用简单的词汇和句子；得体度是指学生能够根据交际场景使用肢体语言和交际用语进行交流。因此，教师要精心设计这些活动，确保活动的趣味性、参与度和真实性。让学生在活动中有话可说、有话想说、有话能说。

综上所述，在实际的口语教学过程中，教师要把握好课堂交际、模拟交际和真实交际的特点，根据教学目标的不同选择创建不同类型的交际场景，展开不同的交际活动，引导学生用英语表达自己的看法和观点，通过真实的活动提高学生的综合语言运用能力。

2）帮助学生克服语言知识和技能障碍

英语口头表达能力的提高是一个缓慢渐进的过程。在这个过程中，学习者往往会遇到诸多困难。Brown（2001）认为，学生在口语表达中可能会遇到以下 10 个方面的障碍，具体有语音群、冗余现象、缩略形式、行为变量、口语体、语速、重音、节奏、语调和互动。而山后地区农村校的学生，还面临着除了语言因素以外的诸多非语言障碍，如词汇量不足、语用知识和文化背景知识匮乏等。教师只有帮助学生努力克服口语习得路上的语言和技能障碍，才能真正促进学生语言能力的提升。

（1）语音。

在语音方面，经过对农村校学生口语语料的分析和教师的课堂观察，学生在准确度方面的问题主要在于加音、吞音、辅音不到位、元音不饱满、重音错位等；在流畅度方面的主要问题在于不能正确运用连读、失去爆破、意群停顿、语调、节奏等朗读技巧。

比如加音问题，学生容易在名词词尾滥加 s 音，His father（s）is a worker

（s）. 在名词或动词时为滥加 d 音，Do you like（d）the flower（ed）？还有滥加词缀的现象，That doesn't interest（ing）me at all.

在吞音问题上，学生容易吞掉单词的尾音，比如 My na（me）is Peter. 吞掉名词复数的 s 音，如 His parent（s）have died. 吞掉比较级或最高级的后缀，如 I'm more clever（er）than you. 吞掉词尾的 k 和 t 音，如 I don'（t）thin（k）I can do i（t）at the momen（t）. 吞掉动词过去式的 d 音，如 He use（d）to live in Beijing.

在元音和辅音的发音问题上，学生经常混淆长元音和短元音/i：/和/ɪ/，如 sit 和 seat，ship 和 sheep 等；混淆元音/æ/和/e/，如 bad 和 bed；双元音发音不到位，混淆/æ/和/ai/，如 back，bike；混淆/aɪ/和/eɪ/，把 file 读成 fell，whale 读成 well；混淆/s/和/θ/，把 think 读成 sink 等。混淆/v/，/f/和/w/，将 leave 读成 leaf，或者将 very 读成 ferry 或 werry。

重音错位也是很常见的。如双音节单词，尤其是动词和名词同形的单词，学生往往无法分辨：record，progress，desert，transport，import，export，object，present，increase，produce，content 等。这些单词作名词时重音在第一个音节，作动词时重音在第二个音节。学生要根据语境判断单词的词性，从而发出正确的读音。如 He broke the record. 句中 record 作名词，重音在第一个音节。长单词的重音也是学生发音的难点，如 natural，meaningful，comfortable. manager，scientist，government，以及结尾含有 – ic 如 scientific，含有 – ion 如 conversation，含有 – ity 的多音节单词如 activity，nationality 等。

而由于英语和汉语发音方式的不同，前者是线式发音（——），后者是点式发音（……），学生在连读上也存在困难。如在同一个意群中，词尾辅音 + 词首元音的连读，put^it^on，get^up；词尾辅音 + 词首半元音/j/，如 Thank^you，Nice to meet^you 等。

学生还不能完全掌握爆破音的发音技巧。英语中一共有 6 个爆破音，分别是/p/，/b/，/t/，/d/，/k/和/g/。当爆破音遇到爆破音时，应该失去爆破。如 what time/wɔt taim/，goodbye/'gudbai/，blackboard/'blækbɔːd/，big party/big'pɑ（r）ti/。而爆破音遇到其他辅音时，不完全爆破，如 best friend/best frend/，keep silent/kiː p'sailənt/，bad luck/bæd lʌk/等。

在朗读句子或者段落时，要想使朗读听起来流畅、自然、便于理解，常常需要停顿。但停顿不是随意的，只能在意群之间进行。意群可以是一个词、一个短语，也可以是并列句中的一个分句或复合句中的一个主句、从句等。大部分学生都知道在标点符号处停顿，但其他情况则需要教师的引导。如词组或短语的停顿，The Lantern Festival/is an important festival/in China. 并列成分的停顿，如 People often go out/and watch the lantern show. 从句的停顿，如 we hear a lot about/how we should change our lives to help save our planet.

　　重读与非重读也是学生朗读中存在的一个普遍问题。在教学中，教师首先要向学生明确，通常哪些单词重读、哪些单词非重读。一般而言，句子中表达实际意义的词，如名词、形容词、实义动词等需要重读；而无实际意义的，如介词、代词、冠词，通常轻轻、快速带过，也就是非重读。例如 This is his father. She looks happy. She is afraid of the tiger. 这些句子中画线的单词为重读单词。当然，为了强调某个信息而重读也是可以的。如在朗读 He runs quickly towards the sea. 这个句子时，强调什么信息，就重读什么信息。如果重读 runs，强调的就是他是跑过去，而不是走过去或者跳过去；如果重读 the sea，强调的就是他是冲着大海跑过去，而不是冲着其他地方。

　　学生朗读的语调也不够地道。这不仅与缺少跟读模仿操练有关，还与教师在教学中对语调的重视程度有关。我们发现，教师在日常教学中更重视词汇、句子等的教学，对课本附录中语音部分的利用率不高。几乎有 80% 的老师没有带领学生听并跟读课本附录中的语音材料，更不谈花时间专门讲解了。以人教版七年级上册第 3 单元为例，课本 73 页就对目标句型的语调给出了指导。如：

　　①A：Is this your ↗ruler?　　　　　B：↘Yes, it ↘is.

　　②A：Is that your ↗schoolbag?　　　B：↘No, it ↘isn't.

　　③A：Are these her ↗books?　　　　B：↘Yes, they ↘are.

　　④These are my ↘keys. Are those your ↗keys?

　　要解决以上问题，教师需要从起始年级开始，预留一定的课堂时间进行音标教学。音标是初中阶段需要学习的语音知识。只有帮助学生学习和掌握好音标，借助音标准确读出和记忆单词，才能为学生开展自主学习奠定基础。教师要利用好课本内容，夯实学生的语音基础。朗读技巧的培养和训练需要落实到每一天的教学中去。只有日积月累，才能逐步做到朗读准确、流畅和有节奏感。才能体现朗读的实际意义，不至于出现语音和语调问题、缺乏韵律感和节奏感等现象（何锋，章玉芳，2012）。

　　（2）词汇。

　　在词汇方面，学生遇到的首要障碍是词汇量匮乏。这就使得学生在表达时容易出现想说说不出的尴尬。教师要帮助学生克服这一困难，不仅要重视平时的词汇教学、夯实基础，还要指导学生进行有效的词汇学习。首先关注学生单词的发音是否准确，其次要帮助学生学会根据单词的发音正确拼写单词，最重要的还是要系统地教授学生记忆单词的策略和技巧，帮助他们从死记硬背的苦海中脱离出来。我们以七年级学生为例，以下是部分学生总结的词汇记忆方法思维导图（图 3.3 ~ 图 3.5）：

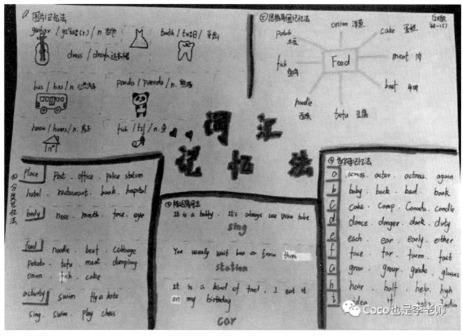

图 3.3 词汇记忆法思维导图 1

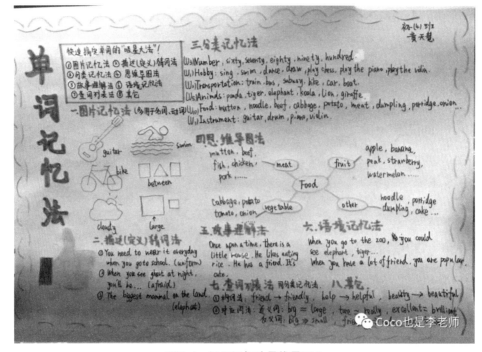

图 3.4 词汇记忆法思维导图 2

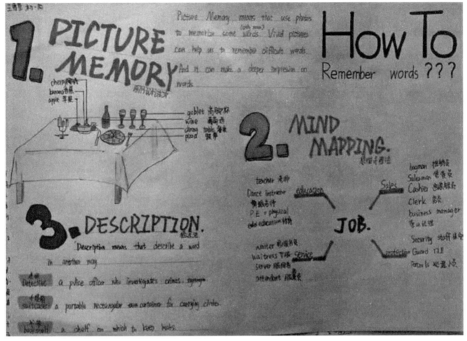

图 3.5　词汇记忆法思维导图 3

可以看到，学生都能够总结出图片记忆法、分类记忆法、思维导图记忆法、描述猜词法等。还有学生想到了故事理解法（通过上下文来推断词义）、构词法（通过词根词缀记忆单词）、对应词法（通过近义词、反义词记忆单词）等。

在这些记单词的方法中，按场景分类记忆有助于学生的口语表达。因为同一个语境下，不管是听力材料还是口语表达，相关词汇出现和使用的频率更高。例如，讨论喝什么饮料时，往往会出现 coffee，Coke，juice，tea，wine 等。我们将《课标（2022 年版）》收录的初中阶段英语课程应学习和掌握的基本词汇 1 095 个，以及二级词汇 505 个按场景进行了分类整理，方便学生记忆和背诵。如天气与温度话题包含以下词汇（表 3.9）：

表 3.9　场景分类词汇表节选

英文	中文	英文	中文	英文	中文
air	空气	rain	雨；雨水	snow	雪
cloud	云	wind	风	storm	暴风
degree	度数	shower	阵雨	temperature	温度
heat	热，高温	smoke	烟	weather	天气

　　词汇方面学生遇到的第二个障碍就是中式英语，例如 "There have five apples on the table. ""Today is very sunny. " 和 "I very love my mom. " 等。这样的中式表达都是学生受到母语迁移影响的表现。而现代外语教学的研究成果表明，在口语交际中，人们并非使用单词和语法来组成句子，而是大量地使用已有的固定表达进行交际。这些固定的表达就是语块（Chunk），也被称为词块（Lexical Chunk）、程式语（Formulaic Language）、固定搭配（Collocation）或者词丛（Clusters）等。它指的是由一组单词共同构成的语言单位，具有出现频率高、有特定的语义表达功能等特点。语言使用者往往将其作为语义整体储存在记忆中，使用时整体提取。国外研究者普遍认为，语块对于增强二语表达的流利度、准确度、创造性和连贯性都有重要的作用。同时，语块还能减轻学习者短时记忆负担，减少听力理解中信息处理耗费的资源（高航，2017）。《课标（2022 年版）》提出，教师要尽量以词块的形式呈现生词，引导学生关注词语的搭配和固定的表达方式，并在围绕主题意义建构结构化知识的过程中，提炼词语的搭配和固定表达，构建词汇语义网，积累词块，扩大词汇量。因此，语块应该成为听说教学的重要语言材料。

　　语块包括以下基本类型：词汇固定搭配、语法固定搭配、习语（Idiomatic Expressions）和程式化话语。

　　词汇固定搭配指的是固定的单词组合，例如 listen to tapes（听录音磁带）、read aloud（大声读）、wear glasses（戴眼镜）等。当这类固定搭配语块中的动词和中文意思一致，比如 read aloud，学习者很容易掌握。但是当其中的动词有明显的同义词或者不固定时，就容易混淆。比如 listen to tapes，学生很容易说成 hear tapes 或 listen tapes。类似的还有 have breakfast（吃早餐）、take a walk（散步）、make one's own decision（自己做决定）等。

　　语法固定搭配指的是由一个开放性词类（可以是名词、动词或形容词等）和介词组合成的固定搭配语块。常见的有 in my opinion（在我看来）、made in China（中国制造）、in the future（未来）、look after（照看）、worry about（担心）、fill in the chart（填表）、be interested in（对……感兴趣）、pay attention to（注意）、in total（总计）、in that case（那样的情况下）等。

　　习语是经过长时间使用而沉淀下来的固定短语或短句。其意义往往不是由组成它的单词的字面意思构成，而是作为一个整体表达的特定意义。在日常交际中，习语语块就像中文的成语，能够使得语言简练有趣。例如 a piece of cake（小菜一碟）、born with a silver spoon in one's mouth（出生富贵）、lucky dog（幸运儿）等。

　　程式化话语指的是具有句子结构的语块。具体又可以分为完整句程式化话语和框架式程式化话语。完整句程式化话语顾名思义就是完整的句子，但这些句子的意义完全固定，需要作为整体来理解、记忆、存储和使用。例如，"What's the weather like?"（天气怎么样?）、"How do you do?"（你好!）、"I can't agree with you more."（我非常同意你的观点）等。框架式程式化话语指的是语块中一部分的形式和意义被固定，但留出了部分内容供补充来形成一个完整的意义表达。如"What about..."（……怎么样?）、I think...（我认为）等。

对于初中阶段山后地区的学生而言，把语块作为材料来学习不仅减轻了记忆的负担，而且有利于听力理解和表达能力的提高。人教版初中英语教材的目录部分也有对语块的摘录。七年级上册目录词汇（Vocabulary）和循环（Recycling）部分总结的语块如下（表 3.10）：

表 3.10　人教版《英语》七上目录部分语块

词汇固定搭配	first/last name, middle school, telephone/phone number, a set of, watch TV, a pair of, book sale, art festival, birthday party, English test, school trip, basketball/soccer game
语法固定搭配	in English, thank you for..., ask...for..., think about, from...to...
习语	good morning, good afternoon, good evening, come on, for sure
程式化话语	Nice to meet you. What about...? How about...? How much...?

九年级全一册目录词汇（Vocabulary）和循环（Recycling）部分的语块如下（表 3.11）：

表 3.11　人教版《英语》九年级目录部分语块

词汇固定搭配	get bored, find out, straight/curly hair, wear glasses, take place, make one's own decision, take photos, thousands of, plenty of, shake hands, make friends, get mad, make an effort, drive sb. crazy, brush one's teeth, wash one's face, get dressed, get up late, senior high (school), take the bus/subway, ride a bike

语法固定搭配	pay attention to…, connect…with, be interested in, be good at, in common, learn from, fall in love with, because of, put on, lay out, end up, be similar to, remind…of, pass by, go along, turn right/left, second/third floor, next to, deal with, in public, be proud of, in person, take pride in, be known for, by accident, without doubt, by mistake, divide…into, look up to, keep…away from, get in the way of, move out, take care of, look after, care about, run after, stick to, shut off, in total, cheer up, clean…off, take off, get used to, to one's surprise, be friends with, leave out, let…down, in common, even though, wake up, go off, stay up, put on, show up, sell out, take part in, turn off, pay for, throw away, pull…down, believe in, be thirsty for, ahead of, separate from, set out, full of, deal with, be proud of, give up, grow up, work out
习语	pardon me, excuse me, from time to time, no matter, all of a sudden, talk back, at the same time, in that case, once in a while, don't mind, feel like, in time, drop by, after all, go out of one's way, make…feel at home, to start with, kick sb. off, pull together, give…a lift, put sth. to good use, clean up, cut down, set up, in a row, make a mess, keep one's cool, first of all, no matter
程式化话语	so…that It is said that… It is believed that… not only…but also not…anymore not only…but also the more…the more, neither…nor

从上面的梳理可以看到，即便是起始年级，教材也强调语块的学习。到了九年级，语块更加丰富。教师在进行听说教学时，不一定要将语块进行分类。但一定要利用好教材，把不同类型的语块作为语言材料输入给学生，鼓励学生整体理解、记忆和输出这些语块。

（3）语用知识和文化知识。

除了语音和词汇障碍，学生在语用知识和文化背景知识方面也存在困难。语用知识指的是在特定语境中准确理解他人和得体表达自己的知识。学习和掌握一定的语用知识能帮助学生在真实的交际场合中，根据交际的目的、正式程度、参与人的身份和角色，选择正式或非正式、直接或委婉等语言形式，得体恰当地与他人沟通和交流，提升语言运用能力和灵活应变的能力。文化知识既包括饮食、服饰、建筑、交通，以及相关发明与创造等物质文化的知识，也包括哲学、科学、历史、语言、文学、艺术、教育，以及价值观、道德修养、审美情趣、劳动意识、社会规约和风俗习惯等非物质文化的知识（教育部，2022）。这些知识背后，渗透的是文化和价值观。听和说是语言交际的重要手段。学生只有具备一定的语用意识和文化意识，才能顺利完成跨文化交际的任务。

　　然而在实际教学中，还存在有"How are you?"学生只会教科书式回答"I'm fine. Thanks."的现象。尤其是山后地区的学生十分缺乏英语语言环境，教师更要通过引入多模态的语料或真实的情境来帮助学生选择得体的语言形式与人交流。以人教版《英语》七年级上册 Starter Unit 1 Good morning! 为例。本单元的主题是见朋友、打招呼。课本上提供的教学内容如下：

Good morning, Alice!

Good afternoon, Eric!

Good evening, Bob!

Hello, Frank!

Hi, Cindy!

How are you?

I'm fine, thanks.

　　如果仅仅局限于课本上的内容，学生在实际生活中并不能灵活处理。比如"Good morning"在口头交际中，经常会省略为"morning"。对"How are you?"的回答还有"Pretty good.""Not bad."等。事实上，回答"I'm fine."反而听起来有点奇怪。如果近况不佳，还可以回答"Not so good.""Not great.""Not so well."等。此外，除了用这个句型来询问好友的近况以外，还有很多更为常见和随意的表达，比如"Hey, how's it going?""What's up?"等。而从文化角度来说，大部分情况下这样的问候并不是代表真的在询问对方的身体情况，而是一种礼貌的询问，就像是另一种说"hello"的方式，以便开启话题。这就要求教师到课本外寻找真实的语料素材，比如电影、短视频等，让学生在真实的问候情境中感悟语用知识和文化知识，从而培养学生的跨文化交际能力。

　　3）通过活动锻炼学生听说能力

　　技巧要真正变成能力，不能停留在课本和考试上。只有在真实的活动中历练，学生才能将课堂上所学的听说技能转化为能力。山后地区的学生在学习英语时以应试为主要动机，认为学好英语主要是为了取得好成绩。要改变这一观念，最重要的是丰富学生英语学习的体验，提供学生建立英语自信的平台，创造学生体验英语文化的环境。多样的英语活动，如英语戏剧、英文演讲比赛、英文歌唱大赛、英语故事会等，符合学生的心理和认知特点，能使学生置身于真实的英语情境中，激发学生的学习兴趣，为学生提供整体习得语言的机会。

以英语戏剧为例，北京一零一中温泉校区 2017 级 3 班全体同学组成的《小王子》剧组，在学校第二届英语戏剧大赛中获"特等奖"，随后又相继获得第十届"希望中国"青少年教育戏剧北京赛区三等奖及"最具风采人气剧目"，为学校斩获一枚铜牌。在这一过程中，学生经历了前期准备、校级决选、北京市决选三个阶段。

前期准备时，学生阅读了大量原著，并在教师指导下选定并创作了剧本《小王子》。剧团成立后，导演组、演员组、服化组、道具组、技术组、场务组也都相继确定，导演从形象、口语、表演等维度进行演员试镜及选定。剧组排练阶段，演员们研读台词，揣摩人物性格并打磨演技，同时结合服化道进行剧组集体排练。

参与学校决选时，英语教师、美术教师和音乐教师都对孩子们进行了具体指导。从单词发音到语音语调，从道具制作到舞台设计，从剧目配乐到声台形表，剧组能力都取得了很大提高。鉴于剧团出色的表现，在尚无校级专业话剧社团的情况下，学校决定大胆一试，选派《小王子》剧团代表学校参加第十届"希望中国"青少年教育戏剧北京市初选。随后成功入围北京市现场决选。

为备战北京市决选，团队又进行了以"向世界表达中国"为主题的中华才艺特训，接受了外籍戏剧专家的指导，不管是在语音语调方面，还是声台形表方面，都取得了长足进步。决选当日，选手们顶住压力，用流利的英文分别介绍了乒乓、剪纸、箜篌、书法和朝鲜舞的渊源，并进行了灵动的才艺展示。舞台上，演员们收放自如，将《小王子》这部文学经典娓娓道来，在仅有的十几分钟时间内最大限度地重现了这个温暖的故事，勾起了大家心底对童年的美好回忆。不久，展评结果公示，《小王子》剧组不负众望，一举斩获第十届"希望中国"青少年教育戏剧北京市三等奖及第十届"希望中国"中英双语文化节"最具风采人气剧目"，为学校赢得了一枚铜牌。

这次经历给学生提供了有价值的语言练习机会，从而全方位提升学生英语学科的核心素养。在语言能力层面，通过反复研读剧本，学生的语音意识和语言理解能力得以增强；学习能力层面，通过个人练习和剧组排练，学生的自主学习及合作学习能力得以提高；思维品质层面，通过对剧本的深刻解读，学生的思维深刻性和批判性得以加深；文化意识层面，通过对剧目内核的理解及真切表演，进一步体会美、创造美，不仅实现了对学生的美育，也实现了跨文化教育和价值观教育。

观看了现场戏剧表演的师生和家长，都对学生在英文戏剧表演中所展现出来的活力、自信和流畅的英语表达能力印象深刻。学生自己也享受其中，对自身、对英语学习的信心都大大增强。这充分说明，以戏剧方式开展语言学习不仅为学生习得语言提供了丰富的语境，也为学生提供了整体习得语言的宝贵机会。学生在丰富的语境中，围绕语言意义，整体感知语音语调，理解语言意义，获得语言知识，体会语言魅力，思考语言所传递的含义，并通过反复练习台词和内化时间，形成整体运用语言进行思维和表达的能力（王蔷等，2016）。这样获得的语言驾驭能力和表现力是一般课堂中所看不到的。

■ 3.2 活动设计与实施

3.2.1 听说前、中、后活动设计

听说课作为初中英语教学的一个重要课型，对于培养学生的听说能力发挥着重要作用，同时也是培养学生思维品质、落实学科核心素养的重要途径（吕国征，2020）。然而通过我们对山后地区英语听说课的观摩和对英语教师的访谈，发现目前还存在两个关键的问题：一是过多关注听力材料信息的提取和听说技巧的训练，而忽视引导学生探究听力语篇所蕴含的主题意义、忽视真实口头交际场景的创设；二是教学目标表述不清晰、层次不清楚、教学活动不能围绕教学目标展开。

为此，我们提出教师在进行听说前、中、后的活动设计时，应该遵循两个原则：一是基于对主题意义的探究；二是基于核心素养的教学目标展开。

1）基于对主题意义的探究

无论是《普通高中英语课程标准（2017年版）》（教育部，2018），还是《义务教育英语课程标准（2022年版）》（教育部，2022），都将主题列入英语课程内容六要素之一，并且处于首要位置。《课标（2022年版）》提出，主题具有联结和统领其他内容要素的作用，为语言学习和课程育人提供语境范畴。在教学建议中，《课标（2022年版）》也要求教师依托语境开展教学，引导学生在真实、有意义的语言应用中整合性地学习语言知识。

而基于主题意义探究的英语听说教学也具有其独特的优势。一方面，在探究所学主题内容时，学生将注意力集中在语篇的主题上，而不是语言的规则上，这有助于减轻单纯学习语言产生的枯燥感，从而提高学生学习的积极性和参与感（程晓堂，2018）。另一方面，学生在对意义的探究过程中，结合了自身的经验和认知，不仅对语篇有更深刻的理解，也能在情感、态度和价值观，以及对世界的理解上有所收获。

语言的使用都是在生活情境中发生和发展的（王蔷，2016）。学生要实现意义的建构，也必须基于一定的情境。教师要改变脱离语境的知识学习和碎片化的

教学方式，在设计活动时片面关注听力语篇中语言知识点的学习或者将教师自己对主题意义的理解强加给学生，都无法帮助学生建构主题意义。基于主题意义探究的听说教学要求教师深度解读听力材料并确定主题，以主题和内容为主线，以意义为核心，以语言为暗线设计教学目标和教学活动。在教学实践中，以听力语篇为意义的载体，以听说活动为途径，以学习策略为手段，用问题链推动主题意义的自主探究，挖掘主题内涵，渗透学科育人。

教师可以通过游戏、讨论、多模态的视听材料等导入情境，通过师生、生生互动和意义协商深入情境，通过联系生活实际的活动关联文本情境，通过创设角色扮演、真实任务等方法来迁移情境。将各个小情境自然衔接起来，形成一条完整的情境链（孟碧君，2022）。换句话说，主题情境的创设和主题意义的探究要贯穿整个听说教学过程：听前创设主题语境，激发学生的学习兴趣，扫清学生的听说障碍；听中设计基于英语学习活动观的阶梯式听说任务，让学生体验、理解、建构、完善主题情境，实现对主题意义的探究；听后引导学生在真实情境中运用语言，创造性地解决新问题，从而升华主题意义，实现学生语言能力、文化意识、思维品质和学习能力的融合发展。

2）基于核心素养的教学目标

通常来说，教学目标可以分为课程总目标、单元教学目标和课时教学目标。这里将从微观层面出发，聚焦听说课的课时教学目标。

在观摩山后农村校英语听说课时，我们发现教师在目标的设定、表述和达成上都存在一定问题。第一，教师对教学目标的设定不清晰。例如，有的教师预设"通过本节课的学习，学生能够听出材料中的细节信息，并概括听力材料的大意"。这个预设并不是教学目标，而是听力技能，甚至于放在任何一节听说课可能都成立。第二，教师对教学目标的表述不明确。例如，教师预设"通过本节课的学习，学生能够掌握用英语问路的技能"，这里的"掌握"是一个模糊的概念，很难量化和检测，类似的表述还有"了解""知道""理解"等。第三，教师所预设的教学目标之间缺乏逻辑，无法体现思维和能力的进阶。换言之，教师没有基于英语学习活动观来制定教学目标。

实际上，在设计教学目标时，学生目前的认知水平和能力是起点。语言输入理论启示我们，要充分了解学生的语言水平、心智特征、兴趣爱好和成长背景等，以生为本，设计恰当的目标和活动。《课标（2022年版）》也强调要"凸显学生主体地位"。因此，教师首先要依据学情来制定教学目标。

其次，英语学科核心素养对教学目标的制定起着引领作用。核心素养是课程育人价值的集中体现，是学生通过课程学习逐步形成的适应个人终身发展和社会发展所需的正确价值观、必备品格和关键能力。英语学科核心素养包括四个方面：语言能力、文化意识、思维品质和学习能力。英语课程总目标也从这四个方面展开：发展语言能力、培育文化意识、提升思维品质、提高学习能力。教师在制定课时教学目标时，也应该从核心素养的四个方面进行考量。

同时，英语学习活动观是制定教学目标的重要依据。教师要秉承在体验中学习、在实践中运用、在迁移中创新的学习理念，在英语学习活动观的指导下，预设指向主题意义探究的学习理解、应用实践和迁移创新等多层次、相关联、循环递进的学习目标，让学生逐步建立、内化和运用新知。

最后，教师在拟定教学目标时，还应将评价贯穿其中。"教—学—评"一体化设计要求我们以评促学、以评促教。教学目标的表述和设定只有可操作、可检测、可达成，才能保证教学活动的顺利实施、教学内容的有效落实。

我们结合《课标（2022 年版）》中的案例 7（8 年级对话语篇教学设计"A Picnic"）进行分析。

通过本课时学习，学生能够：

（1）获取 Julie 和 Uncle Dan 在电话对话中谈到的野餐计划和安排，包括出发时间、集合地点、参加人，以及各家需要准备的食物和餐具等信息，完成留言条；

（2）基于电话留言条，讲述两家的野餐计划，关注、提取、归纳并内化电话中请求对方转达信息的语言表达方式；

（3）运用相关的语言表达方式，与同伴角色扮演打电话，谈论班级的野餐计划，并完成留言条。

在以上案例中，每一个目标都将行为主体指向了"学生"，体现了以学生为主体的原则。

"获取……""完成留言条""讲述……""运用……""谈论……"等表述符合语言能力 7~9 年级学段分项特征；得体、有效地使用电话用语和记录电话留言符合文化意识学段目标"能初步了解英语的语用特征，选择恰当的交际策略"；运用所学语言，谈论班级的野餐计划，体现了思维品质学段目标"能根据语篇内容或所给条件进行改变或创编"；与同伴角色扮演打电话，则体现了学习能力学段目标分项合作与探究特征。也就是说，以上教学目标充分渗透了英语学科核心素养的四个维度。

此外，目标 1 中"获取……"和目标 2 中"关注、提取"属于英语学习活动观学习理解类活动，即感知与注意、获取与梳理；目标 2 中"归纳并内化……"属于应用实践类活动，即描述与阐释、内化与运用；目标 3 中"运用……谈论班级的野餐计划……"则超越了语篇、联系了学生的生活实际，让学生在真实情境中完成交际任务，解决问题，学以致用，属于迁移创新类活动，即想象与创造。三个目标相互关联、循环递进，使用的行为动词具体，学习内容明确，体现了英语学习活动观和"教—学—评"一体化的理念。

综上所述，教师在设计听说教学活动时，应基于对主题意义的探究，围绕逻辑连贯、可操作、可检测的教学目标展开。下面我们将从听说前、中、后的活动设计具体阐释。

1. 听说前活动设计

在以主题意义为引领的英语课堂教学中，导入环节起着创设主题语境的作用。在导入活动中，教师可以基于学生的真实生活体验来引入主题语境，也可以使用契合主题的素材来创设主题语境。在与学生互动的过程中，围绕目标话题，实现激发学生学习兴趣或扫清学生听说障碍的目标，从而为听的环节做好语境和目标语言的铺垫。

1）创设主题语境，激发学习兴趣

在导入阶段，教师可以利用图片、视频等多模态形式，采用符合主题的与生活实际相关联的问题引入话题，通过问卷、讨论、头脑风暴等活动让学生置身其中，引发共鸣或者留下悬念，激发学生探索主题意义的兴趣。

（1）听前联系生活实际。

以人教版《英语》八年级上册 Unit 1 Where did you go on vacation? Section A1b 的听说课为例。听力材料包涵 3 个内容结构类似的对话语篇，内容是同学之间互问假期生活，包括去哪儿、做了什么、和谁去的、是否愉快等。教师可以在本节课上课之前，请学生准备一张假期生活的照片。在开始 1b 的听力之前，教师呈现问题"Where did you go on vacation?"。教师先分享自己假期生活的照片并描述。接下来，教师利用 1a 提供的语块提问"Who stayed at home?""Who went to the beach?""Who went to the mountains?"，请学生分享他们假期生活的照片。这样不仅导入了话题、铺垫了语言知识，还调动了学生参与课堂的积极性，课堂氛围热烈。

（2）听前预测。

以人教版《英语》九年级 Unit 13 We're trying to save the earth! Section B 1c – 1d 的听说教学为例。本单元的话题是环境污染与环境保护（Pollution and Environmental Protection）。该听力材料是 Jack 和 Julia 之间的对话，讨论的是在生活中如何保护环境、节能减排。在此之前，学生已经熟悉了两个人物 Susan 和 Jason，他们讨论了现有的环境问题、污染的原因和解决办法。因此，为了保持主题的连贯性，教师将听力材料中原本的 Julia 和 Jack 换成了原来在 Section A 部分出现的 Susan 和 Jason，同时对听力音频做了重录。教师再次引入学生熟悉的人物 Susan 和 Jason，并呈现 2d 部分 Susan 拎着购物袋的照片，请学生预测对话内容以及 Susan 在环保方面做出的努力，完成下面的表格（表 3.12）。

Predict and tick：

表 3.12　人教版《英语》九年级 Unit 13 听说活动

Things Jason and Susan talk about	Things Susan is doing now	Things Susan will do in the future	Things Susan would never do
___√___ turning off the lights			
____ turning off the shower			
____ not using paper napkins			
____ taking your own bags when shopping			
____ not riding in cars			
____ riding a bike			
____ recycling paper			

接下来，教师可以请学生听录音并核对自己的猜测。学生通过预测说话者在环保方面做的事情，激活了主题相关的语言。教师通过改编听力材料，激发了学生听听力的兴趣，也增强了单元设计的整体性和关联性。

（3）听前讨论。

以人教版《英语》九年级 Unit 7 Teenagers should be allowed to choose their own clothes. Section B 1a–1d 的听说教学为例。该听力语篇围绕 Peter 和父亲的谈话展开。Peter 因为错过班车，只能走路上学，并因此迟到，不被允许参加数学考试。父亲建议 Peter 课后与老师沟通。

在进行 1c 的听力活动之前，教师可以对课本 1a 的活动进行改编，请学生完成下面的调查问卷（表 3.13）。通过互问互答，学生不仅激活了话题相关的背景知识，而且对彼此的经历充满好奇，讨论气氛高涨。接着教师请学生分享自己的问卷调查结果，并追问"Are you allowed to fail tests?"等，从而为 1c 的听力做铺垫。

表 3.13　人教版《英语》九年级 Unit 7 听说活动

Do you ever…	Me	My partner
get to class late?		
study with friends		
finish a test early		
worry about failing a test		
argue with your teacher		

（4）听前头脑风暴。

以人教版《英语》八年级上册 Unit 5 Do you want to watch a game show? Section A 1b – 1c 的教学为例。1b 的听力是一个对话语篇，内容是 Mark 邀请 Jack 晚上一起看电视，二人讨论看什么节目以及对这些节目的看法。在进行听说活动之前，教师可以利用最新的电影或火爆的电视节目图片引入话题，然后请学生头脑风暴不同种类的电视节目。教师可以在讨论过程中适当帮助学生拓展电视节目类型的相关表达，如 quiz show, documentaries, science fiction 等，同时可以追问"What do you think of talk shows?" "What do you think of talent shows?" 等引入话题。

2）基于主题意义，提供语言和知识支架

教师可以在导入环节用歌曲、提问、游戏等活动，启动学生的视觉、听觉、触觉等多种感官，帮助学生扫清词汇、句型、文化知识等障碍。

（1）歌曲引入，复习主题词汇。

以人教版《英语》八年级下册 Unit 1 What's the matter? 中 Section A 的听说教学为例。课本中 1a 部分呈现了身体各部位的词汇，其中大部分都是学生比较熟悉的，如 hand，ear，leg，eye 等。如果单纯复习这些单词难免有些枯燥，教师可以围绕这个单元的主题健康（Health）引入动画歌曲 "Head, Shoulders, Knees and Toes"。学生边唱歌边跳健身操，通过多重感官复习身体部位的词汇。接下来，教师可以趁热打铁，和学生玩 Touch and Say 的游戏，从而进一步复习和拓展身体部位的词汇。

（2）图片引入，呈现主题词汇。

以人教版《英语》七年级下册 Unit 2 What time do you go to school? Section A 1a – 1c 的听说教学为例。该听力材料是一个对话语篇，内容为采访 Rick 的日常作息，如起床时间、吃早餐的时间等。在开始听录音之前，教师可以搭设支架。先请学生观察一组图片，内容是教师自己的作息安排。接下来教师介绍自己的作息安排。例如，教师指着自己起床的图片，引导学生完成句子 "I usually…at…"，然后将句子板书在黑板上：

I usually get up at 6:00.

I usually brush my teeth at 6:10.

I usually get dressed at 6:30.

I usually eat breakfast at 7:00.

I usually go to work at 7:20.

句中词组 get up, brush teeth, get dressed, eat breakfast 以及时间的表达都是在接下来的听力内容中会出现的。最后，教师回到图片，依次提问学生图片上的时间，如 "What time do I usually get up?" 等，帮助学生熟悉 what time 引导的特殊疑问句，理解听力内容。

（3）歌曲导入，呈现主题词汇。

以人教版《英语》八年级上册 Unit 3 I'm more outgoing than my sister. 为例。在 Section B 的听说部分开始之前，教师可以用符合本单元主题的歌曲 Shining Friends 来引入话题，创设主题情境。在欣赏完歌曲之后，教师随即提问 "What are shining friends like?"。学生自由发言，教师在互动中继续追问 "Does he/she care about your feelings?"，并通过幻灯片呈现 make…laugh, is talented in, a good listener, is good at 等单元目标语言，从而帮助学生扫清生词障碍，为下一步 1c 的听力做语言准备。

（4）歌曲导入，熟悉目标句型。

以人教版《英语》八年级上册 Unit 10 If you go to the party, you'll have a great time! 为例。本单元以举办聚会为线索，主要谈论事件的结果，尤其用到了 If 条件句的句型。为了让学生提前适应 If 条件句的表达，教师可以在开始 Section A 1a–1c 的听说教学之前，询问学生今天心情如何，然后引入歌曲 If you are happy。这首歌的歌词简单好记，如 If you're happy happy happy, clap your hands. If you're angry angry angry, stamp your feet. 等。通过这一形式学生很快可以将 If 条件句的表达融会贯通，从而让后面的听说活动更好地聚焦主题内容而非语言形式。

（5）视频导入，熟悉文化知识。

以人教版《英语》九年级 Unit 2 I think that mooncakes are delicious! Section B 1a–1d 的听说教学为例。1b 的听力内容是中国学生 Wu Yu 和 Jane 关于万圣节习俗的对话。教师可以先用课本上万圣节的图片导入，让学生猜测这是哪一个节日。接下来提问学生 "What do you know about Halloween?"。随着学生的发言，教师呈现一段美国人庆祝万圣节的视频，并让学生边看边做笔记。这样不仅激活了学生关于万圣节的背景知识，而且解决了可能的文化背景知识障碍。

2. 听说中活动设计

在设计听说活动时，教师要充分考虑听说教学的特点，把语言知识学习和听说策略有机融合在对主题意义的探究中，做到语言学习、听说策略训练和主题意义探究三者的平衡（黄正翠、彭德河，2019）。在此基础上，教师可以开展学习理解和应用实践类活动，通过问题链的探究，发展思维能力；通过分类整合信息，促进知识结构化。

1）问题链探究，发展思维能力

以人教版《英语》九年级 Unit 12 Life Is Full of the Unexpected Section A 部分

1a－2c 的听说课为例。本单元的主题是 Unexpected Events，要求学生运用过去完成时谈论过去发生的意外事件。听力语篇是 Mary 和朋友有关她一个糟糕的早晨的讨论。对话中，两人主要谈论了 Mary 因为睡过头而遭遇的一系列不如意的事情，包括错过班车、上学迟到、把书包忘在家里等。听力文本如下：

Boy：Hi, Mary. You look so tired.

Mary：I am. I had a bad morning.

Boy：Really? What happened?

Mary：Well, first of all I overslept. By the time I got up, my brother had already gotten in the shower.

Boy：Oh, what a pain!

Mary：So, after he got out of the shower. I took a quick shower and got dressed. But by the time I went outside, the bus had already left.

Boy：Oh, no!

Mary：Oh, yes! So I ran all the way to school. But when I got to school, I realized I had left my backpack at home.

Boy：No wonder you look stressed.

教师可以设计以下教学活动（表3.14）：

表3.14 人教版《英语》九年级 Unit 12 教学设计

听说活动	设计意图
➢ 听前预测 教师请学生浏览课本1a的图片，根据图片猜测： ①Did Mary have a good day or a bad day? ②What happened to her? ➢ 听第一遍 教师请学生验证自己对于问题①的推测 ➢ 听第二遍 教师请学生验证自己对于问题②的推测，并在每一幅图片旁边做笔记 ➢ 听第三遍 教师请学生对照录音材料，跟读模仿语音语调 教师请学生根据自己的笔记，复述 Mary 的一天	聚焦主题，培养读图和预测能力，激发学习兴趣，减轻听力焦虑 归纳文本大意 获取细节信息 训练朗读技能，深化文本理解、缓解口头复述焦虑，内化目标语言和语法

在上面的听说活动中，教师充分给予了学生听力策略的指导：包括通过观察图片、从主题意义角度预测文本大意和事实性细节，泛听获取听力文本大意，精听获取听力材料的事实性信息，听并记录关键词，再到跟读录音强化新知，最后复述故事内化新知，既帮助学生形成了主题意义引领下的新的知识结构，又将听

说技能的训练落到了实处，提高了学生的听说能力。

再以人教版《英语》九年级 Unit 13 We're trying to save the earth! Section A 2a‒2c 的听说教学为例。该听力材料是一个采访，采访者就环境问题向 Jason 和 Susan 进行提问，并谈到造成这些环境问题的原因。听力文本如下：

Interviewer：Today we're talking to Jason and Susan about environmental problems. Jason and Susan，can you tell us about some of the problems you've seen?

Jason：I think one problem is that the air is badly polluted. I hardly ever see blue skies anymore.

Susan：Yes，and I used to see the stars clearly.

Interviewer：What do you think has caused this problem?

Susan：Well，there are more cars on the road these days.

Jason：And factories that burn coal also pollute the air with a lot of black smoke.

Interviewer：What other problems do you see?

Susan：I guess there's too much rubbish and waste in the streets.

Jason：Yes！Every day people are throwing away things like wooden chopsticks，plastic bowls and plastic bags.

Susan：They're also littering in public places，for example，during picnics in parks. This is turning beautiful places into ugly ones.

Interviewer：You're right. There are serious problems for our environment. Next，let's talk about the things we can do to help.

教师可以将听说活动设计如下（表 3.15）：

表 3.15　人教版《英语》九年级 Unit 13 教学设计

听说活动	设计意图
➢ 听前热身 　教师呈现图片，引出 land pollution，air pollution，noise pollution 和 water pollution，并请学生谈论自己对这些污染的了解	创设情境，调动学生对于环境问题的背景知识
➢ 听并记录 　学生在听录音时，边听边做笔记，回答问题 ①What pollutions did Jason and Susan talk about? ②What are the causes of these pollutions? ③What are they mainly talking about? ④What will they talk about later? ⑤How can we help solve these problems?	问题①和②是低阶思维问题，要求学生获取听力语篇的关键信息； 　问题③是归纳类型的高阶思维问题，问题④是推断类型的高阶思维问题，旨在帮助学生深入理解文本 　问题⑤是思辨类型的高阶思维问题，需要学生联系生活实际，提出解决问题的办法

通过以上问题链的方式，教师逐步引导学生建立基于主题意义的语言知识框架，即 problems—causes—solutions。学生在听说活动中充分调动自己关于环保问题的背景知识，主动学习，在思考和讨论中形成环保意识，实现了深度学习。

2）分类整合信息，促进知识结构化

在设计听力任务时，教师可以利用概念图、表格、思维导图等呈现出主题和语言之间的内在逻辑关系，将知识结构化，从而帮助学生建立新知。

以人教版《英语》八年级上册 Unit 3 I'm more outgoing than my sister. Section B 1c 部分的听说课为例。该听力材料是一个采访类文本，采访者就好朋友的话题对 Molly 和 Mary 进行了采访，主要关注了几个问题：

- Who is your best friend?
- What do you like about her?
- Is she different from you in any way?
- Is she a lot like you?

听力对话文本如下：

Interviewer：Who's your best friend, Molly?

Molly：Peter.

Interviewer：Why do you like him?

Molly：Because he likes to do the same things as I do. He's popular, too, and he's good at sports.

Interviewer：So, is he different from you in any way?

Molly：Well, yes, I like to study. I study harder than Peter. He plays baseball better than me.

Interviewer：OK, I see…

Molly：Oh, and he speaks more loudly than me. I'm a little quieter. But I'd say we're both pretty outgoing.

Interviewer：How about you, Mary? Who's your best friend?

Mary：My best friend is Lisa.

Interviewer：What do you like about her?

Mary：Well, she's a good listener, and that's important to me.

Interviewer：Is she a lot like you?

Mary：Some people say we look similar. We're both tall, and we both have long, curly hair. But Lisa is quieter than me. I'm always talking. She's also smarter. I'm more outgoing.

可以看到，对话主要围绕 who, why, how 三个方面展开采访，关注朋友之间的相同点和不同点。因此，教师可以请学生听录音，根据下面的思维导图（图3.6）做笔记：

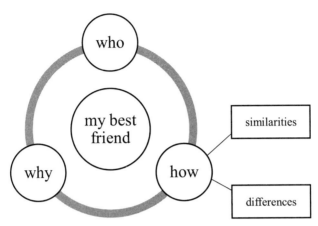

图 3.6　人教版《英语》八年级上册 Unit 3 思维导图

　　这不仅能够锻炼学生听的能力，更能帮助学生将"好朋友"话题的相关知识结构化，为口语输出活动搭建脚手架。

　　以人教版《英语》八年级下册 Unit 1 What's the matter? Section A 2a - 2b 的听说教学为例。该文本由 5 个形式和内容相近的短对话构成，主要谈论的是疾病的症状、原因及对策。听力文本如下：

Conversation 1

Girl 1：You don't look well. Your face looks a bit red.

Girl 2：Yeah，and my head feels very hot. What should I do?

Girl 1：Maybe you have a fever. You should take your temperature.

Girl 2：Yes，you're right.

Conversation 2

Girl 1：What's the matter?

Girl 2：I didn't take good care of myself. I didn't wear enough warm clothes yester-day. Now I have a cough and a sore throat.

Girl 1：You should drink some hot tea with honey.

Girl 2：That sounds like a good idea.

Conversation 3

Girl：You look terrible！What's the matter?

Boy：I think I ate too much at dinner last night. It was an all-you-can-eat meal at the restaurant. But now I have a stomachache.

Girl：That's too bad. You shouldn't eat so much next time. Right now，you should lie down and rest.

Boy：I guess I should.

Conversation 4

Girl：What's wrong with your face?

Boy：It's not my face. It's my tooth. I have a toothache.

Girl：You should see a dentist and get an X - ray.

Boy：But will it hurt?

Girl：No，and if you don't go to the dentist now，it'll hurt even more later！

Conversation 5

Girl 1：Oh，no！What happened?

Girl 2：I was making dinner just now and I cut myself by accident.

Girl 1：Oh，that looks serious. You should put some medicine on it. Here，let me help you.

Girl 2：OK，thanks.

在设计听中活动时，教师可以将以上语篇处理成表格，请学生听材料，填写表格（表 3. 16）。

表 3.16 人教版《英语》八年级下册 Unit 1 听中活动

	Symptoms/Reasons	Illnesses	Advice
Conversation 1			
Conversation 2			
Conversation 3			
Conversation 4			
Conversation 5			

此外，课本还提供了相应的图片（图 3.7）。教师可以在听前引导学生预测，尝试根据图片描述症状、疾病，并给出自己的建议。然后听对话排序、听对话填表格。这样不仅降低了听力的难度、调动了学生的生活常识，在填表的过程中也将听力材料中的知识结构化，形成 "症状—疾病—建议" 的知识网，从而建构了健康主题下的新知体系。

除了以主题内容为线索的知识结构化，教师还可以在听中利用表格帮助学生将语言知识结构化。以人教版《英语》八年级上册 Unit 10 If you go to the party，

Listen and number the pictures [1-5] in the order you hear them.

图 3.7　人教版《英语》八年级下册 Unit 1 课本图片

you'll have a great time！Section A 2a – 2b 的听说活动为例。该听力材料为对话语篇，内容是 Nelly 和 Mark 在讨论举办班级晚会的时间以及晚会上的活动安排。听力文本如下：

Nelly：Hi，Mark. I want to have a class party. Will you help me?

Mark：Sure Nelly. I can help you. So when shall we have the party?

Nelly：Let's have it today after class.

Mark：No，today is too early. If we have it today，half the class won't come.

Nelly：OK，let's have it tomorrow then.

Mark：Hmm…There's a test the day after tomorrow. Students will leave early to study for the test. Why not have it on the weekend?

Nelly：OK，let's have it on Saturday afternoon. We can all meet and watch a video.

Mark：No，I don't think we should watch a video. Some students will be bored. Let's play party games.

Nelly：OK，good idea. Can you organize the party games?

Mark：Sure，I can do that. And can you make some food for us?

Nelly：Yes，no problem.

可以看到，Nelly 和 Mark 在讨论中进行了多次的协商。比如谈到举办晚会的时间，Nelly 提了两次想法，Mark 都不同意，但都给出了理由。学生在听对话时不仅可以就内容进行大意和细节的探究，还可以将其中表达同意、不同意、给出理由的功能句型罗列出来，完成下面的表格（表 3.17）：

表 3.17 人教版《英语》八年级上册 Unit 10 听力活动

	Agree	Disagree and reasons
Mark		
Nelly		

在这个活动中，学生分类梳理了表达同意和不同意他人观点的语言功能项目，同时学到了在否定他人观点时要给出充分理由以便对方能够接受这一交际策略。教师通过听填表格的活动帮助学生将零碎的语言知识系统化，发展了学生的交际能力。

3. 听说后活动设计

在完成对材料听的处理和基本的口头回答以后，教师可以根据需要决定是否跟读听力文本，培养学生的语音语调。当这一系列基本的听说活动结束后，教师可以通过游戏、提问、续编、讨论等活动，帮助学生内化目标语言，发展高阶思维和解决问题的能力。

1）花样内化语言，创意迁移知识

学生虽然通过听获取了听力文本的细节和大意，又通过朗读、跟读等巩固了语音和语调，但要真正内化目标语言，还需要在脱离文本的情况下，能说出来、用起来。此时教师需要设计多样的输出活动，如接龙复述、角色扮演、拍视频等。

以人教版《英语》九年级全一册 Unit 12 Life is full of the unexpected. Section A 1a – 2c 听说课为例。1b 的听力内容讲述的是 Mary 因为起晚了没赶上车，跑去学校发现书包忘在家里。2a，2b 部分的对话继续讲述了 Mary 回家取书包上学迟到的故事。听力文本如下：

Section A 1b

Boy：Hi, Mary. You look so tired.

Mary：I am. I had a bad morning.

Boy：Really? What happened?

Mary：Well, first of all I overslept. By the time I got up, my brother had already gotten in the shower.

Boy：Oh, what a pain!

Mary：So, after he got out of the shower. I took a quick shower and got dressed. But by the time I went outside, the bus had already left.

Boy：Oh, no!

Mary：Oh, yes! So I ran all the way to school. But when I got to school, I realized I had left my backpack at home.

Boy：No wonder you look stressed.

Section A 2a，2b

Boy：So then what did you do，Mary?

Mary：Well，I ran home to get my backpack. But when I got home，I realized I had left my keys in the backpack.

Boy：You're kidding!

Mary：So I ran back to school without my keys or my backpack. But by the time I got back to school，the bell had rung.

Boy：Oh, no!

Mary：And by the time I walked into class，the teacher had started teaching already. She asked for our homework，but of course I didn't have it.

可以看到，以上两个听力文本是一个完整的故事链。课本还提供了与故事情节相匹配的图片 9 张（图 3.8）。教师可以在 PPT 上展示 9 幅图，请学生 3 人一

图 3.8　人教版《英语》九年级全一册 Unit 12 听后活动

组，每人 3 幅图片，接龙复述 Mary's bad morning。对于语言还比较薄弱的班级，教师还可以在图片旁边标注提示词。

图片和教师所给的提示词为学生完成接龙复述提供了必要的支架，降低了活动的难度，能够有效帮助学生顺利完成训练和内化目标语言、提升逻辑思维和口头表达能力的目标。

再以人教版《英语》八年级上册 Unit 1 What's the matter? Section A 2a–2c 的听说教学为例。课本听力原文如下：

Conversation 1

Girl 1：You don't look well. Your face looks a bit red.

Girl 2：Yeah，and my head feels very hot. What should I do?

Girl 1：Maybe you have a fever. You should take your temperature.

Girl 2：Yes，you're right.

Conversation 2

Girl 1：What's the matter?

Girl 2：I didn't take good care of myself. I didn't wear enough warm clothes yesterday. Now I have a cough and a sore throat.

Girl 1：You should drink some hot tea with honey.

Girl 2：That sounds like a good idea.

Conversation 3

Girl：You look terrible！What's the matter?

Boy：I think I ate too much at dinner last night. It was an all-you-can-eat meal at the restaurant. But now I have a stomachache.

Girl：That's too bad. You shouldn't eat so much next time. Right now，you should lie down and rest.

Boy：I guess I should.

Conversation 4

Girl：What's wrong with your face?

Boy：It's not my face. It's my tooth. I have a toothache.

Girl：You should see a dentist and get an X–ray.

Boy：But will it hurt?

Girl：No，and if you don't go to the dentist now，it'll hurt even more later！

Conversation 5

Girl 1：Oh, no！What happened?

Girl 2：I was making dinner just now and I cut myself by accident.

Girl 1：Oh，that looks serious. You should put some medicine on it. Here，let me help you.

Girl 2：OK，thanks.

该听力文本呈现了 5 段关于健康的对话，A 表现出不适，B 询问原因并给出建议。为了帮助学生内化语言，教师可以设计一个角色扮演活动，将 5 段对话中的发烧、感冒、胃疼、牙疼、受伤等写在纸片上，请学生两两一组抽签，根据抽到的病症编写对话。小组练习后，教师请学生上台抽签表演。以下是某组学生抽到"catch a cold"之后角色扮演的对话内容：

A：What's the matter，Peter？ You don't look well.

B：Well，I have a cough and my head feels very hot.

A：That's too bad. Maybe you have a fever. Let me take you to the doctor. She will take your temperature.

B：OK. Thank you.

通过抽签进行角色扮演，将原本呆板生硬的活动变得好玩起来。学生因为不清楚会抽到什么内容，在准备阶段会更加努力熟读对话。能够熟练掌握对话的同学才会自信地走上台前，基于抽签内容进行创编。在提高学生参与积极性的同时，帮助学生巩固了目标语言。

以人教版《英语》八年级上册 Unit 8 How do you make a banana milk shake？以 Section A 1a－2c 的听说课为例。两个听力文本均为对话，其中一个是两个男孩做香蕉奶昔，另一个是两个女孩做水果沙拉。原文如下：

Section A，1b

Boy 1：I'm hungry！Let's make a banana milk shake.

Boy 2：How do you make a banana milk shake？

Boy 1：Well，first peel three bananas.

Boy 2：Three bananas？

Boy 1：Yes. Then cut up the bananas.

Boy 2：OK，I'm finished.

Boy 1：Now put the bananas and ice-cream in the blender. Then pour the milk into the blender.

Boy 2：Is this enough milk？

Boy 1：I guess so. Next，turn on the blender. Finally，pour the milk shake into a glass and drink it.

Section A，2a，2b

Girl 1：Let's make fruit salad.

Girl 2：OK. Do you have bananas?

Girl 1：Yes，I do. How many bananas do we need?

Girl 2：We need three bananas.

Girl 1：That sounds about right. What else?

Girl 2：Watermelon.

Girl 1：How many watermelons?

Girl 2：Oh，only one small watermelon. And we need some honey.

Girl 1：How much honey do we need?

Girl 2：Let's see. Two spoons.

Girl 1：Right. What else?

Girl 2：Apples.

Girl 1：How many apples do we need?

Girl 2：Two should be enough. And yogurt.

Girl 1：How much yogurt do we need?

Girl 2：A cup. Now what else do we need? Oh，do you have any oranges?

Girl 1：I think so. How many oranges do we need?

Girl 2：Only one. This is going to taste great！

课上教师已经引导学生总结了描述制作过程需要用到的顺序词，以及烹饪用具、食材及用量。听说课后，教师请学生利用周末时间选择水果沙拉或香蕉奶昔等，不仅动手制作，还要在制作过程中进行讲解，请父母协助拍成视频，作为周末作业。学生也可以选择自己喜欢的菜肴来拍摄视频。以下是其中一位学生制作戚风蛋糕的视频脚本：

Do you know how to make an orange chiffon cake? Follow me and you will never forget. First，prepare three oranges，and cut each into two pieces. Then，squeeze out 70 grams of orange juice. And then we're going to prepare the eggs. Prepare 5 eggs and separate the white and yolk of the eggs. Weigh 20 grams of sugar and set aside. Pour the egg yolks，orange juice and sugar into an empty bowl. Stir quickly clockwise. Sift 110 grams flour into a bowl. After that，pour the egg white and sugar into an empty bowl. Pour the white，sugar into a bowl three times and stir well until it turns into meringue. Mix the meringue and egg yolks thoroughly. Finally pour into the mold. Place molds in the oven at 170 degrees and bake for 50 minutes. After baking，take out the mold and invert until cool. A delicious chiffon cake is just waiting for you.

在上面的视频脚本中，学生能够熟练运用本单元的目标语言，并根据所选内容拓展了相关表达。虽然在视频中，学生的发音还有些许问题（如 flour，thoroughly）等，但此时学生不仅在自己做蛋糕，更在用英语描述这一过程。可以说，该活动既锻炼了学生的动手能力、视频制作能力，为学生提供了展示的平台，更让学生学会用英语做事情，真正将所学语言用了起来。

以上接龙复述、角色扮演、拍摄视频等花样语言实践活动，将原本枯燥的复述过程变得有趣，并在游戏和体验中帮助学生运用所学知识，内化了目标语言。

2）评价反思文本，发展思维品质

教师还可以针对听力语篇中的人物、内容细节提出追问，引导学生思考、分析、判断、评价和反思，深入探究主题意义，形成正确的价值观，发挥文本的育人价值。

以人教版《英语》九年级全一册 Unit 12 Life is full of the unexpected. Section A 1a－2c 听说课为例。两篇听力材料以对话形式呈现了 Mary 因为睡过头而上学迟到，又忘带书包、忘带钥匙的糟糕早晨。在进行跟读复述之后，教师可以提出以下问题，请学生思考讨论：

①Was Mary good at dealing with unexpected things?

②Why or why not?

③What would you do if you are Mary?

④What suggestions will you give Mary?

⑤What can we learn from Mary's story?

学生在评价 Mary 遇到意外事情的处理方式时，能够设身处地设想如果自己遇到类似情况应该如何应对。同时，在给 Mary 提建议时，有同学说到 Mary 应该定好闹钟，应该在出门时检查自己的物品是否带齐，应该养成早睡早起的习惯等。在谈到从 Mary 身上汲取什么样的经验教训时，有同学说到 Mary 错过车自己跑去学校，没有撒谎和摆烂，是个爱学习的好学生。这些都无形中对学生养成良好的生活习惯、形成正确的价值观念产生了积极影响。

以人教版《英语》八年级上册 Unit 3 I'm more outgoing than my sister. Section B 1c 部分的听说后活动设计为例。在听说活动中，教师已经引导学生总结出了以 my best friend 为主题的知识结构图，并板书了核心语言点：

the same as…/both/like/look similar

be different from…

学生在跟读录音之后，能根据上面的思维导图复述听力材料中 Mary 和 Molly 的好友是谁、为什么、和他们的相似点与不同点。此时教师请学生按思维导图整理一段关于自己好朋友的描述，并在小组内口头交流。以下是其中一名学生写的内容：

My best friend is Guo Yapeng. I like him because we share the same hobbies. We both like playing basketball and he is good at it. I'm taller than him but he plays basket-ball better than me. But I study harder than him, so I sometimes help him with this math.

教师邀请部分学生在全班分享后，可以继续追问以下问题，启发学生思考：

①Is it important for a good friend to be the same or different? Why or why not?

②Do you truly care about your best friend?

③Do you know about his or her hobbies?

④Are you a good listener?

⑤How can you be a better friend?

在讨论中，学生对朋友这一主题有了思辨的认识，同时也反思自己怎样才能做一个更好的朋友。通过反思和表达，学生内化了本单元的主题意义，对人际交往有了更深刻的认识。

3）创设真实情境，解决真实问题

除了对主题进行思辨讨论，教师还可以根据单元内容设计情境问题，引导联系生活实际，以项目组的形式展开讨论，解决实际生活中的问题。

以人教版《英语》八年级上册 Unit 10 If you go to the party, you'll have a great time! Section A 2a–2d 的听说教学为例。两段对话围绕 class party 展开，分别讨论了举办聚会的最佳时间、食物、活动内容等。听力文本如下：

Section A，2a，2b

Nelly：Hi，Mark. I want to have a class party. Will you help me?

Mark：Sure Nelly. I can help you. So when shall we have the party?

Nelly：Let's have it today after class.

Mark：No，today is too early. If we have it today，half the class won't come.

Nelly：OK，let's have it tomorrow then.

Mark：Hmm…There's a test the day after tomorrow. Students will leave early to study for the test. Why not have it on the weekend?

Nelly：OK，let's have it on Saturday afternoon. We can all meet and watch a video.

Mark：No，I don't think we should watch a video. Some students will be bored. Let's play party games.

Nelly：OK，good idea. Can you organize the party games?

Mark：Sure，I can do that. And can you make some food for us?

Nelly：Yes，no problem.

Section A，2d

Jeff：Hey，Ben. For the party next week，should we ask people to bring food?

Ben：No，let's order food from a restaurant. If we ask people to bring food，they'll just bring potato chips and chocolate because they'll be too lazy to cook.

Jeff：OK. For the games，do you think we should give people some small gifts if they win？

Ben：I think that's a great idea！ If we do that，more people will want to play the games.

Jeff：Yes，the games will be more exciting，too.

在前面的听说活动中，教师已经引导学生获取了对话的大意和细节，并总结出对话主要围绕举办聚会的时间、食物、活动展开讨论。教师可以请学生头脑风暴，在举办聚会时还需要考虑哪些细节。有学生提到邀请哪些人、举办的地点、谁来主持等。由此形成了如图 3.9 所示的气泡图。

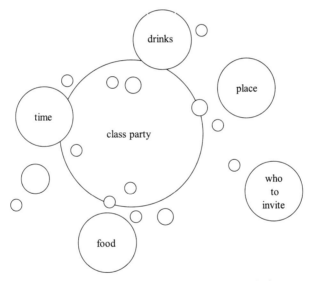

图 3.9　人教版《英语》八年级上册 Unit 10 气泡图

接下来，教师导入情境：元旦即将到来，班级要举行聚会。请同学们分组讨论举办班级聚会的时间、地点、食物、饮料等细节内容。讨论结束后，请小组代表向全班汇报。以下是其中一个小组的汇报内容：

"We decide to hold the party on Friday because it's the last day of the week，so most students and teachers can come. It's going to be a big party. We will ask people to bring food. Snacks are okay，but we hope you can cook some dishes so everyone can taste. We can't drink alcohol，so we will buy some juice and coffee. There will be games for both students and teachers. It will be held in our classroom so everyone can find the place easily. We do hope you can come and enjoy the party！"

通过对真实情境问题的讨论，学生不仅内化了听力材料的语言，还懂得了如何策划班级聚会，培养了解决实际问题的能力。

再以人教版《英语》九年级 Unit 6 When was it invented? Section A 2a – 2c 的听说教学为例。对话中 Carol 向 Alex 描述了三个有趣的发明（包括 shoes with lights，ice-cream scoop，shoes with special heels）。听力文本如下：

Section A，2a，2b

Alex：Hi，Carol. Wow，what are those?

Carol：Hello，Alex. Oh，these are some of the interesting inventions that I'm writing about for my English homework.

Alex：I see…What's that，then?

Carol：They're shoes with lights. You use them for seeing in the dark when you get up at night.

Alex：Oh，that's a cool idea! I always hit my toe on something on the way to the bathroom at night.

Carol：Next is a special ice-cream scoop. This is my favorite invention. It runs on electricity and becomes hot.

Alex：I know what it's for. It's used for serving really cold ice-cream.

Carol：Yes，that's right! The last invention I'm going to write about is shoes with special heels. You can move the heels up and down.

Alex：What are they used for?

Carol：Well，you can change the style of your shoes. You can raise the heels if you are going to a party or lower them if you are just going out for shopping.

教师在处理好听力文本和听后跟读活动以后，可以引导学生形成 problem—invention—usage 的知识框架。在此基础上，教师将学生分成 4 人一组，就生活中遇到的某个问题展开联想和想象，讨论出一种发明来解决这个问题，并向班级汇报。其中一个小组的讨论结果如下：

The invention we're going to talk about is a mini-backpack. When we go to school, we always have to carry a lot of books and papers. That makes our schoolbag large and heavy. It's not good for our health. This mini-backpack is different. It is the size of our largest book. It is made of special materials. It can be used to hold books without getting larger or heavier. And when you want to use the books, you can open the bag and the books are just the same size as before. If we have schoolbags like that, we will love school a lot more.

该小组根据听力内容联想到了自己上学时书包太沉的问题，并通过讨论给出了解决方案，在描述中灵活运用了目标语言 be made of 和 be used for，既锻炼了语言运用能力，又创造性地解决了生活中的问题，培养了想象力和探索精神。

3.2.2　听说教学评价

在英语教学中，"教"是指教师基于英语学科核心素养，组织和实施教与学的活动，实现学科育人目标的过程；"学"是指学生在教师的指导下，参与各种语言学习和实践类活动，将英语学科知识和技能转化为自身核心素养的过程；"评"是指教师依据教学目标来确定评价的内容和标准，通过组织和引导学生完成多样评价活动来检测教与学的效果（教育部，2018）。

《课标（2022 年版）》指出，教学评价对促进学生核心素养的发展发挥着重要的作用。一方面，教学评价能帮助学生不断体验英语学习中的进步和成功，更加全面地认识和发现自我，从而保持和提高学习英语的兴趣和信心；另一方面，评价有助于教师获得教学的反馈，根据学生学情反思自己的教学行为和效果，从而不断提高自己的教学水平和专业能力。因此，评价是教与学中不可或缺的组成部分，对教师的教和学生的学都起着重要作用（蒋京丽，2021）。

在实施教学评价时，《课标（2022 年版）》还给出了具体的原则。其中之一就是以学生核心素养的全面发展为出发点和落脚点。评价的目标和方式要与课程目标相一致，评价的结果要为后续的教学决策提供依据。在本书第 1 章中，我们已经讨论过学业质量标准是检验课程目标达成与否的手段。教师在制定评价标准时，要参考课程标准，根据教学目标和活动的设计，对学生的听说表现进行描述。

以人教版《英语》七年级上册 Unit 1 My name's Gina. 为例。在参考课程内容，依照六要素整合的语言学习要求，参照学业质量水平描述后，该单元的教学目标如下（表 3.18）：

表 3.18　人教版《英语》七年级上册 Unit 1 单元教学目标

序号	质量描述
1 – 1	能听懂"介绍自己和问候他人"的语篇，准确记录说话人的姓和名、电话号码
1 – 2	能根据人物的对话内容，判断说话者的身份和关系
1 – 3	能根据不同的人物关系和交际语境，选择合适的用语打招呼和自我介绍，询问电话号码

在此基础上，教师可以继续细化，将评价标准制定如下，并在单元学习开始时呈现出来（表3.19）：

表3.19 人教版《英语》七年级上册 Unit 1 单元评价标准

- I can note down first names and last names of speakers;
- I can note down the telephone numbers of speakers;
- I can infer the relationship of speakers by listening to their conversation;
- I can greet teachers properly;
- I can greet new friends properly and ask for their telephone numbers;
- I can introduce my first and last name to others;
- I can tell people my telephone number clearly in English;
- I'm not afraid of speaking with strangers and I can make friends quickly by talking to them.

以上标准既包括听的表现、说的能力，还包括了学生在面对交际情境时的情感态度和策略描述。学生可以对照上面的标准，督促自己学习，并检验自己在本单元结束后是否能够达到学习要求，从而反思自己的学习过程和效果。换句话说，当学生知道标准之后，评价就从"检查"变成了"引导"，对教学形成了积极的反拨作用。

关注了课程内容的同时，对学生学习的评价还应该发挥学生的主体作用，评价的方式和手段也应该体现多渠道、多视角、多层次和多方式的特点。将形成性评价与终结性评价相结合、定性评价和定量评价相结合。让评价全面、准确和灵活，促进学生的"学"和教师的"教"（教育部，2022）。

传统的教育评价以"对于学习的评价"（Assessment of Learning）即终结性评价为主。学生往往为了提高成绩而死记硬背、机械练习。这样不仅不能提高语言的综合运用能力，反而会让学生失去学习的兴趣。当前的教育评价强调"建立促进学生全面发展的评价体系"，将"对于学习的评价"（Assessment of Learning）、"为了学习的评价"（Assessment for Learning）和"作为学习的评价"（Assessment as Learning）相结合。"为了学习的评价"主要用于改善教与学，通过提供描述性反馈发挥评价的诊断作用，收集的信息也可以帮助教师改进教学。而"作为学习的评价"是在教学和学习的过程中置入评价，使评价成为学生学习的一部分，强调学生在教师的指导下，监督和评价自己在学习中发挥的作用。在听说教学中，三种评价方式相结合才能够最大限度发挥评价对教与学的促进作用。

1. 对于学习的评价 Assessment of Learning

作为课堂教学的重要组成部分，对于学习的评价通常是指终结性评价或者阶段性评价。这类阶段性评价可以由任课教师自主命题，也可以是与人工智能相结合的考察。

1）教师自主命题

教师在结合学习要求，设计阶段性学习评价内容时，要有以下两个原则：首先是内容与近期所学相关联，尽量做到"学什么，考什么"。在平常的英语考试中，学生普遍有一个感受，就是课本所学和最后考试的内容相距甚远，以至于学生没有学习积极性，认为反正学了也不考，学不学都无所谓。为了让评价真正起到对教与学的促进作用，教师在设计命题内容时，要充分考虑阶段性学习的内容，尽量在话题、语言知识、学习策略等方面与所学内容保持一致。其次，试题的材料要尽可能采用真实的语料，体现真实的语言运用或交际情境，从而帮助学生提高在现实交际场景中运用语言的能力。

以下是参考北京中考英语听说命题要求，设计的八年级下学期期中阶段性听说考试题。内容基于人教版《英语》八年级下册 Unit 1 – 5。

一、听后选择（共 15 分，每小题 1.5 分）

听对话或独白，根据对话或独白的内容，从下面各题所给的 A、B、C 三个选项中选择最佳选项。每段对话或独白你将听两遍。

请听一段对话，完成第 1 至第 2 小题。

1. What's the matter with Peter?

A. He has sore eyes.

B. He has a sore throat.

C. He has a sore back.

2. What's the woman's advice?

A. He should drink enough water.

B. He should lie down and rest.

C. He should drink some hot tea with honey.

第 1 至第 2 题听力原文

W：You don't look well. What's the matter with you，Peter?

M：Well，I talked too much yesterday. And I didn't drink enough water. Now I have a sore throat.

W：That's too bad. Right now，you should drink some hot tea with honey.

M：I guess I should.

【设计意图】以上两道题与课本 Unit 1 What's the matter? 紧密关联。该单元的话题为健康和急救，要求学生能够谈论健康方面的问题和意外，并给出合理的建议。题目 1 考查了说话人 Peter 的身体状况，需要学生识别出 sore throat；题目 2 考查了针对这一健康问题给出的建议，drink some hot tea with honey 出自课本的听力原文。

请听一段对话，完成第 3 至第 4 小题。

3. When is the after-school study program?

A. Two weeks from now.

B. One week from now.

C. One month from now.

4. What could Mary do?

A. She could call up 10 students and ask them to come.

B. She could put up some signs.

C. She could hand out notices after school.

第 3 至第 4 题听力原文

W：Mary, we need to come up with a plan to tell people about the after-school study program.

M：Yeah, but I'm hungry, Peter. Let's have lunch first.

W：No, we need to start now. The program is only one week from now.

M：You're right. So what can we do first?

W：Let's make some notices. I'll hand them out after school. And you could call up 10 students and ask them to come.

M：That's a good idea!

【设计意图】以上听力内容是关于课后学习项目的宣传。这和课本 Unit 2 I'll help to clean up the city parks. 紧密相关。对话中 after-school study program 就来自课本 Section A，1b 的听力材料。其中用到的短语，如 come up with，make some notices，hand sth. out，call up 等都来自课本听力。甚至对话之间的话轮转换和情节变化也是参考 Section A，2a 和 2b 的对话编写的。这样与课本内容高度相关的试题能够让山后农村校学生对学习充满动力、对考试充满信心。

请听一段对话，完成第 5 至第 6 小题。

5. What's wrong with Peter?

A. He can't get on with his family.

B. His parents are giving him too much pressure.

C. He doesn't have free time to do anything he likes.

6. What will Peter do to solve the problem?

A. He will talk to his parents and tell them his feelings.

B. He will do more housework around the house.

C. He will write his parents a letter.

第 5 至第 6 题听力原文

W：You look sad, Peter. What's wrong?

M：Well, I can't get on with my family. My parents are under too much pressure. They fight a lot, and I really don't like it.

W：Why don't you talk to them and tell them how you feel.

M：I did. But it didn't work. Relations between my parents have become difficult.

W：Maybe you should write them a letter. They'll take it serious.

M：I don't think so. I'm not good at writing letters.

W：Hey, I know. Maybe you could do more jobs around the house so that they have more time for proper communication.

M：You're right. I'll do it. Thanks for the good advice, Alice.

【设计意图】 以上听力材料为对话语篇，其中 Peter 因为父母经常吵架而不开心，另一人给 Peter 提出了几条建议，最终 Peter 决定在家多做家务，让父母有时间沟通。这一话题对应的是课本 Unit 4 Why don't you talk to your parents? 本单元主要是谈论问题，并给出建议。题目 1 考查了 Peter 面临的问题，题目 2 考查了 Peter 最终采纳的建议。该对话改编自课本 Section A，2a 和 2b 的听力以及 Section B，3a 的阅读（如下）。这样的命题不仅有效考查了所学语言点，巩固了课本所学的目标语言，还能让学生重视平时和课本知识的学习，体现了教考结合。

Section A，2a—2b

Boy 1：Hey, Peter, what's wrong?

Boy 2：I had a fight with my best friend. What should I do?

Boy 1：Well, you could write him a letter.

Boy 2：I don't think so, although it's a good idea. I'm just not very good at writing letters.

Boy 1：Maybe you should call him up.

Boy 2：No, I don't want to talk about it on the phone.

Boy 1：But you really should talk to him so that you can say you're sorry.

Boy 2：Yes, I know I should, but it's not easy.

Boy 1：Maybe you could go to his house.

Boy 2：I guess I should, but I don't want to surprise him.

Boy 1：Hey, I know. You could take him to the ball game.

Boy 2：But the ball game is next week. I don't want to wait until then to talk to him.

Section B, 3a

Dear Mr. Hunt,

My problem is that I can't get on with family. Relations between my parents have become difficult. They fight a lot, and I really don't like it. It's the only communication they have. I don't know if I should say anything to them about this. When they argue, it's like a big, black cloud hanging over our home. Also, my elder brother is not very nice to me. He always refuses to let me watch my favorite TV show. Instead he watches whatever he wants until late at night. I don't think this is fair. At home I always feel lonely and nervous. Is that normal? What can I do?

Sad and Thirteen

Dear Sad and Thirteen,

It's not easy being your age, and it's normal to have these feelings. Why don't you talk about these feeling with your family? If your parents are having problems, you should offer to help. Maybe you could do more jobs around the house so that they have more time for proper communication. Secondly, why don't you sit down and communicate with your brother? You should explain that you don't mind him watching TV all the time. However, he should let you watch your favorite show. I hope things will be better for you soon.

Robert Hunt

请听一段对话，完成第7至第8小题。

7. What do we know about Mr. Scott's son?

A. He always come home late.

B. He is only about one month old.

C. He drinks milk and smokes.

8. What is the relationship between the two speakers?

A. Old friends.

B. Family friends.

C. Husband and wife.

第 7 至第 8 题听力原文

W：I had no idea you had a son, Scott.

M：Oh, he is perfect. He never comes home late.

W：And he doesn't hang out with bad friends?

M：Not at all. In fact, he spends all of his time with his mother and me.

W：And he doesn't drink or smoke either?

M：No. His favorite drink is milk and he's never smoked in his life.

W：Well, that's amazing. How old is he? He sounds like a mature young man.

M：He'll be one month old this Friday!

【设计意图】以上对话语篇改编自二十一世纪学生英文报·初一第 732 期 Reading Fun 栏目的文章 Best son in the world。对话中男士吹嘘自己有一个完美的儿子——他不和坏朋友出去玩,从不夜不归宿,从不抽烟喝酒——最后男子才说出他的儿子这周五满月。该对话与课本 Unit 3 Could you please clean your room? 单元话题相关。这一单元的内容是关于子女征求父母同意做某事,如 go out for dinner, stay out late, 以及 get a ride 等。同时,该对话作为一则笑话,能使原本测试的气氛变得轻松,让学生在听英语的同时享受听懂英语带来的乐趣,从而感受到学英语的成就感。

请听一段独白,完成第 9 至第 10 小题。

9. What is TRUE according to the speech?

A. The panda train started to run on March 8th.

B. Passengers can order Sichuan food on the train.

C. Workers will give panda toys to passengers.

10. Why does the speaker give this speech?

A. To give information about the panda train for panda fans.

B. To describe the service on the panda train.

C. To attract people to Sichuan.

第 9 至第 10 题听力原文

Good news for panda fans！China's first panda-themed tourist train started to run on March 28th. The train runs from Chengdu in Sichuan to Zunyi in Guizhou. It has giant panda pictures inside and outside. Passengers can try a panda-shaped cake. Workers who carry panda toys will welcome them. The train also has great service. It has a dining room，dance hall，and mahjong room. In the dining room，people can order Sichuan food. With 12 cars，the train can take 252 passengers. Two or three passengers share one room with a washroom. They can enjoy a three-day trip on the train.

【设计意图】 以上独白语篇同样改编自二十一世纪学生英文报・初一第 732 期 Magic World 栏目文章 *What is the panda train*？。改编后的听力材料符合学生当前的知识能力和认知水平，同时紧扣当前时事，开阔了学生的视野。题目 9 考查了独白内容的细节，题目 10 考查的是说话人的发言目的。两道题目的命题从听细节到听意图，对学生的听力理解能力提出了要求。类似这样课本外的真实语料能激发学生学英语的兴趣，培养学生在真实情境中理解语言的能力。

What is the panda train？

Good news for panda fans！China's first panda-themed tourist train（熊猫专列）started to run on March 28.

The train runs from Chengdu in Sichuan to Zunyi in Guizhou. It has giant panda pictures inside and outside. Passengers（乘客）can try a panda-shaped cake. Workers who carry panda toys will welcome them.

The train also has great service. People call it a "mobile（移动的）star hotel". It has a dining room，bar（酒吧），karaoke room，dance hall，and mahjong room. People from Sichuan are known for their love of mahjong. In the dining room，passengers can order Sichuan food.

With 12 cars，the train can take 252 passengers. Two or three passengers share one room with a washroom. They can take a shower on the train. The train also has a smart service system（系统），long tables for enjoying scenery，5G internet，and a song-ordering service.

Passengers can enjoy a three-day trip on the train. After arriving，they will visit tourist sites（景点）in Guizhou，such as the Site of the Zunyi Conference.

If the train does well，it might travel to other parts of the country，according to a local railway company（当地的铁路公司）.

二、听后回答（共 10 分，每小题 2 分）

听对话，根据对话内容笔头回答问题。每段对话你将听两遍。

请听一段对话，完成第 11 小题。

11. How often does Jim work in the old people's home?

第 11 题听力原文

W：Hi，Jim. I heard you're working in an old people's home.

M：Yes. I volunteer there once a week，and help out with things like reading the newspaper to the old people.

【设计意图】本题考查了 How often 引导的特殊疑问句及其回答。Jim 谈到自己在老人院做志愿者，一周去一次，给老人们读报纸。这一话题内容来自课本 Unit 2 I'll help to clean up the city parks. 该单元的主题是提供帮助（offer help），其中 Section A 2d 对话就谈到了去老人院做志愿者、给老人读报纸的情节。课本原文如下：

Helen：Hi，Tom. I'm making some plans to work in an old people's home this summer.

Tom：Really? I did that last summer!

Helen：Oh，what did they ask you to help out with?

Tom：Mm… things like reading the newspaper to the old people，or just talking to them. They told me stories about the past and how things used to be.

Helen：That sounds interesting.

Tom：Yeah，a lot of old people are lonely. We should listen to them and care for them.

Helen：You're right. I mean，we're all going to be old one day，too.

请听一段对话，完成第 12 小题。

12. What was Tom doing when the sandstorm came?

第 12 题听力原文

W：A big sandstorm hit Beijing yesterday evening. What were you doing when the sandstorm came, Tom? Were you reading books?

M：No, I wasn't. I was shopping with my mom.

【设计意图】本题考查的是人物行为，需要用过去进行时态来回答。这与 Unit 5 What were you doing when the rainstorm came? 话题密切相关，知识点也完全契合。充分体现了"学什么考什么"的原则，也能够检测学生是否能够熟练听懂和运用过去进行时。

请听一段对话，完成第 13 小题。

13. Why can't the girl stay out late?

第 13 题听力原文

W：Dad, could I go out for dinner with my friends tonight?

M：Sure. But don't stay out late.

W：Could I stay out until eleven? We might get something to drink after the movie.

M：No, you can't. You have a basketball game tomorrow, remember?

W：Oh, OK. No problem.

【设计意图】这道题考查了 why 引导的特殊疑问句，需要学生听出女孩不能晚归的原因。对话内容是女孩征求爸爸的意见，问能不能出去和朋友玩并晚点回家。这与 Unit 3 Could you please clean your room? 单元话题征求同意（ask for permission）是一致的。同时对话也基本改编自 Section A 2a 和 2b 的听力材料。以下是课本听力原文：

Peter：Hey, Dad?

Dad：Yes?

Peter：Could I go out for dinner with my friends tonight?

Dad：Sure, that should be OK.

Peter：Could I go to the movies after that? My friends said the new action movie is really good.

Dad：I guess so. But don't stay out late.

Peter：Could I stay out until eleven? We might get something to drink after the movie.

Dad：No, you can't. You have a basketball game tomorrow, remember? You need to have a good rest.

Peter：Oh, yeah. Well, could you give me a ride to town now? If I take the bus, I'll be late.

Dad：I can't, Peter. I have to do some work now.

Peter：Oh, OK. No problem. I'll call Alan. Maybe his dad can give me a ride.

请听一段对话，完成第 14 小题。

14. Where did the man work during the 2008 Olympic Games?

第 14 题听力原文

W：I want to be a volunteer at the 2022 Winter Olympic Games.

M：Really? I've been a volunteer at the 2008 Olympic Games.

W：What did you do then?

M：I went up to strangers on the street and taught them English.

【设计意图】这道题考查了 where 引导的特殊疑问句，需要学生听出地点 on the street。对话中两人讨论了做志愿者的事情，扣紧了课本 Unit 2 I'll help to clean up the city parks. 单元话题提供帮助（offer help）。同时，对话中 2022 年冬奥会也紧跟时事，将课本话题和内容延伸到课外，发散了学生的思维，提高了学生的语言运用能力。

请听一段对话，完成第 15 小题。

15. What is the school "Clear Your Plate" campaign for?

第 15 题听力原文

W：Hi Peter, what are you doing?

M：I'm putting up notices for the school "Clear Your Plate" campaign.

W：That sounds interesting. What is it for?

M：We want to ask students to help save food.

【设计意图】这道题考查的是目的意图，即"光盘行动"的目的是什么。对话中用到的 put up notices 来自课本 Unit 2 I'll help to clean up the city parks. 单元目标语言。同时，"光盘行动"（"Clean Your Plate" campaign）紧跟时事，联系了生活实际，能够帮助学生将所学内容与真实生活相连接。

三、听短文，记录关键信息（共 5 分，每小题 1 分）

How to Remember Names

Some common ways	• Write the name down as soon as possible. • Repeat the person's name loud at least three times 16. _____ you talk together. 　■ For example, 17. _____ of saying "Where do you live?" you can say "Where do you live, Jack?" • Introduce the person by name to someone else right away.
Some 18. _____ ways	• Think of a story using the person's name. • Think of a rhyme（押韵）for the person's name. 　■ For example, think to yourself, "Jack has a nice jacket." to ____ 19 ____ Jack in a nice jacket.
Remembering names takes work and 20. _____ .	

听后记录听力原文

Does this ever happen to you? Someone introduces you to a friend, you hear his or her name, and then two minutes later, you forget it. Or you go to the same restaurant every day and the owner always says "Hello" to you but you can never remember her name. If this happens, you are typical—actually most people have the problem remembering names.

Here are some common ways that can help people remember names.

• Write the name down（with a little information about the person）as soon as possible.

• Repeat the person's name loud at least three times **while** you talk together. For example, **instead** of saying "Nice to meet you." say "Nice to meet you, Jack（or Sue or whatever the person's name is）." Instead of saying "Where do you live?" you can say "Where do you live, Jack?"

• Introduce the person by name to someone else right away.

There are other ways which may seem a little **strange**. However, try them.

 ● Think of a story using the person's name. For example, think to yourself, "Jack has a nice jacket." to **imagine** Jack in a nice jacket.

 ● Think of a rhyme（押韵）for the person's name. For example, think to yourself, "Jack would look nice in black." Imagine Jack wearing black clothes.

All these ways have one thing in common. You must pay attention to the people you meet. You can't just meet someone, nod your head, say hello, and walk away. Remembering names takes work and **practice**.

【设计意图】以上独白改编自外文期刊，内容是一些有助于记住别人名字的办法。所考查的词汇包括 while, instead, strange, imagine 和 practice。其中单词 while 出自课本第三单元，imagine 出自课本第二单元，instead 出自第四单元，strange 出自第五单元，practice 是学生之前就掌握的。这道题考查了学生听并记录的能力，尤其是对所学词汇听辨和拼写的考查，能够对学生背记课本词汇起到一定的激励作用。

四、短文朗读。（共 8 分）

现在，你有 90 秒钟的时间浏览短文并做录音准备。

I woke up at 6：30 a. m. yesterday. While I was making my breakfast, my sister was listening to the radio. As I was eating, the radio news talked about a car accident near our home. My sister and I went out right away to have a look. When we got to the place of the accident, the car was in bad shape from hitting a tree. But luckily, the driver was fine. The roads were icy because of the heavy snow from the night before. What were you doing when the accident happened?

下面请准备录音。听到录音提示音后，在 2 分钟内完成朗读。

【设计意图】上面的短文朗读语篇改编自课本 Unit 5 Section A, 4b 的短文填空语段。该文段意义结构完整，句式比较丰富，长句和短句相结合，有特殊疑问句、转折等语言现象，能够有效考查学生的语音、语调、重音、连读、不完全爆破、意群停顿、流畅度等，同样体现了学考结合。

从以上案例可以看出，当教师进行自主命题以考查学生的听说能力时，一方面应该以课本话题为线索，以课本语言知识为内容，适当对课本听力和阅读语篇进行改编，这样既可以考查学生阶段所学，促使学生在平时的课堂学习中积极参与，还能对教师的教给出有价值的反馈。另一方面，教师可以围绕课本话题，选取符合学生认知特点和语言学习能力的真实语料，拓宽学生的视野，帮助学生提高在真实交际中的综合语言运用能力。

2）人工智能测评

鉴于中考听说机考的形式，在平时的阶段性测试中，也不免采用自动化测试软件对学生进行听说测评。采用机考的方式不仅能让学生提前熟悉中考听说的形式，避免考试焦虑，而且能够提高听说考试的工作效率，为教师和学生提供明确的量化依据。在需要的情况下，可以生成校级、班级和学生个人的测试评估报告，帮助教师和学生清楚地了解、分析测试结果，从而调整教和学的策略，发挥评价对英语教学的导向作用。

以山后某校初三年级的一次机考为例。这次听说考试旨在检测学生在听和说方面的能力，其中听的能力要求包括：①能获取事实性具体信息。②能根据所获取的信息进行简单推断。③能理解说话者的意图、观点和态度。④能理解所听语段的主旨要义。⑤能针对所听语段的内容记录简单信息。说的能力要求包括：①能与他人交流所听语段中的关键信息。②能传达所听语段中的相关信息。③能运用所学语音知识完成朗读。④能在口头表达中进行适当的自我修正。⑤能在口语表达中做到语音准确、语调自然、节奏适中。

某测试机构在考试结束后很快为学校提供了成绩分析报告，内容包括成绩分析和典型分析及教学建议。在成绩分析部分，报告给出了全校分数概况、各题型答题分析、各分段人数分布图、各班平均分对比以及各班高分段人数比例分布情况。在典型分析及教学建议部分，报告给出了各小题的平均得分率，针对各题型的典型问题进行了分析并给出了建议。

以各题型得分情况为例，报告显示听后选择题得分率最高，为82.5%，听后记录题得分率最低，仅有44.00%。

在听后选择题中，第7和第8小题的平均分较低。其中，第7小题是综合推断题。学生需要根据所听内容归纳主旨，结合上下文"The new hospital was the first opened for women and children."和"set up the first medical school for women"推断她为妇女的医学教育做了很多贡献（She did a lot for the medical education for women.）。第8小题是主旨要义题，题目问 Why does the speaker give this talk？要求学生能够根据关键信息"invite you to write an article"判断出说话的意图。

在听后回答题中，第13小题平均分最低。报告显示138人作答后只有76人得到满分，主要原因在于学生没有捕捉到关键信息或者答非所问。建议教师一方面向学生进行考点的阐释，如对关键信息的捕捉技巧；另一方面安排练习，关注教材中给出问题的形式，并在课堂中进行讨论。

学生在做听后记录题型中，出现了单词拼写错误、单词形式错误的现象。主要原因在于：①听清并理解答案但单词没写对，或者写对了基础单词却错了形式；②没听清也不理解答案单词是什么，误写其他单词。例如将 characters 写为 charactors，将 prepared 写为 prepare 等。还有学生记不住内容、抓不到或抓错关键信息，或填错信息位置等。建议教师在词汇教学中关注学生的发音是否准确，帮助学生根据发音正确拼写单词，并教授学生记忆单词的策略和技巧。学生在做题时要充分理解表格信息，关注留空部分所在的句子或者短语，利用题干定位法定位答案。

在听后转述题型中，报告显示学生的主要问题在于转述时要点信息未抓取到，出现原文中没有的信息，单词发音不标准，时态、人称和数有问题，出现卡顿、上下文意思不连贯等。建议教师要加强答题的策略指导，在平时听说练习中教会学生通过关键词来把握故事情节。学生在平时叙述前应将短文流畅地叙述一遍，如果遇到不会组织的地方，不宜停顿太久，应该立刻用自己最熟悉、最有把握的句型把要点说出来。叙述时保证全篇人称、时态、数要一致。

在短文朗读题型中，学生的作答比较理想，但也存在有学生声音太小、发音不标准、不清楚、朗读没有节奏的情况。建议教师预留一定的课堂时间进行基础的音标教学，规范学生的作答习惯，多做跟读和朗读。学生在平时训练时应积累自己容易读错的单词，并找出错误类型，如加音、吞音、辅音不到位、元音不饱满等问题；注意划分节奏，实词重读、虚词弱读、划分意群、适当停顿。

有了以上量化分析的数据和质性分析的建议，教师在后期的听说教学中就更有针对性，学生在日常的听说训练中也更有方向性。但自动化测试软件虽然能够作为初中英语日常教学的辅助手段，为学生的英语学习提供过程性评价，也有其局限性。比如，在对听后回答第 13 小题的失分原因分析时，报告显示是因为学生没有捕捉到关键信息或者答非所问。原题如下：

题目：Where are the speakers?

听力原文：

M：Amy，what do you think of this painting?

W：Well，to be honest，I don't understand what the artist is expressing.

M：Me neither. It seems strange that a sad man is holding a red hat.

W：Perhaps the man needs to cheer himself up，I guess.

M：Maybe. Well，let's move on to other works of art.

但报告给出的只是表面原因，究其根本，是学生对艺术类话题的词汇和背景知识储备量少，没有理解对话内容。因此，教师再度分析考试结果后，可以适当补充艺术类话题的语料，帮助学生熟悉相关词汇，如 artist，works of art，gallery， museum 等，从而帮助学生克服学习中的难点。

另外，虽然听力部分的测评由机器完成比人工阅卷更准确、客观和便捷，口语部分的测评却相对复杂。每个人的发音音质不同，差异较大，即便是同一个人在不同时间或环境下的发音也会有所差别。再考虑到表达时语速、音调、音量等音素，测评的答案就不能唯一了。而人机对话测评口语是基于逻辑分析的模糊测评，评分大数据上相对公平公正，个体上可能会有差别（蒋京丽，2019）。例如教师在回听学生的朗读录音时发现，有些学生在读错之后，又将句中这个单词用正确的发音重读了一遍，然而依然被扣分。

综上所述，在利用人工智能进行英语听说教学评价时，教师要用好语言测试提供的分析反馈，发挥该评价对教学的积极反拨作用。同时对于口语测评部分针对学生问题进行个性化的质性分析，采取各种措施，促进英语听说训练，全面提高学生的听说能力。

2. 为了学习的评价 Assessment for Learning

《课标（2022 年版）》要求教学评价将形成性评价与终结性评价相结合。为了学习的评价通常强调的是过程性评价。在教学过程中，教师应该把握即时评价具体化、评价渠道多样化、评价内容立体化、评价主体多元化的原则。

1）即时评价具体化

所谓即时评价，指的是教师在课堂教学时，当场给学生作出的口头评价；或者在批阅学生的听说作业时，即时给出的点评。这类即时点评对于培养学生即兴口头表达能力、提升学生的课堂参与度起着关键作用。但往往教师在点评时给出的是 Good!，Well done!，Nice try!，Great!，Wonderful! 等模糊的评论。这样的评论千篇一律，无法对学生起到积极的引导作用。教师要提供一些具体的指导意见，例如具体好在哪里，从而准确反映学生的课堂表现，创造出更好的教学效果。教师可以参考"lifeboat 评价法"（周培蓓，2021）。"lifeboat 评价法"包含Loudness（音量）、Intonation（语调）、Fluency（流畅度）、Emotion/Energy（情感/能量）、Body Language（肢体语言）、Orientation（互动定向）、Articulation（发音）、Trust（信心）共 8 个方面。具体的评价语言见表 3.20。

表 3.20　Lifeboat 评价法

Loudness	• You speak loudly. That's great! • I can hear you well. I think everyone can hear you well. • You can make yourself heard. • If you can speak louder next time, I think that will be better. • It's good to make yourself heard. But if you can raise your voice a little bit, I think I can hear you in a more comfortable way. That would be perfect!

续表

Intonation	• You speak good English. • You have very good pronunciation and intonation. • You sound like a native speaker.
Fluency	• You speak very fluently. • You give a smooth speech. • You sound like a native speaker. • You speak too fast. I find it a little hard to catch you. • If you can slow down a little bit, that would be better.
Emotion/Energy	• You can speak with emotion. • I am attracted to your speech. • Your speech is full of energy and passion. • Your show needs more energy and passion.
Body Language	• You use some gestures when you talk. • You use good/proper body language. • Your body language helps to express your meaning.
Orientation	• You look at the audience in the eye. • It's great for you to interact with your audience with questions. • The quiz/activity/game after your show improves the interactions. • The story connects the audience well. • The... helps us better understand your show.
Articulation	• You speak very clearly. I can understand you well. • You can express your ideas in a clear way. It's easy to follow and understand. • Some of the words in your show do not sound good, for example... (You'd better pay more attention to the word.) • I can't quite understand what you expressed. I think your pronunciation needs to be improved. (I suggest that you should get more chances to listen, speak and practice.)
Trust	• You speak confidently. • You really trust yourself. • You are an open and brave speaker. • You know how to get rid of the stage fright, you did a good job. • You've tried your best to present in a natural way, and you made it. • You stayed calm even when meeting something unforeseen in the middle of the speech. You are something!

以上评价方法能够帮助教师从不同角度和层次对学生的发言给出即时的反馈，同时语言丰富、内容精准的评价，能够对学生口头的表达起到积极的引导作

用。当然，教师可以结合具体的任务选择其中几个评价的维度。例如，在学生口头回答问题时，教师可以就 loudness，fluency 和 articulation 等给出点评。在学生进行口头演讲时，则可以加入更多维度。

2）评价渠道多样化

《课标（2022 年版）》指出，教学评价应该体现多渠道的特点。多元智能理论也启示我们，应通过多样的活动发展学生在不同智能领域的能力。只有设计不同的评价活动，学生才会有更多发展的可能，才能看到自己的亮点，在英语学习中充满获得感。因此，教师在日常的听说教学中，应该从多种渠道评价学生的听说表现。

（1）口头自我介绍。

以起始年级为例，在开学第一节课中，教师不仅可以介绍课程内容、初中三年的学习计划、课堂要求等，还可以请学生自制 Name Tent，包含以下内容（表3.21）：

表3.21　自我介绍活动1

- Write your name in the middle and draw a picture around it.
①Write one goal you wish to accomplish.
②Write two subjects you like.
③Write three words that describe you.
④Write four activities you like to do in your free time.

学生准备好后，利用每节课前 10 分钟，请学生做口头自我介绍。上台的学生在介绍的同时，台下的学生要填写表 3.22，完成记录：

表3.22　自我介绍活动2

My Classmates				
Name	1 goal he/she sets	2 subjects he/she likes	3 words to describe him/her	4 activities he/she likes to do

当全班同学都完成介绍后，教师请学生写一篇短文，介绍自己的班级和同学。

在上面的活动中，学生经过课下的准备，能够就自己的目标、喜爱的学科、性格特点、兴趣爱好进行发言，做到有话可说。当台上的学生在说的时候，台下的学生边听边记录，将听的内容落实到笔头。最后的习作更是将听说落实到写上，全方位提高了学生的听说能力。

（2）真实的口语活动。

对于高年级学生或者以上自我介绍活动完成后，教师还可以利用课前 3～5 分钟时间，请学生口头演讲。演讲的内容可以是结合单元主题的，也可以是关于学生兴趣爱好的，比如"我最喜欢的……"。以下是部分学生的演讲稿：

①My favorite song.

Nowadays, music plays an important role in our daily life. Today I'd like to share my favorite song to you.

My favorite song is *Gold Steps*, which is sang by Neck Deep. They are a rock band and I like them very much. I prefer some loud rock music to cheer me up when I'm down. This music also have cheerful lyrics and exciting rhythm. When I first listened to it, I've been love it very much. It is a song to encourage people when they are in a hard time. If you want to give up, this song may help you pick up yourself and go on, believe the hope is up ahead.

At last, I recommend you to listen this song. If you want to get some energy to face the difficulties in life, then you may like this song.

②My favorite music.

My favorite piece of music is *You Can Be What You Want to Be*, a song written by famous rapper Jiang Yunsheng.

The song is about people who fight hard even though they are poor. It tells us that whatever your situation is, you have to make an effort. The process may be difficult, but the result is always brilliant. This rap is different from the others, while most raps are loud and rhythmic. But this one is mild and full of warmth. When I am low, I listen to the music and get inspired by it. I used to be down and sad for weeks only because of a really small problem, but after I listen to this song, my heart released. Then I realize that my problems are less serious and feel more better. I'm even more optimistic and composed when I'm in the face of crisis!

As the saying goes, music is the medicine of the breaking heart. I'd like to recommend this song to you, it doesn't matter whether you like raps or not, this is a great one to have a try. People of any age can listen and enjoy. Now go and feel the moving music, I am sure you'll like it!

③My favorite movie.

Today I'm going to recommend my favorite movie to you, which called *The Intern*.

The movie attracted me by its special main character Ben—one old man in his seventies. I had always thought that the main characters of the film would not be this age group, because the moment the audience see them, they seem to conclude that the film is very boring. But after watching this movie, my ideas was completely changed.

What can people do when they are old? I guess many people's answer will be "nothing". But Ben proved that this view is totally wrong. Ben has a successful career as the vice president of a famous printing company. In our mind, most old people are slow, stubborn, boring and conservative, but Ben is totally different. He has clear eyes and he goes out to exercise or goes to the Starbucks to have a cup of coffee and read newspapers every morning. After retirement, he is still passionate about life. He travels around the world, plays golf, reads books, goes to the movies, and even learns Chinese. So I guess that's why when he saw an advertisement for a senior intern at a new e-commerce company, he signed up for an interview at the next moment. Because he still wants to use his waste heat.

I didn't think he could adapt to the job at first because he was very different from others. However, he is considerate, polite and sociable at work. And his years of experience in the workplace allows him to give advice to the boss. Surprisingly, but also like a matter of course, he did his work pretty well. So I think what I like about this movie is that it changes our stereotypes about old people. Ben is good at observation, modest, humorous. He will never use his age as an excuse, but tries his best to make up for his lack of learning ability with his own experience. It can be said that Ben is a representative of maturity.

Why I recommend this movie to you guys is because that I hope you can all learn to be a person who will be still curious about the world and keeps expanding his width in his limited life, just like Ben. The population of our country is getting older and maybe one day older people will enter the workplace again. However, I think if we can do as Ben does, regardless of age, full of passion for life all the time, maybe aging is not so terrible. If we see the streets full of old people walking confidently under the sun, we probably would not think they are old. Just as the introduction of the movie said, experiences never gets old.

一方面，这样的演讲活动能为具备不同智能的学生提供展示的舞台。比如有一位学生在分享自己最爱的歌曲时，甚至带来了自己的吉他，边弹边唱，收获了班级同学的热烈掌声。另一方面，这类活动也能让不同语言水平的学生都得到锻炼和发展。上面的三篇演讲稿出自同一个班级的学生在同一时期的创作，但三篇文章无论是从词汇和句式的丰富度，还是内容和思想的深度来说，都是一篇更比一篇强。在现场演讲时，学生更是表现出了自己不同的口语水平。但通过演讲和分享，每一位学生都在说英语时更自信了，学习英语的动力也更强了。

（3）小组合作展示。

教师还可以将英语听说学习融入课堂活动之中，即 team based learning（团队学习）。在团队协作中，学生不仅要就内容进行意义的协商、对材料进行检索和阅读，还能够锻炼人际交往和团队合作能力。

以人教版《英语》八年级 Unit 2 How often do you exercise? 单元为例。本单元的话题是谈论做事的频率（talk about how often you do things）。教师请学生 5 人一组，自选内容（如看电影、锻炼、阅读等），对班级同学进行问卷调查，并根据调查结果制作 PPT，在课堂上进行汇报。以下是选择了"饮食习惯"作为调查内容的小组所作的汇报：

Hi, boys and girls! The topic of our group's speech is about "Class 4 Grade 8 Students' Eating Habits". And the leader of our group is Zhang Yutong. Team members are Chu Wenyan, Xu Jingen, Wu Qingyuan and Li Mingxi. So here's our talk.

Last week we asked our students about their eating habits. Our question were about breakfast, snacks and fast food. Here are the results.

We found that only thirty five percent of our students eat breakfast a few times a week. Sixty five percent eat breakfast every day. And no one hardly ever eat breakfast.

We probably know that today many students like snack more than the meal. But luckily, there is only thirty percent of our students eat snack every day. Forty percent have it only 1 - 3 times a week. And twenty-five percent hardly ever touch the snack. Only Mr. Bowen Xing (five percent) in our class eats snack nearly before every the meal and all year round. So he is strong and big.

The answers to our question about eating fast food were also interesting. Only five percent of student never eat junk food. Fifteen percent eat junk food one to three times a week. Seventy percent eat junk food three to five times a week! And ten percent eat junk food every day! It's a serious problem. But according to our results, we found a worse problem. You know what is fast food actually appeared in the school canteen! Many of our students paid for it. We asked to our classmates, if it's good or bad. Sixty percent students said "No, it's not good for us." But the remaining 40 percent said "yes I do". You surely have seen the long queue（队伍）in front of the "fast food way". Although the fast food is delicious, don't forget they are expensive and make your fat. So start to stop providing fast food. As we can, eat less of them.

Based on this survey, we can see that most of the students are in good physical and mental health. But I still want to make some suggestions there. Although snacks and junk food can make us feel full quickly, the best way to solve hunger is to eat a regular meal. Eating regular meals will help us balance our nutrition and avoid symptoms such as obesity. But remember "Habits are not formed in a day", so start to develop good eating habits before it's too late!

在以上口头汇报中，学生分工明确，每人汇报调查结果的一项内容；同时在汇报的最后，针对调查的问题给出了合理的建议；在准备演讲稿和制作 PPT 的过程中，学生将口头表达的内容落实到写，其信息技术能力也得到增强。可以说，这类活动不仅能够锻炼学生的听说能力，更全面发展了学生的综合素养。

3）评价内容立体化

多元评价，不只是通过不同活动评价学生表现，还应该在活动中将评价的内容立体化，即从不同角度评价学生表现。

以学生角色扮演课本对话为例，教师可以准备以下评价量表（表 3.23）checklist 供学生参照。分析学生学习量表后就会发现，在进行角色扮演时，不仅要注重自己的发音是否正确，语调是否自然，还需要保证内容的完整性以及角色扮演时的表现力。这就使得角色扮演不再是机械的模仿和操练，学生需要理解对话内容，体会角色形象，才能演得绘声绘色。

表 3.23　角色扮演评价量表

	Category	Stars
Pronunciation	Do they get the pronunciation right?	☆ ☆ ☆ ☆ ☆
Intonation	Do they get the right intonation?	☆ ☆ ☆ ☆ ☆
Content	Do they read without missing any information?	☆ ☆ ☆ ☆ ☆
Performance	Do they act like the roles they play?	☆ ☆ ☆ ☆ ☆
	Total	

课堂展示是一项能在真实任务中发展学生英语沟通技能的活动。不仅如此，课堂展示还能锻炼学生的胆量，帮助学生为未来的教育和职业生活做准备。在以往评价学生课堂展示时，教师往往着重于学生的口头表达准确性，以至于一些语言水平不高的学生得不到鼓励。为了发展学生的综合素质，也为了鼓励更多学生开口说英语，教师可以在评价时加入除语言技能外的其他评价维度，如流利度、肢体语言、内容、视觉支持等。具体可以参考表 3.24。

表 3.24 课堂展示评价量表

Category	Excellent 3	Good 2	Needs improvement 1	Score
Pronunciation	Clear pronunciation and intonation with few errors	Some word pronunciation errors but can be understood	Many word pronunciation errors and can't be understood	
Fluency	The presenter communicates directly with the audience without reading from prepared notes	The presenter refers to written notes sometimes but is generally communicative	The presenter read from ppt or prepared notes without communicating with the audience	
Content	Great ideas with many supporting details	Well-structured content but needs some more examples	The content is not relevant enough and little evidence is provided	
Body Language	Excellent physical presence and effective body language	The presenter used some body language to communicate	Little use of eye contact or body language	
Visual Props	The ppt is well-designed and helpful to the presentation	Some photos and slides are not clear enough	Uses no slides or photos to help the presentation	

　　教师还可以根据任务的具体内容对评价量表进行定制。以人教版《英语》九年级 Unit 6 When was it invented? Section A，2a - 2c 的听说教学为例。在听力活动后，教师请学生就生活中遇到的问题和困难展开联想和想象，讨论出一种发明来解决这个问题，制作海报，并向班级汇报。此时教师在提供学生评价量表时，除了考虑发音准确性、语言流畅度、肢体语言等外，还可以加入创意维度，即对该发明的创意程度进行评价；加入海报维度，即海报是否能够展示出该发明的用途。

　　从不同角度评价学生在某一活动中的表现能够将学生从唯知识的传统学习思路中解放出来。加入了内容、主题、思维、信息技术等综合视角后，评价能够引导学生更多关注意义的表达、思维的碰撞和技能的提升，从而真正"用英语做事情"，提高交际能力，发展核心素养。

　　4）评价主体多元化

　　在以往的听说教学中，评价的主体往往是教师或者测评软件。《课标（2022年版)》指出，教学评价应该充分发挥出学生的主体作用。为了提高学生学习的积极性和目标达成度，教师可以多元化评价的主体，引入学生自评、同伴互评和小组互评等。

以学生自评为例，教师可以请学生在演讲后，完成以下自评表（表3.25）。

表 3.25　学生自评表

Speaking Self-Assessment Checklist Name：　　　　　　　　　　　　　　　　　　Date：			
Category	Always	Sometimes	Not yet
I looked at the audience.			
I spoke with good volume.			
I spoke clearly with expression.			
I stayed on the topic.			
I spoke at a good pace（not too fast or too slow）			
I was really good at			
I had difficulty with			
Next time，I'm going to try to improve			

在表3.25中，评价的项目以"I"为主语，能让学生在评价时切身关注到自己的表现，体现了以学生为主体的原则。评价的维度从观众互动、音量、清晰度、聚焦话题、语速等方面考量。这里教师可以参考句式，加入其他维度，如 I did well in pronunciation. 或 I used some examples to support my opinion. 等。此外，自评表还请学生自我反思在哪方面做得很好，在哪方面还有困难，以及下一次如何改进。这样的设计能够帮助学生形成主动反思的学习习惯，调动学生学习的内驱力，促进学生的自我监督性学习，从而培养学生的自主学习能力。

除了自评，教师还应该帮助学生开展相互评价。以学生口头演讲为例，教师可以请台下的同学给做演讲的学生评价。评价量表可以参考表3.26。

表3.26　学生互评表

Speaking Peer Assessment Checklist			
Name：　　　　　　　　　　　　　　　　　　　Date： Person presenting：　　　　　　　　　　Topic being presented：			
Category	Never	Sometimes	Always
The presenter made eye contact and tried to engage with the audience.			
The presenter spoke clearly and loudly enough for everyone to hear.			
The presenter spoke at an appropriate pace for the audience to understand.			
The presenter spoke about the topic in detail and showed that they had a clear understanding of the topic.			
One thing I enjoyed from the presentation was：			
One thing that could be improved on was：			

　　在表3.26中，学生首先从演讲者与观众的互动情况、发音是否清楚洪亮、语速是否合适、内容是否充实等方面对同学的表现进行评价。接下来，学生根据自己聆听演讲的感受，思考自己最喜欢同学演讲中的哪一方面，还有哪一个部分可以改进。这样的设计能够帮助学生发现同学的亮点，并发展解决问题的能力。同时，在相互评价中学生不断反思、取长补短，同学之间互相激励、共同发展，提高了课堂的参与度和学生学习的积极性。

　　在小组展示活动中，教师还可以根据需求引入小组自评、组内互评和组间互评。以小组评价为例，评价量表如表3.27所示。

表3.27　小组自评表

Group Self-Assessment Checklist
Name：　　　　　　　　　　　　　　　　　　　Date： Group members：　　　　　　　　　　Topic being presented：
As a team，decide which answer best suits the way your team worked together. Then，complete the remaining sentences.

	Never	Sometimes	Always
We finished our task on time, and we did a good job!			
We encouraged each other and we cooperated with each other.			
We communicated effectively with each other.			
We each shared our ideas, then listened and valued each other's ideas.			
We did best at			
Next time we could improve at			

在表3.27中，学生以小组为单位自评。评价维度包括：是否按时完成任务，是否相互鼓励与合作，是否有效沟通，是否分享、聆听、尊重他人的想法等。这对于发展学生团队协作的能力具有重要意义。此外，量表还引导学生以小组为单位主动反思，在哪些方面做得好、下次在哪方面继续改进。学生在完成量表的过程中一定是经过共同讨论的，这无疑能够促进合作学习，实现学生的共同发展。

组内互评也是一种能引导和促进学生积极参与小组活动的有效手段。以小组讨论为例，教师可以设计如下评价量表（表3.28）。

表3.28　小组成员互评表

Group Peer Assessment Checklist Group member：			Date：		
As a team member, he/she…			Never	Sometimes	Always
has a positive attitude about the task.					
stays focused on the task in group discussions.					
always listens to, shares with, and supports others. Tries to keep everyone working well together.					
provides work of high quality.					

在表3.28中，学生给自己的小组成员做评价，内容包括：对待任务的态度，讨论中是否能专注，是否能互相聆听、分享和支持，完成的工作是否有质量等。有了相互评价，学生在参与小组活动时态度更积极、讨论更专心、任务的完成度也更高。

最后，小组互评对学生的小组展示活动也起着重要的促进作用。教师可以参考以下评价量表（表3.29）。

表 3.29　组间互评表

Group Peer Assessment Checklist	
Group Name：　　　　　　　　　　　　　　　　　　Date：	
Category	Points
All group members participate equally. （4'） All group members participate. （3'） Some group members participate. （2'） Only 1 or 2 group members participate. （1'）	
All group members speak clearly and are easy to understand. （4'） Most group members speak clearly and are easy to understand. （3'） Some group members speak clearly, but are difficult to understand. （2'） Only 1 or 2 group members speak and can be understood. （1'）	
All group members speak to the entire audience. （4'） Most group members speak to the entire audience. （3'） Group members speak to only part of the audience. （2'） Most group members speak only to part of the audience. （1'）	
Information is presented in an organized way. （4'） Information is mostly presented in an organized way. （3'） Information may be only partially organized. （2'） Information is presented in a disorganized way. （1'）	
Oral presentation includes many details. （4'） Oral presentation includes some details. （3'） Oral presentation includes few details. （2'） Oral presentation includes few or no details. （1'）	
Presentation is visually organized and complete. （4'） Presentation is organized and complete. （3'） Presentation is complete. （2'） Presentation is disorganized or incomplete. （1'）	

在表3.29中，学生为其他小组的表现打分，包括：是否全员参与，是否表述清晰，是否面对全体观众，信息是否有组织、演讲是否有细节、展示是否完整有条理等。通过小组间的相互点评，小组成员能够更清楚努力的方向。为了赢得高分，甚至能在发音、表述等方面互帮互助，从而发挥合作学习的作用，让学生共同成长。

在上面的评价中，学生不只是参与者，还是合作者。教师还可以让学生成为各类评价活动的设计者，让学生商议评价标准，自己制定评标。通过参与评价设计、自评、互评等，学生的学习积极性被调动起来，并在相互评价中互相借鉴，总结经验，规划学习。

3. 作为学习的评价 Assessment as Learning

作为学习的评价也是一种形成性评价，它强调对学习的证据进行反思，引导学生通过元认知过程评价自己的学习并进行自我调整。一般情况下，如果学生对自己的学习目标十分明确，其自我评价往往是准确和诚实的。因此，教师要和学生一起讨论学习成果，在学生学习过程中提供反馈和指导性问题，帮助学生设定清晰的学习目标。一旦学生掌握了元认知技能，他们就可以自主调整学习，并表现出自我反思、自我监控和自我调整。在日常的学习中，除了完成老师交代的任务以外，还能从被动学习者变成主动学习者。

最典型的学习评价方式就是档案袋评价（Portfolio），又被称为"学生成长记录袋评价"或"学生学习档案评价"。这是一种通过收集学生在学习过程中的作品和数据，真实全面展示学生学习过程和学习成果的评价方法。它可以反映学生在某一段时间内、某一个方面的技能发展、努力情况和进步情况。在初中英语听说教学中，以下项目可以纳入学生的学习档案。

1）每日朗读录音

在起始年级或者学生听说能力有限时，教师可以请学生按照课程进度，每日在家长监督下朗读课文，并将朗读录音发到微信群。

开始时可以由老师来点评，以人教版《英语》七年级上册 Starter Unit 1 – 3 为例，很多学生认为内容很简单，但朗读起来却还存在一定问题。教师听录音后在群内点评："整体语速很好，发音清晰。注意 quilt 的发音，再听一遍跟读一下哦！"或"录音收到，作业交的很及时，点赞哦！再听一下原文，是 it's pen 还是 it's a pen？"。教师的反馈其实就是对学生进行朗读标准的指导，能够帮助学生理解什么样的朗读是合格的甚至优秀的朗读。

接着，教师将学生的录音按日期命名，放进以学生姓名命名的文件夹。经过一周的练习后，教师请学生回听自己第一天的录音音频，感受自己的进步情况。

经过一个月的练习和点评之后，教师请学生参照老师点评的方式，轮流给同学的朗读或背诵做点评。有学生点评如下："大家好！我是 KK。下面我将从规范性、准确性、流畅性三个角度来点评小组成员的背诵作业，和大家一起进步。A 同学更流畅了，发音也比较标准，比上次好！继续加油！B 同学要注意 thought，write，decision 的发音，其他的都很好！C 同学整体很流畅，语速也很好。只有 2 个单词发得不准，一个是 knocked 敲门，第一个字母 k 不发音哦。还有人物的名字是 Percy Buttons，不是 Bercy。继续加油哦！"从学生的点评中可以看出，他们已经明确了背诵的标准，并能够用这样的标准来指导其他同学的背诵。

本学期结束时，教师可以请学生回听历次的朗读和背诵音频，并写下自己的学习体会。有同学这样写道："听到自己第一次朗读的音频，感觉好丢脸。当时读得又慢还不标准。好在现在知道怎么读对、读好了。我觉得就是要多跟读，然后反复听一下自己的录音，看看跟课本录音有什么差距。老师让我们点评其他同学的背诵作业的时候，一般都要听好几个人的，听着听着就听熟了。我觉得这个过程不仅提高了我的英语口语，还提高了我的听力。当老师的感觉也很棒！"

不只是录音音频，教师还可以利用手机等设备，给学生的演讲展示做记录。例如，教师可以每学期开展一次自我介绍活动并保存学生当堂演讲的视频。当教师告知学生下学期还将请大家做一次自我介绍时，学生学习的目标感会更强，也会有意识地准备下一次演讲内容。以同样一名学生七年级入学时和七年级下学期开学的自我介绍为例：

入学自我介绍：Hi，my name is A. I'm a student. I'm 13 years old. My birthday is April，5th. I like playing the piano and I can cook. My favorite animal is panda because they are cute. Emm…I also like tigers. I think they are cool. My family has 3 people，my father，my mother and I. Do you want to be my friend?

七年级下学期自我介绍：Hi everyone，my name is A. I'm a 13 - year-old student. I'm from Beijing. It's a beautiful city. In my free time，I like playing the piano and cooking is also part of my life. Sometimes I go hiking with my family because it's good for my health and also relaxing. I'm a positive and bright girl. Do you want to be friends with me?

从上面的案例中可以看到，同一名学生在经过一学期的英语学习之后，其自我介绍就有了很大变化。在语言方面，学生的用词变复杂了，如 13 - year-old，free time，go hiking 等；句式更丰富，如 sometimes I go hiking with my family because it's good for my health and also relaxing.；逻辑更清晰，不再是刚入学时想到什么说什么，而是集中介绍自己的兴趣爱好；思想更深邃，学生介绍中加入了对自己的性格描述，如 a positive and bright girl。此外，从视频中学生的现场表现来看，学生的发音更清晰、表达更流畅，身体语言也更为自然。

这样的档案袋记录能直观地展现学生在一段时间内的变化。当学生回过头回顾时，也会为自己的进步而感到充满成就感，从而不断调整自己的学习策略，增强英语听说的动力和信心。

2）配音作品

配音作为语音训练的一种形式，是让学生在示范下进行口语练习。在配音的过程中，学生要先听原视频中人物的发音、语调、语气和节奏，然后再模仿人物角色，完成配音作品。在这一过程中，学生用声音塑造人物，用声音体会人生。教师既可以指定视频请学生完成，也可以让学生自选视频完成配音。学生可以根据自己的兴趣选择不同难度、题材和时长的视频素材。有同学喜欢漫威电影、有同学热爱迪士尼电影，还有同学酷爱英音纪录片，配音软件可以满足学生多样化的需求和不同层次的口语水平，真实的语料和场景还能够激发学生练习听说的热情。教师可以设计以下自评表（表3.30），引导学生制作优秀的配音作品。

表 3.30　配音作品自评表

Dubbing Self-Assessment Checklist Name：　　　　　　　　　　　　　　　　　　　Date：			
Category	Criteria		Points
Video Length	< 1 min	5	
	1 – 2 mins	8	
	> 3 mins	10	
Difficulty Level	Beginner	5	
	Intermediate	8	
	Advanced	10	
Performance	发音与口型不匹配，不标准，表达不流畅	3	
	发音有个别不标准，表达基本流畅，能理解影片表达的感情，有一定的表现力	5	
	发音标准洪亮，配音与人物口型一致，对影片理解到位，引人入胜	10	
Total			

完成配音作品后，学生可以在班级群内相互分享。教师可以利用早读等时间请全班同学共同赏析配音作品。实践表明，学生对配音活动充满热情，在听同学的配音时也格外专注。经过一个学期的练习，有学生已经可以从只能配三两句话的视频过渡到能完成一个两分钟的作品，还有同学能声情并茂演绎电影《小妇人》的经典片段：

Meg：Jo.

Jo：We can leave. We can leave right now. I can make money. I'll sell stories，I'll…

I'll do anything. I'll cook，I'll clean，I'll work in a factory. I can make a life for us.

Meg：Jo!

Jo：And you，you should be an actress. And you should have a life on the stage. Let's just run away together.

Meg：I want to get married.

Jo：Why?

Meg：Because I love him.

Jo：You will be bored of him in two years，and we will be interesting forever.

Meg：Just because my dreams are different than yours doesn't mean they're unimportant. I want a home，and a family. And I'm willing to work and struggle. But I want to do it with John.

Jo：I just hate that you're leaving me. Don't leave.

Meg：Oh，Jo. I'm not leaving you，and besides，one day it will be your turn.

Jo：I'd rather be a free spinster and paddle my own canoe. I would.

Meg：I can't believe childhood is over.

Jo：It was going to end one way or another. And what a happy end!

在这段配音中，学生一人分饰两角，一边演绎出 Jo 挽留姐妹的迫切心情，一边表现出 Meg 的温柔坚定，甚至将哽咽说话的情绪都表达了出来。不论是语速、语言的难度和表现力，都体现出该学生驾轻就熟的听说能力。经过这样的练习，学生在真实的交际场景中才懂得用不同的语气、语调和语速来表达情感，从而真正提高交际能力。将这样的作品放进学生的成长记录袋，能让学生体会到学英语的乐趣，从而增强说英语的信心，也能让教师看到学生成长的足迹，教学相长。

3）听写作业

对于高年级或听说能力较好的学生，教师还可以鼓励他们进行听写练习。对于教师而言，听写既是日常听说教学中一种有效的教学手段，又是一种可靠的检测方法。对学生来说，听写是学习一门外语最为有效的训练方法。这是因为听写并不只是听和写，而是英语综合能力的运用。听写的过程涉及多方面的能力和知识，如语音知识、词汇知识（单词的发音、拼写、词汇量）、语法知识、听力理解能力、语篇表达能力、书写的速度、短时记忆能力和心理素质等。在短时间内将听到的信息快速处理和归纳并落实到笔头，能够促进学生听力理解能力的提高。通过听写词汇和句子，学生能更快地记住单词、理解语法现象。以句子为单位进行听写，还能加强学生的语感，提高整体理解语言的能力。在听写时进行口头的重复，能帮助学生纠正语音、提高口头表达能力。

教师在指导学生进行听写时，可以从单词先开始，慢慢过渡到词块、句子和语篇。在学生开始自主听写时，教师要帮助学生筛选出适合自己的听写材料，鼓励学生边听边说边写，将听写的内容积累到一个本子上，从而记录自己的进步。以下是某初三学生的听写本（图 3.10）：

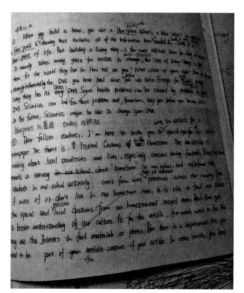 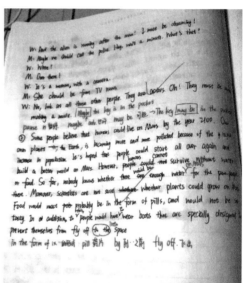

图 3.10　学生听写图片

从图 3.10 中可以看到，学生的听写不仅有对话，也有独白。学生能够听出语篇中绝大部分的信息，说明学生基本能够理解文章的大意。学生对照原文，修改了自己听写中的不足之处，同时积累了其中的单词、词组和语块。例如，学生通过听写，除了区分 may be 和 maybe，还给出了例句 The key may be in the pocket. 和 Maybe the key is in the pocket.，证明学生已经完全理解了两者的区别。学生在访谈中谈到："听写其实挺痛苦的，有时候就是听不出来，而且开始很花时间。但是收获也很大。我感觉我的听力就是这么练出来的，我的语音也比以前好了，说英语更快了。有时候除了听写，我还自己听听广播，就发现自己不害怕听这些语速快的音频了。然后我已经听写了一个本子，感觉很有成就感，高中我还会坚持下去！"

3.2.3　纠错反馈

除了评价，教师的反馈对学生的学习也起着重要的调控作用，尤其是对学生口头表达中出现的错误的反馈。这是因为语言学习不是一蹴而就的，而是一个动态渐进的创造性的发展过程。语言学习者在这一过程中需要不断学习新的语言规则，逐步建构起目标语的语言体系，其中难免会出现语言错误。有学者将这一时期的语言称为"中介语"，即在结构方面处于母语和目标语中间的语言知识系统。使用中介语的过程就是不断试验和犯错以及验证和纠错的过程，也是外语学习的必经阶段。

对于山后地区农村校的学生而言，课堂教学是他们学习英语听说的主要途径。因此，教师能否提供有价值的反馈，有效纠正学生在学习中（尤其是口语表达中）出现的语言错误对学生的英语学习质量和效果至关重要。教师既要对学生所犯的错误采取理解和宽容的态度，又不能够对所有错误置之不理。选择了恰当的纠错反馈策略，就能让错误在学习者语言学习中产生积极有益的作用（王栋，盛佳飞，2021）。

1. 纠错反馈的类型

纠错反馈，本质上是师生互动的过程。本书所谈的纠错反馈，具体指的是在课堂教学中以口头形式指出学生所输出的目标语与标准目标语之间的差距。Lyster & Ranta（1997）将教师的纠错反馈分为以下六大类，分别为明确纠错、重述、要求澄清、元语言提示、引导和重复。

明确纠错指的是教师直截了当地当场指出学生所犯的语言错误，并呈现出正确的形式，从而帮助学生改错。例如，教师一般会说"We should say…""That's not correct."然后说出或者板书出正确的表达。

重述是指教师不明确指出学生所犯的错误，而是将正确的形式重新表述一遍。学生会将自己的表述和教师所提供的正确形式进行对比，从而找出错误。这种方法能够节约时间，同时保护学生的自信心，不中断交流。

要求澄清是教师在没有理解学生话语的情况下，要求学生再说一遍。教师通常说"Sorry，can you repeat it again?"或者说"Excuse me，louder please."等委婉地提示学生自我纠错。

元语言提示是指教师不指出学生的错误所在处，而是通过评价，如"I think there's something wrong in this sentence. Can you say it again?"，让学生意识到并自我纠错。

引导指的是教师用提问的形式引导学生注意自己的语言错误，比如学生在改用动词过去式的时候用了动词原形，教师会提示说："Sorry，what's the past tense of…?"，从而引导学生用正确的形式来表达。

重复则是指教师通过改变声调，比如重读"We buy some books yesterday."句中的"buy"让学生意识到自己的表述问题，然后加以纠正。

2. 纠错反馈的原则

不管是哪一种纠错方式，都需要根据实际情况灵活运用。除了考虑纠错的方式，教师在实际教学中还需要把握以下三个原则：①学生自我纠错优先；②意义纠错优先；③结束纠错优先。下面我们用具体案例来阐释这三个原则。

首先，当学生在口头表达中出现错误时，要以学生自我纠错优先。口头交际时，人们难免会出现口误。尤其是初学者在课堂上面对众多听众，更容易因为紧张而犯错。这时教师不要立刻打断，急于给出正确的示范或者提示，应该耐心等待，把发现错误和纠正错误的机会留给学生自己。比如以下的教学片段：

T：What's your name?

S：My name Helen. No，sorry，my name is Helen.

在上面的对话中，学生开始没有使用动词 be 来表示谓语关系。但她很快便意识到了这个问题，马上进行了自我修正，重新表述为 my name is Helen. 再比如：

T：Mike，what's this in English?

S：It's a orange. It's an orange，an.

在这个教学片段中，学生由于着急回答老师的问题，在 orange 前误用了冠词 a。但他立刻进行了自我纠正，重述为 It's an orange，并着重强调了 an，以证明自己在冠词使用上是有充分理解的。

以上两个案例充分体现了优先让学生自我纠正的好处。一方面，学生能自我纠错，说明已经对这个知识点有所掌握，比如第二个案例中的冠词。给学生自己纠正的机会不仅能够帮助他内省和巩固所学内容，内化语言，还能够让教师了解学生对该知识点的掌握情况，对教学进度和内容做出调整。另一方面，学生自己找出自己的错误，而不是由老师当面指出，能有效地保护好学生的"面子"和自尊心。尤其是在课堂上，山后地区的学生本就对说英语不够自信。如果学生能不怕犯错，勇于表达，并自我修正，这对他的英语学习将起到鼓舞作用。因此，教师在课堂教学中不要急于指出学生的错误，而是耐心等待一下，给学生自己一个纠错的机会。只有在确认学生自己没有纠错的能力，如眼睛看着老师发出求救信号，或者根本意识不到自己的错误时，教师再做出纠正。这不仅把课堂的话语权交给了学生，也让教师从一个指导者变成了协助者，师生关系更加和谐。

其次，并不是所有的错误都需要纠正，教师应该坚持意义纠错优先的原则。在日常交际中，即便是母语者也难免出现口误。学生作为外语学习者，其口语表达更是一个不断试错、逐步接近目标语的过程。但教师要明确知道的是，语言交际的目的是传达意义。相比于语法错误，语义错误更容易影响交际的顺利进行。比如下面这个教学片段：

（学生在进行看图说话的练习）

S：Gina's books is everywhere—in her bed，on the sofa，and under the chair.

T：In her bed?

S：Sorry，on her bed.

T：OK. So Gina's books are everywhere—on her bed，on the sofa and under the chair.

在上面的对话中，学生开始时出现了两处错误，即谓语动词 be 应该用复数形式，保持主谓一致。但相比于这个语法错误，in her bed 表达的意义是不符合图片内容的。因此，教师通过重复学生的表述，并提高声调，来提示学生自我纠错。学生也马上意识到了这个问题，随即进行了纠正。教师最后又将学生的表达用正确的形式带领全班同学复述了一次，既解决了语义问题，又无形中解决了语法问题。再比如：

（学生在口头失物招领）

S：If this is you pen，go and ask you teacher about it.

T：OK. If this is your pen，go and ask your teacher about it or for it?

S：Oh yes，for it. Ask your teacher for it.

T：Good. Now everyone，if this is your pen，ask your teacher for it.

在这个案例中，学生也犯了两处错误，一个是语法错误 you pen 和 you teacher 应该用形容词性物主代词 your；另一处是语义错误，ask sb. about sth. 有向某人问好或者向某人询问某事的意思。这里学生想表达的是"到老师那儿去领"，也就是 ask sb. for sth. 。这时，教师没有把关注点放在语法错误上，而是重了一遍学生的话语，委婉给出了正确的语法形式，并以疑问的方式提示学生 ask sb. about sth. 的错误用法。学生很快意识到这个问题，马上修正了这个说法，并自然而然地给出了 your teacher 的表达。教师最后又将整个句子的正确形式完整复述了一遍。学生不仅表达出了自己想传达的意义，也在无形中强化了正确的语言表达。

通过以上案例可以看到，相较于语法错误，语义错误在实际交际过程中更为重要，在纠错时应以语义为先。同时，在学生犯了多处错误的时候，比如上面案例中的语法和语义错误，如果教师对几处错误都随即打断学生，处处进行纠正，无疑会有损学生说英语的信心，导致学生不敢开口。更严重的是，频繁纠正学生的语法错误会让学生将表达的重心放在语言的形式上，而不是意义的使用上。因此，教师应果断遵循意义优先的纠错原则，帮助学生用语言做事情。

最后，关于何时纠错，答案是显而易见的，教师应该在学生发言结束后纠错。这里一方面考虑到教师应耐心等待学生说完，即使出错也应该给予学生自我纠错的机会。另一方面，学生如果在表达时被打断，既容易因为紧张而导致更多的错误或者忘记要表达的内容，另一方面其说英语的信心也会受打击。因此，教师应该留给学生充分思考的时间，纠错最好在学生表达了一个完整的意义之后进行。例如：

T：Tell us about you and your partner's favorite sports.

S：I like playing basketball and tennis. I think they are fun. My partner Mike like playing basketball too. But he don't like playing tennis. So we often go and play basketball after school.

T：OK，your partner Mike likes playing basketball right?

S：Yes，that's right. But he doesn't like playing tennis.

在上面的教学片段中，教师并没有急于打断学生进行纠正，而是等到学生说完之后，用疑问和提高声调的方式重复学生的话，提示学生问题所在。学生也马上意识到三单的问题，对教师的提示表示了认可，并纠正了自己三单否定形式的表达。这样的做法既保护了学生表达的欲望，又给到学生自我纠错的机会，课堂气氛也更轻松。

纠错是课堂教学中的重要环节，恰当的纠错反馈能将学生的错误巧妙转化为有价值的教学资源。在听说教学中，教师要根据不同的学情采用不同的教学方式，因材施教，也要遵循学生自我纠错优先、意义纠错优先和结束时纠错优先的原则。尤其是面对山后地区英语学习信心不足的学生时，教师更要充分考虑学生的情感因素，理解包容并耐心引导学生发现并改正错误。当学生表达得当或者自我纠错成功时，应及时给予正面、积极的肯定，增强学生口头表达的信心，从而真正提高教学效果，发展学生的听说能力。

▨ 3.3　特色教学与资源开发

3.3.1　读听说联动的教学实践

北京市第一零一中学　毛筠

初中英语教师普遍认为听说能力，特别是口语表达能力是最不容易提升的，只有掌握听说，才能真正运用所学语言。读和听是输入，说是输出，有足够的输入，才能有足够的输出，然而，在教学实践中，笔者发现教材中听的输入略显不足，所以在听读说能力培养的课堂教学中，读、听和说三种技能结合起来同步学才是正确的学习方法，三者之间互相补充又互相促进。

根据初中英语教学的要求和现状，笔者提出了围绕初中生英语听说能力培养，主要采取以听力为基础，以阅读材料为指导，并将它们作为口语表达的基础，促进学生英语综合能力提高的读、听、说联动教学法，并撰写了相应的教学案例。这些教学案例的核心是：先进行课内听力教学、课内外阅读教学，并将其作为口头表达的基础，在听和读的基础上，马上进行同步的口头表达教学。同时，以口头表达或写作教学的结果（学生口语录音或写作文章），作为对"读、听、说"联动教学效果的检验，从而达到"读、听、说"教学的联动，促进学生英语综合能力的提高。

笔者的教学对象是北京市第一零一中学初三 9 班、10 班 A 层。该班英语起点较高，但是经过三年的初中学习，学生逐渐形成了良好的听说能力提升的学习习惯；有较好的用英语表达的欲望；喜欢课堂环节紧凑、有序。三年来，通过读写联动、听说联动等教学实践，学生在听力、阅读与写作方面有了很大进步；口语表达能力相对于听、读、写的能力，较为逊色，但经过一段时间有意识地在课堂教学中的培养，也在逐步提高。

不过也有一小部分学生学习很努力，但是效果与付出不成正比。通过初步诊断，显然是学习方法不当，学习信心有所不足，特别是口语表达的信心不足。

以人教版《英语》八年级下册 Unit 5 What were you doing when the rainstorm came? Section A 1a，1b，1c，2d 为例，笔者开展了"读、听、说"联动的教学实践。

1. 挖掘教材听力文本内涵

通常一个单元分为七个课时处理（Section A 三个课时；Section B 三个课时；还有一课时的练习课），笔者在每个单元的教材处理上都会根据需要进行适当的删减与补充，以及顺序上的调整。

本节课是一节以听说为载体的语法课。笔者将 Section A 的教学内容根据过去进行时的时间状语进行了调整，第一课时主要是过去某一点的时间状语（如 at 7:00 last night）；第二课时主要是 when 和 while 引导的时间状语从句；第三课时为阅读教学。经过这样的整合，降低学生在第一课时的学习难度，教学重点相对比较突出，易于攻破。

从话题角度来说，第一课时相对单一，教学目标为设定学生能听出、谈论过去某一时刻发生的事情，学生对此话题比较熟悉，笔者把与 1a - 1c 话题与语法一致的 2d（对话表演）提前学习并改为听力材料，两次听力输入内容互相关联、层层递进、螺旋拓展；第一次听力输入要求学生简单处理信息并进行模仿性的口语输出；第二次听力输入是对第一次听力内容的拓展，听后要求学生对信息进行多层次处理，然后进行控制性的口语输出，此外，在模仿性输出的基础上，增加了与实际生活相关联的创造性口语输出训练。

第二课时进行故事讲述，用熟悉的时态去讲述过去的经历，难度逐步上升，但只要本节课打好基础，第二课时自然是水到渠成。

此外，本节课笔者还补充了两篇阅读小篇章。一则可以通过这两篇文章来进行时态练习；二则，这两个文段可以为学生的进一步口语表达奠定基础。此外，笔者还加入一些难度较大、培养学生思维能力与初步推断能力的任务。如模仿电视人进行新闻播报、写出所听材料的主旨、归纳补充阅读的大意并在此基础上为文段写一个结尾等。让学生通过阅读，根据作者的实际，把握作者的态度，写一个结尾。这样既能训练阅读技能，又能为写作做准备，使学生能写出篇章结构结尾好、主题突出的文章。

2. 整合课内外课程资源

现行教材中，在每个单元都有一个口头表达和话题写作的内容，但相关的阅读材料要么太短、要么太长、要么与写作任务结合不密切，远远满足不了学生的阅读需求，更谈不上口头表达和写作参考。根据笔者所摸索的"听、读、说"联动教学法：在深入挖掘教材文本内涵之后，针对教材中听读材料的不足，笔者有意识地按照阅读理解教学的训练要求和方法，给学生们补充一些和本单元话题相关的课外阅读和一些拓展训练来完成口头表达和写作教学任务，从而实现听、读、说话题及其材料的联动。

本课要求学生能够从听力文段中听出过去某一时刻（at the time of the rainstorm/at 7：00 last night）正在发生的事情；学生能够用过去进行时谈论和写出过去某一时刻（at the time of the rainstorm/at 7：00 last night）发生的事情。从听力、阅读主旨的设问到文章中间具体细节的讨论及文章结尾的推断，笔者不拘泥于书中课本听力任务的设置，而重在对听、读、说的整体理解和把握，为下一步的演讲和写作奠定基础。

为了达到在本节课学生能够准确地运用所学的语言知识，口头笔头谈论他们在过去某一时刻正在经历的事情这一教学终极目标，笔者采用了两篇听力材料、两篇补充阅读（语言输入）的方式，通过谈论过去某一时刻正在发生的事情，从单句到文段（语言内化并输出），提高学生在真实的情景下运用语言进行交际的能力（图3.11）。

3. "听、读、说"联动教学实践

（1）除课本听力任务 1b，2a 和 2b 外，还把课本上的 2d 设计成了听力任务（表 3.31）。

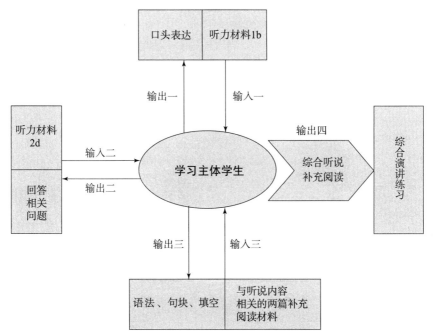

说明:

输入与输出一、二在传统听力教学过程中,嵌入了诸如归纳听力材料大意、模仿新闻播报、看表格复述并创作等任务;输入与输出三、四为听读联动后增加的教学过程。从学习信息过程分析,增加了 2 个输入环节,同时信息输入与输出的强度大大增强。

图 3.11　听、读、说联动教学模型

表 3.31　人教版《英语》八年级下册 Unit 5 2d 听说活动 1

What was Linda doing at 7:00/8:00/9:00 last night?			
	7:00	8:00	9:00
Linda			
You			
Your partner			
...			

1st *Listening*:

2nd *Listening*:

What's the listening passage mainly about?

Why did Mary call Linda so many times?

How did Mary solve her problem?

（2）除课本上的说的任务，笔者还补充了比较有难度的说的任务。例如，让学生模仿天气播报员播报新闻（图3.12和图3.13）；让学生小组合作，填表、问答并转述同伴在过去的某一时刻做了某事。

1c: Suppose you are a reporter. Report what the people in 1a were doing at the time of the rainstorm.

Yesterday's rainstorm:
1. do my homework, at home
2. read, at the library
3. wait for the bus, at the bus stop
4. walk home from the supermarket

At the time of the rainstorm…

Hello! This is Bill from CCTV. Here is a report about yesterday's rainstorm. Many people were caught in the rain … However, some were luckily staying indoors…

图3.12　人教版《英语》八年级下册 Unit 5 听说活动1

（3）为培养学生原汁原味的语音语调，笔者嵌入了一个原版动画片的剪辑和原版青春偶像剧的视频音频剪辑（图3.13）。

playing dancing swimmingsinging running

What were they doing on the beach yesterday morning?
They were singingand dancing.

图3.13　人教版《英语》八年级下册 Unit 5 听说活动2

（4）为了避免听的输入的不足，笔者还补充了两篇课外阅读文章，其中一篇是《新概念英语》改编（图3.14），以培养学生口语表达严谨且逻辑性强的能力。

Reading and speaking practice – 2

Last Sunday morning Sally's family were all at home. Sally's parents were in the

图 3.14　人教版《英语》八年级下册 Unit 5 听说活动 3

kitchen. They _____ . Her mother _____ a meal. And her father _____ his dog through the windows. The dog _____ after a cat in the garden. The sun _____ . What a lovely day! Sally _____ under the tree, and she _____ a book. She thinks reading enriches the mind. Her brother, Jack, is a sports lover. He _____ a tree. Can you see some birds in the tree? They _____ .

How happy they were!

（5）创设情境做演讲，培养学生的语言表达能力。本课的最终任务是让学生运用听力和补充阅读中的目标语言，有条理、逻辑清晰地描述，如图 3.15 所示。

图 3.15　人教版《英语》八年级下册 Unit 5 听说活动 4

基于以上分析，建构课程资源，培养初中生英语听说能力的总的方针是根据学生实际情况，遵循学生身心发展的普遍规律，按照学生的认知水平和能力，从学生实际生活经验出发，由易到难，逐级铺设台阶，合理整合教材、安排教学内容，注重学生学习英语的过程。本课强调学以致用，通过设置真实情境，在课堂上为学生"架起课堂与实际生活的桥梁""系起课堂与外国文化的纽带"：即笔者在语法教学中，为了提高教学效率，重视学生对学习过程的参与，即"感知、发现、总结、练习、运用"。笔者在教学过程中围绕本节课的交际目的和语言项目，设计出可操作性强的、任务化的课程，在保持学生学习兴趣的同时，提高课堂学习的效率。突出以学生为主体的教学活动，使学生通过多种课堂学习方式，特别是"听、读、说"联动教学方法，运用一定学习策略，最终完成系统的任务链，达到学习掌握并运用语言的目的。

3.3.2 模拟联合国课程开发与实践

北京市第一零一中学 张越

【摘要】"模拟联合国"是青年学生们扮演不同国家的外交官，模仿联合国及相关国际机构议事规则，围绕国际热点问题所召开的会议。作为英语教学的实践性训练，模拟联合国课程不仅集英语学习的听、说、读、写四项语言能力为一体，还可综合锻炼学生的文化意识思维品质和学习能力，从而全方位提升学生英语学科核心素养。本文以为期一年的模拟联合国课程经验为依托，从基础篇、技能篇、实战篇、拓展篇四大模块出发，对模拟联合国课程的开发与实践进行了系统梳理和总结，以期为今后的英语课程教学及模拟联合国课程建设与实施提供一定借鉴。

【关键词】模拟联合国；英语教学；核心素养；实施策略

一、背景分析

《义务教育英语课程标准（2022 年版）》指出，英语课程要培养的学生核心素养包括语言能力、文化意识、思维品质和学习能力等方面。语言能力是核心素养的基础要素，文化意识体现核心素养的价值取向，思维品质反映核心素养的心智特征，学习能力是核心素养发展的关键要素。核心素养的四个方面相互渗透，融合互动，协同发展。教师应注重在发展学生英语语言运用能力的过程中，帮助他们拓展国际视野，增进国际理解，逐步提升跨文化沟通能力、思辨能力、学习能力和创新能力，帮助他们树立人类命运共同体意识和多元文化意识，形成开放包容的态度，加深对祖国文化的理解，增强爱国情怀，坚定文化自信，树立正确的世界观、人生观和价值观。

进一步提升学生英语学科核心素养是当今英语教学的刚需所在，模拟联合国活动恰恰为此提供了契机。模拟联合国的本质是角色扮演。青年学生们扮演各国外交官，以联合国会议的形式，通过阐述观点、协商对话、政策辩论和投票表决等亲身经历，熟悉联合国的运作方式，了解人类所面临的共同问题，思考自身可以发挥的作用，是一个培养外语外交人才的平台。这项活动可极大激发学生外语学习的热情，综合锻炼学生各项语言技能，潜移默化提升学生国际理解力，锻炼学生批判性思维，并培养自身学习能力，从而综合培养学生英语学科核心素养。

目前的模拟联合国研究主要聚焦于大学阶段模拟联合国活动的展开，针对中学生模拟联合国活动的研究并不多，且研究主要集中在模拟联合国活动的德育功能，以及其对政治、历史学科核心素养的提升。少数聚焦英语学科的模拟联合国实践研究主要包括模拟联合国培训策略研究和实践研究，后者主要聚焦于听、说、读、写等具体语言技能的培养。通过以上学习发现，目前对指向核心素养的初中模拟联合国课程开发与实践的研究较少。因此，本文以为期一年的模拟联合国课程经验为依托，以培养英语学科核心素养为指向，对模拟联合国课程的设计与实施进行了系统梳理和总结，以期为后续模拟联合国相关研究提供有效经验。

二、模拟联合国双语课程开发的意义

模拟联合国双语课程的开发与实施，对课程建设、教师和学生三方面都大有裨益。首先，从课程建设角度来看，本研究可从模拟联合国基本知识、模拟联合国策略和模拟联合国课程建构等方面为学校开展模拟联合国课程提供建议。其次，从教师发展角度来看，模拟联合国双语课程开发旨在引导实验教师通过浸入式研究共同体，共同提炼提升学生英语学科核心素养的方法和策略，研发优秀教学案例，为一线教师提供可借鉴的模式与方法，促进中学英语教师的专业发展。最后，从学生角度来看，开设模拟联合国双语课程不仅可借助双语教学平台突破模拟联合国语言壁垒，又可使学生在模拟联合国活动中，细心聆听，勇敢表达，求同存异，辩证思考，积极合作，相互借鉴，从而在此过程中综合提升语言能力、文化意识、思维品质和学习能力，从而全面提升英语学科核心素养。

语言能力层面，学生在角色扮演的过程中，需要通过背景文件阅读、立场文件写作、开场演讲、磋商辩论、工作文件及决议草案撰写等系列活动，逐步推进会议议程，同时在真实情境中锻炼英语语言能力。这其中，演讲、磋商等环节需要学生不断听取他方意见，并有理有据地表达己方观点，进而综合提升其听说能力；背景文件阅读等环节则需学生充分理解文件，加深对本议题的理解，从而锻炼其阅读能力；立场文件、工作文件及决议草案的撰写等环节，则是对学生写作能力的集中锻炼。

文化意识层面，模拟联合国是学生了解世界格局的一扇窗，它帮助学生了解全球文化多样性。模拟联合国活动为学生传递更多国家的优秀文化，不断提升创造性的交际能力，以及进行跨文化交流搭建了良好的舞台，可帮助学生积累文化经验，提高包容共处、相互尊重、开放借鉴的意识。同时，它也无形中培养了学生的国家认同意识，有助于坚定文化自信，增强责任心，唤起使命感，从而有助于培养出兼具家国情怀和全球意识的学生。

思维品质层面，学生自主表达本国观点，还需根据不断生成的新的情境问题，随机应变，与他国代表辩论、磋商，求同存异，合作共赢。在此过程中，学生需积极运用和不断调试思考策略，是对逻辑能力和思辨能力的综合考察，而这些因素都会直接影响利益同盟的组建和协议缔结。与此同时，投身模拟联合国工作的学生，在社团工作和模拟联合国大会组织管理过程中，也将大幅度提高策划执行、沟通协调、突发事件处理等各项综合能力。

学习能力层面，学生代表不同的国家，就不同委员会下的不同议题进行讨论。在教师引领下，他们将充分进行自主学习，如进行信息检索和立场文件写作，学会通过多渠道获取、阅读、分析、比较、归纳和整合国家及议题背景资料，自主高效地开展以英语语言为工具的跨学科深度学习。同时，在磋商等环节，他们又将充分进行合作学习，求同存异，辩证思考，通过沟通与辩论，找到解决问题的最优解。

三、有效的模拟联合国双语课程实施策略

笔者对模拟联合国社团学生进行了前瞻性调研及个人访谈，调研内容涵盖英语学科核心素养、中国英语能力等级量表、中国学生发展核心素养、国际学生评估项目（PISA）全球胜任力评价等多维度。结果显示，学生最想在认识模拟联合国的基础上，借助听、说、读、写等活动充分掌握模拟联合国的相关技能，从而在模拟联合国实践中学以致用，继而提升国际理解力及全球胜任力。据此，笔者以本校学生学习需求为出发点，进行了以下四个模块的课程设计及实施。完成相应学习后，教师通过过程性评价及终结性评价对学生的课程学习进行评估。

（一）基础篇

1. 认识联合国与模拟联合国

社团大部分学生对联合国相关内容知之甚少，对模拟联合国大会的认知也停留在基础层面。因此，教师在第一堂课中通过知识问答、播放视频等方式让学生了解联合国的历史、构成、《联合国宪章》等基本信息，同时可借助导图让学生明确模拟联合国大会的意义、规格、组织流程等。如此，学生对联合国和模拟联合国大会才能具备科学系统的认知，进而为后期学习奠定基础。

2. 模拟联合国核心词汇学习

模拟联合国大会通常会设置多语种会场，但在初中英语教学实践中，主要锁定的工作语言是中文和英文。模拟联合国大会具有规范的流程，每环节都涉及大量的专业术语，如"立场文件（Position Paper）""磋商（Caucus）""三分之二多数（Two-thirds Majority）"等。对于首次接触模拟联合国的同学而言，对模拟联合国大会中英对照术语的学习是重中之重。教师在授课时可结合模拟联合国大会流程对术语进行分类讲解，同时可借助小组 PK 等灵活多变的形式，让本模块不局限于一堂词汇课，从而更加丰富生动。

3. 常见国际组织学习

在日常学习生活中，国际组织对于学生而言并不陌生，但这种认知多半零零散散，不成系统。在本模块中，教师可对各国际组织进行简单分类，如先介绍联合国主要机构，如世界卫生组织（WHO）、联合国环境规划署（UNEP）、联合国教科文组织（UNESCO）等，再介绍其他区域性国际组织，如欧盟（EU）、北大西洋公约组织（NATO）、东南亚国家联盟（ASEAN）等。讲解时，可重点介绍各组织机构网站、宗旨、成员国等信息，同样可借助图片和视频等更为直观的资源作为辅助。

（二）技能篇

1. 信息检索（Information Research）

在获得席位后，信息检索是模拟联合国活动的正式开端。教师要引领学生借助各类资源，进行国家信息检索及议题检索。此时，除了了解该国家的政治、经济、地理、文化等要素外，也要充分发掘该国和本议题的联系，思考在推动议题时可发挥怎样的作用，又有哪些潜在的合作伙伴等。总之，只有在连环问题的推动下，学生才可能对该国家在此议题上的信息有更多的掌握，对一切立场有更明确的把握。常见的信息检索资源包括主办方发布的背景文件（Background Guide）、相关书籍刊物，以及各大网络资源等。网络资源层面，学生可充分借助联合国官网、各国际组织官网、所属国家官方网站等搜索信息，亦可通过国际主流媒体官网、谷歌学术等网站进行信息检索。教师可带领学生在机房进行实操，保证学生可灵活运用多种搜索形式，获取最官方、最有时效性的信息。

2. 立场文件写作（Position Paper Writing）

本任务课前要求学生在做好充分的信息检索后，进行立场文件写作，系统介绍议题背景、本国立场及以往措施，并重点提出可行的解决方案。立场文件写作时学生经过信息检索和大量阅读后，科学、系统地向大会呈现代表国家观点的首份文件，也是后期开场演讲的基础所在，因此是模拟联合国大会的重中之重。在开展本模块教学时，教师可下发真实的背景文件，带领学生一起学习以此文件为依托的立场文件例文，充分感知其结构和范式。课后可布置相应作业，让学生在真实的立场文件写作中，充分掌握这项技能。

3. 开场演讲（Opening Speech）

模拟联合国活动中，学生扮演不同国家外交官角色，通过演讲、游说、辩论等方式尝试对议题提出充分的解决方案。演讲能力是这些活动的基础，是直接向大会及其他国家代表传达己方立场观点并提出可行性方案的重要活动。因此，合理训练学生逻辑缜密的演讲能力是模拟联合国训练的重要模块。演讲是一门艺术，学生通过经典演讲的学习，可以学习演讲技巧，并通过演讲实践提高自身的语言能力和社会交际能力。在教学中，教师可首先借助绕口令、趣配音等活动激活学生学习兴趣，巩固语音语调基础。在此基础上，教师可借助名人演讲模仿等活动，作为教学的辅助。名人演讲往往语言优美、逻辑缜密、言语激昂，语音语调等也都是上乘。通过赏析、模仿名人演讲，学生可综合提高语言运用能力，同时在潜移默化中提升个人领导力。

4. 磋商（Caucusing）

模拟联合国活动中，各个国家代表往往会花费大量时间进行磋商，通过一系列讨论，纵横捭阖，进而实现本国利益的最大化，同时积极推进会议议程，为所探讨议题提供可行性建议。磋商分为有主持核心磋商（Moderated Caucus）和自由磋商（Unmoderated Caucus）。前者类似针对主议题下某一特定小议题的意见交换。在本环节中，通过关注发言国家的立场和兴趣点，不同国家利益集团（Bloc）将逐步形成。自由磋商则适用于不明确有哪些具体小议题可供探讨的情况，或者国家集团形成后，各国家代表充分讨论形成工作文件（Working Paper）等情况。但是，不管是有主持核心磋商还是自由磋商，都涉及大量的辩论和游说，因此，教师在教学中可结合相应议题，开展各种微型辩论赛，进而逐步精进学生的辩论技能，为合理进行磋商做好准备。

5. 决议草案撰写（Draft Resolution Writing）

决议草案是模拟联合国大会的出口，是各位国家代表齐聚一堂，经过数天的演讲、辩论及合作，形成相应的国家集团，并在共同探讨得出系列工作文件的基础上，继而形成的规范的结果性文件。决议草案在通过大会投票后，就将成为决议案，成为大会的最终成果。因此，决议草案的撰写不仅需要充足的内容，更需要规范的范式。决议草案的内容主要包括序言性条款和行动性条款，言简意赅地传达议题背景及可行性解决方案。在本模块教学中，教师可借助真实案例，给予学生真实写作的机会，并通过自评、同伴互评、教师面批等方式，一步步提高写作质量。

6. 着装要求及礼仪（Dress Code and Etiquette）

充分了解模拟联合国大会的着装要求及礼仪也是各位国家代表必备的"软技能"之一。模拟联合国大会是各位同学扮演各国外交官，在国际会场进行意见交换的正式场合。因此，与会的国家代表都应着正装，男士应着西装领带和皮鞋，女士则应着西装和高跟鞋，化淡妆为宜。参会期间应充分注意与会礼仪，如遵守会场秩序、尊重他国代表文化信仰等。本项技能的训练可通过播放模拟联合国大会视频带学生细细观察，亦可通过角色扮演或微短剧的形式来做出示范，以加深学生印象，将着装要求及礼仪内化于心。

（三）拓展篇

1. 每日新闻播报：国际新闻分享

首先，利用课前 10 分钟，组织学生进行双语国际新闻分享及探讨。学生在此之前需要做大量功课，从日常关注 China Daily、CGTN 等多个双语新闻平台，到筛选自己感兴趣的国际新闻并认真剖析多方视角，再到双语向同学播报此新闻并分享自己观点，不仅可锻炼信息检索能力、思维认知能力，更能在分享与问答环节锻炼公众演讲能力及辩论能力，而这两项能力对于模拟联合国大会的开场演讲及磋商都极为重要。此外，此活动需要主讲人与观众进行积极互动，还可综合培养学生的应变能力，锻炼良好的心理素质。

2. 小小外交官：世界国家分享

本任务课前要求学生通过网络搜集相关资料，针对某个国家进行自主学习，使其形成自身的看法，借助多媒体完成相应的课前展示，并提交相应的调研小论文。该活动意义如下：首先，检测学生自主学习能力以及信息检索能力；其次，锻炼学生的思辨能力及个人演讲能力；最后，锻炼学生的书面表达能力，而这也是模拟联合国大会的重中之重，与立场文件撰写、演讲稿撰写、工作文件及决议草案起草都有着直接关系。

3. 国际热点讲座

国际热点讲座主要由社团政治学科教师带领同学们共同完成。模拟联合国活动与国际关系及时政热点关系密切，因此，教师通过开展系列国际热点讲座，可帮助学生对错综复杂的国际局势有更深刻的了解，同时也可激发学生从多角度深入了解、分析当今国际社会利益争端，时刻保持对国际热点的敏感度，主动进行国际政治相关知识的自主学习与探讨。通过本模块学习，学生和老师通过探讨国际时事，提升自我认识，完善自身思维，进而提升对世界格局的敏感性，充分锻炼自己的外交思维。

4. 社交晚会活动

有着不同文化背景的外交官进行交流时，需要对彼此文化、习俗、社交礼仪、宗教文明等方面进行了解。作为学生喜闻乐见的模拟联合国活动之一，社交晚会的开展将对学生国际理解力的培养大有裨益。在社交晚会中，各国代表齐聚一堂，教师可安排各位代表对本国文化、艺术、饮食、服饰等进行展示，同时可借助才艺展示和知识竞赛等增强趣味性和互动性。在自然的环境中理解和体会文化，不仅可帮助学生打破固有认知模式、突破思维定势，在良好的氛围中形成对世界各国文化的立体认同感，更有助于学生学会尊重和包容文化差异性，实现国际理解力的综合提升。

（四）实战篇

1. 模拟实战

模拟实战是指在正式参加校外各级别模拟联合国大会前，教师在校内展开的模拟实战，主要用来让学生熟悉会议流程，为参加校外大会充分积累经验。模拟联合国实战部分主要包括前期准备、活动进行，以及总结提升三阶段。前期准备阶段，教师需安排好会议时间、地点、摄影摄像等基本工作，同时，积极做好委员会拟定、议题拟定、国家席位设置及分配、背景文件撰写及发放、立场文件修改等学术准备工作。活动进行中，教师团队应作为主席团，带领学生充分做好开场演讲、磋商、投票等各个环节的仿真模拟，并积极做好议题引领、学术指导等工作，使学生真正感受到正参与其中。总结提升阶段，教师可收集师生各方反思及感受，着重反思不足之处，借助模拟实战后的一手经验，为参与校外各级别大会打好基础。

2. 全真实战

学校之外，学生需要在更大的模拟联合国舞台展现自身实力，学以致用。在全真实战中，指导老师应充分做好学生的学术指导，在信息检索、立场文件写作等层面给予建议和帮助，同时要关注学生每个会期的状态和表现，及时提出建议和反馈，预测会议走向，引导学生为接下来的会期做更灵活的准备。大会结束后，指导教师也应及时与各位与会代表积极沟通，共同复盘整场会议情况，从更宏观的角度重新审视议题和会议结果。这将加深学生对于议题的思考，同时科学地积累经验，为成为一名更优秀的"模联人"做准备。

四、效果及评价

本研究的模拟联合国双语课程实施策略是富有成效的。荣誉层面，笔者曾带领学生参加 2021 及 2022 世界青少年模拟联合国大会，收获经验的同时，也收获了世界青少年模拟联合国大会"优秀团队""优秀指导教师"等称号。部分同学因表现突出，受邀参加世界青少年模拟联合国大会·高级别会议，在与会期间关注全球问题，胸怀世界未来，贡献智慧，精诚合作，为推动 2030 可持续发展议程贡献了智慧和力量，在会议中所展露的能力和风采获得了大会主席团的高度赞赏和认可，因此被授予"世界青少年领导力特别提名"。

教师评价层面，大家集体认为通过模拟联合国活动，学生对英语乃至政治、地理等学科的学习兴趣提升显著。模拟联合国活动作为课堂学习的补充，不仅让学生在自然的语言环境中获取了知识，锻炼了能力，还为其提供了学以致用的平台，拓宽了视野，能够充分了解当今世界动态和真实需求。不仅综合提升了学生英语学科核心素养，对中国学生发展核心素养的提升也起到了积极效果，更有助于学生国际胜任力的提升。

学生评价层面，通过后续调研及访谈，参与模拟联合国课程的大部分学生认为参加模拟联合国对自身英语学习及视野提升有较大促进，特别体现在词汇学习及听、说、读、写能力方面，以及模拟联合国专属技能方面。与此同时，通过模拟联合国活动对英语、政治、历史、地理等多学科的融合，学生在增长知识的同时也提高了学习竞争力。此外，模拟联合国大会的开展有助于学生学以致用，将所学知识融于世界议题的解决中，在活动中进一步认识自己、认识世界。计应然同学表示，"回顾短暂的几天线上模拟联合国时光，我们曾在面对陌生的同学与老师时胆怯，也曾攥紧拳头无畏地走上台前阐述自己的观点；我们曾在夜深人静之际埋头撰写文件，也曾为捍卫所代表的国家立场与其他代表进行激烈的磋商或辩论。忘不了第一次参加磋商时一口气读完长篇立场文件后激动的心跳；忘不了伙伴们稚嫩的脸庞，洋溢着对知识的渴望，从旁听者到参与者和建设者，从参加会议到享受会议。纵使结果并不完美，但我们有能力冷静下来，专注于总结经验。这次的模拟联合国活动让我们受益匪浅。"吴路瑶同学说，"模拟联合国不是个人的演讲秀，而是和一群热爱英语的朋友关注世界议题的头脑风暴；模拟联合国也不是一方独大的单边主义，而是深入调研打破壁垒的多边协商；模拟联合国更不是追求个人名利的角斗场，而是不断打破知识边界参与全球共治的历史担当！"

五、结语

模拟联合国活动是对英语课堂教学的有效补充，有助于培养学生英语学科核心素养。本文以模拟联合国双语课程实施经验为依托，以培养英语学科核心素养为指向，对模拟联合国课程的设计与实施从基础篇、技能篇、拓展篇、实战篇共四大模块进行了系统梳理和总结，对今后模拟联合国课程的开展提供了一定借鉴。

模拟联合国活动的有效开展，对课程建设、教师及学生等多层面均有积极影响。经过一年的实践，本研究不仅可为今后模拟联合国课程的系统实施提供了一定抓手，也促进了教师的专业化发展，最重要的是综合提升了学生的英语学科核心素养，同时促进了英语能力、中国学生发展核心素养及国际胜任力多维度的提升。总之，指向核心素养的模拟联合国活动与英语教学的有机结合有助于我们更好地培养人才，使青年一代拥有更宽广的国际视野，为其走向全世界打下良好基础。

3.3.3 资源开发与工具应用

北京市上地实验学校　李岩
北京市第一零一中学　李文

摘要：听说是跨文化沟通中重要的交际手段，听说能力的培养是初中英语教学的重点内容。但海淀区山后学校普遍存在学生听说基础薄弱、教师对听说资源的利用和开发不够等问题。基于语言输入和输出理论，笔者提出基于教材和课堂的"四位一体"的初中英语听说课程资源开发和利用模型，试图建立听说课程资源体系，以提升海淀区山后学校学生的英语听说能力，落实英语学科核心素养。

关键词：初中英语听说；海淀区山后学校；课程资源开发与利用

《义务教育英语课程标准》（2022 年版）（以下简称《课标（2022 年版）》）指出，英语课程内容由主题、语篇、语言知识、文化知识、语言技能和学习策略等要素构成，这六要素也是构成核心素养发展的内容基础。其中语言技能包括听、说、读、看、写等方面的技能及其综合运用，为学生获取信息、建构知识、表达思想、交流情感提供途径。如今，随着跨文化交际的日益频繁，尤其是英语听说考试的实施，如何切实提高学生的英语听说能力更是成为初中英语教学的重点和热点问题。但在实际教学过程中，笔者发现农村校学生面临的英语听说能力发展困难更大、挑战更多。这一方面与长久以来重读写、轻听说的意识有关，另一方面在教学过程中也越来越多暴露出听说课程资源开发不足、体系不完整的问题。有鉴于此，笔者尝试以语言输入和输出理论为基本视域，针对农村校的特点，建立有效的初中英语听说课程资源开发和利用模型。

一、农村校学生英语听说能力现状

英语听说能力主要表现为听说技能和听说策略两个方面（Celce-Murcia，M.，2001）。听力技能具体包含语言知识（如语音、词汇、语法）、语用及语篇知识，口语技能可以从流利度和准确度两个维度来衡量。

笔者以北京海淀北部某初中农村校初一学生为研究对象，采用问卷调查和半结构性访谈的方式了解学生的听说能力现状。结果表明：65% 的学生没有熟练掌握小学词汇，80% 的学生根据音标拼读单词有困难。在听说习惯方面，学生普遍依赖于课堂听说练习，只有 13.7% 的学生课后会观看英文电影或听英文歌曲。有跨文化交流经历的学生只占到 5%，大部分学生因为听不懂或者表达能力欠缺而害怕用英语交流。由此可见，农村校学生普遍存在听说基础薄弱、缺乏听说环境等问题。

为进一步了解听说教学资源的现状，笔者对该校 4 名英语教师进行了访谈，从中了解到教师对教材内容进行了较为有限的听说练习改编尝试，且没有系统的听说课程资源可供利用，感到在教学中难以营造充分的听说教学环境。

二、语言输入和输出理论对本研究的启示

美国著名语言学家克拉申（Krashen）的输入假说（Input Hypothesis）认为，学习第二语言应像小孩习得母语一样。儿童语言能力是在对许多简化语言码的分析中无意识产生的，是接受大量输入以及输入时产生经验的结果（孟建国，朱建；2002）。Swain 在此基础上提出了"输出假设"（Output Hypothesis），认为学习者只有通过可理解性的语言输出，才能使二语既流利又准确（卢仁顺，2002）。

因此，要想培养农村校学生的英语听说能力，关键在于拓宽可理解性输入渠道，重视可理解性输出练习。

三、基于教材和课堂的"四位一体"听说课程资源开发与利用模型

《课标（2022 年版）》指出积极开发与合理利用课程资源是有效实施英语课程的重要保证。针对农村校学生听说能力现状，在语言输入和输出理论的指导下，笔者提出基于"教材内""教材外""课堂上""课堂下"的"四位一体"听说课程资源开发与利用模型，如图 3.16 所示。

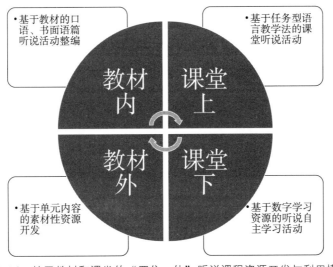

图 3.16　基于教材和课堂的"四位一体"听说课程资源开发与利用模型

（一）教材内：基于教材的口语、书面语篇听说活动整编

《课标（2022 年版）》提出，教师要基于学生已有基础和学习需求，挖掘每个语篇有价值的学习内容，对教材内容进行科学、合理的重组或取舍，实施精准教学。

针对农村校学生基础薄弱的特点，教师可以将教材口语和书面语篇进行适当改编，以确保教学目标的达成和学生学习效果的最优化。以人教版《英语》七年级上册 Unit 3 Is this your pencil？为例，本单元教学的核心结构为名词所有格 mine，yours，his，hers。教材 Section A 部分原有听说活动如下（图 3.17）：

1b **Listen and number the conversations [1-3].** 听录音，为对话编号

☐ A: Is this your pencil?
  B: Yes, it is. It's mine.

☐ A: Is that your schoolbag?
  B: No, it isn't. It's his.

☐ A: Are these your books?
  B: No, they aren't. They're hers.

2d **Role-play the conversation.** 分角色表演对话

Teacher: Hi, Anna. Are these your pencils?
Anna: No, they're Bob's.
Teacher: And is this his green pen?
Anna: No, it isn't. The blue pen is his.
Teacher: What about this dictionary?
Anna: It's Helen's. And the green pen is hers, too.
Teacher: And the eraser? Is that yours?
Anna: Yes, it is.
Teacher: Thank you for your help, Anna.
Anna: You're welcome.

图 3.17　人教版《英语》七年级上册 Unit 3 课本听说活动

教师改编后的听说活动如下（表 3.32）：

表 3.32　人教版《英语》七年级上册 Unit 3 改编听说活动

I Listen and fill in the blanks：听后填空（1b）
● Conversation 1
Girl：Are these _____ books?
Boy：No, they aren't. They're _____ .
● Conversation 2
Woman：Is that your _____?
Boy：No, it isn't. It's _____ .

续表

• Conversation 3

Boy：Is this your _____？

Girl：Yes, it is. It's _____ .

IV Listen and fill in the blanks：听后填空（2d）

Teacher：Hi, Anna, are these your _____？

Anna：No, they're _____ .

Teacher：And is this his _____ pen?

Anna：No, it isn't. The _____ pen is _____ .

Teacher：What about this _____？

Anna：It's _____ . And the green pen is _____ , too.

Teacher：And the _____？ Is that _____？

Anna：Yes, it is.

Teacher：Thank you for your _____ , Anna.

IV Role-play the conversation.

　　显然，教材原本的 1b 活动只涉及对目标语言的识别能力考查，2d 活动仅限于口头练习。改编后的 1b 和 2d 听说活动加强了对核心词汇的听写能力考查，巩固了本单元的核心词汇。

　　教师还可以对课本较为简单的书面语篇进行听说活动的改编。以人教版《英语》七年级上册 Unit 8 When is your birthday? Section B，2b 课文为例，教材活动如图 3.18 所示。

Read the school notice and list the activities and the dates.

阅读一则学校通知，列出文中活动和日期。

Dear students,

We have some interesting and fun things for you this term. On September 21st, we have a school trip in the afternoon.

October is a great month. On the 12th and the 15th, we have two ball games, soccer and volleyball.

School Day is on October 22nd. Your parents can come to our school. Next month, we have an art festival. It's on November 3rd. We have an English party on November 30th. And on December 3rd, we have a book sale in the school library.

This is a really busy term! Have a good time!

图 3.18　人教版《英语》七年级上册 Unit 8 课本活动

Dates	Activities

图 3.18　人教版《英语》七年级上册 Unit 8 课本活动（续）

教师将书面语篇改编为听说语篇，活动设计如表 3.33 所示。

表 3.33　人教版《英语》七年级上册 Unit 8 改编听说活动

Ⅰ. Listen and fill in the table.

Dates	Activities
_____ 21st	_____
October 12th and _____	Ball games：_____ and _____
October _____	_____
_____ 3rd	_____
_____ 30th	_____
_____ 3rd	Book _____

Ⅱ. Report the activities and dates first to yourself, and then to your partner.
The following structures may help you.
On…, we have…/We have…on…

改编后的听说活动解决了书面语篇过于简单的问题，同时为学生提供了本单元语言目标（Talk About Dates）的听说练习。

此外，对于教材中无法回应《课标（2022 年版）》能力要求的听说活动也可以进行科学改编。如《课标（2022 年版）》要求 8 年级学生在语言技能方面，能够获取和梳理口语语篇的主旨要义和关键细节，推断对话者之间的关系。以人教版《英语》八年级上册 Unit 9 Can you come to my party？Section A，2a 和 2b 为例，教材原本的 2a 和 2b 活动都涵盖了 who can't go to the party 这一细节问题，却没有对概括主旨和推断能力的考查（图 3.19）。

教师对以上活动进行了适当改编（表 3.34）。改编后的听力活动关注到了学生听并获取大意的能力、听并推测人物关系的能力，增加了口语练习活动，更符合该学段对学生听说能力的要求。

Listen and circle can or can't.

1. Jeff (can / can't) go to the party.
2. Mary (can / can't) go to the party.
3. May (can / can't) go to the party.
4. Mei Ling (can / can't) go to the party.
5. Paul (can / can't) go to the party.

 Listen again. Who can't go to the party? Why? Complete the chart.

Names	Reasons

图 3.19　人教版《英语》八年级上册 Unit 9 课本活动

表 3.34　人教版《英语》八年级上册 Unit 9 改编听说活动

Ⅰ. Listen and answer the questions.
1. What is Anna doing? ＿＿＿＿＿＿＿＿＿
2. What's the possible relationship between Anna and the speakers?

＿＿＿＿＿＿＿＿＿＿＿＿＿＿＿＿＿＿＿＿＿＿＿＿＿＿＿＿＿＿＿＿＿＿＿＿

Ⅱ. Listen again. Who can't go to the party? Why? Complete the chart.

Names	Reasons

Ⅲ. Perform the role play with your partner.

通过对教材的深入研读，基于学情和课标，对教材口语、书面语篇进行有效开发和利用，能够更有针对性地提高农村校学生初中英语听说能力。

（二）教材外：基于单元内容的素材性资源开发

《课标（2022 年版）》还鼓励教师突破教材的制约，充分挖掘教材以外的真实、完整、多样的英语材料，尤其是与单元主题情境相匹配的学习材料。针对农村校学生语音知识薄弱的特点，笔者所在的教师团队基于教材对语音知识的阐述，研发出以绕口令为特色的音标教学校本教材，旨在帮助学生准确读出和记忆单词，为学生开展自主学习奠定基础。部分章节如表 3.35 所示。

表 3.35 音标教学校本教学节选

Exercise 1

一、英语音标学习——前元音

/i:/ eat bee feel he feet me pea sea heat

/ɪ/ it big listen fit hill sit hit

/e/ bed bread pen beg get wet tell bet lesson

/æ/ match and cap black bad cat hat bag catch

二、朗读下面的绕口令：

1. A cheap sheep is cheaper than a cheap ship.

一只便宜的绵羊比一艘便宜的船更便宜。

2. Bill was beating a big beast with his big fist, and his big fist was badly bitten by the big beast.

比尔正用他的大拳头打一头大野兽，但他的大拳头被这只大野兽狠狠地咬了一口。

3. Ted sent Fred ten hens yesterday so Fred's fresh bread is ready already.

特德昨天给弗莱德送去了十只母鸡，所以弗莱德的新鲜面包已经准备好了。

4. Whether the weather be fine or whether the weather be not.

Whether the weather be cold or whether the weather be hot.

We'll weather the weather whether we like it or not.

无论晴天或阴天，无论是冷或是暖，不管喜欢与否，我们都要经受风霜雨露。

5. A fat fat cat catches a fat fat rat.

一只大肥猫抓住了一只大肥老鼠。

6. Can you can a can as a canner can can a can?

你能够像罐头工人一样装罐头吗？

为进一步加强学生朗读时对重音、意群、语调与节奏的把握，笔者所在团队设计了与单元教学内容匹配的"每周一歌"教学活动，让学生在优美的歌曲中体会重音、语调和节奏的表意功能，运用语音知识更好地表达自己的意图和态度。例如，在人教版《英语》八年级上册 Unit 8 How do you make a banana milk shake? Section B 以感恩节为主题的单元教学中，笔者使用了以下歌曲作为课堂导入和结束活动表 3.36。

表 3.36 人教版《英语》八年级上册 Unit 8 听说活动

I. Sing along with the vocal version of this song.

Things I'm Thankful For

There are many things I am thankful for

续表

Ⅰ can find them near and far

There are many things I am thankful for

Let me tell you what they are

I'm thankful for the earth

I'm thankful for the sea

I'm thankful for my friends

…

Ⅱ. Write out your list of things you are thankful for and sing your own words accompanied by the instrumental version.

此外，英语报刊题材广泛、信息多样，为学生提供了鲜活地道、真实丰富的语言材料。为拓宽农村校学生英语听说途径，教师还可以依托单元主题语境，将报纸上的文章改编为听说活动，帮助学生复现词汇、巩固所学、促进知识建构和思维发展。如就人教版《英语》九年级 Unit 13 We're trying to save the earth! Section A 3a 保护鲨鱼的主题教学，笔者补充了 21 世纪学生英文报·初一版第 749 期 "Protect Our Animal Friends" 语篇，并将其改编为听说活动，如表 3.37 所示。

表 3.37　人教版《英语》九年级 Unit 13 补充听说活动

Ⅰ. Listen and answer the questions.

1. What is the speech mainly about?

2. Why did the speaker give the talk?

Ⅱ. Listen and complete the missing information.

● Giraffes

Over the last 30 years, the number of giraffes has _____ by 40 percent. There are now fewer than 100,000 giraffes in the world today. Giraffes are losing their _____ because of human activities such as _____ .

● Sharks and rays

Working together, more than 300 researchers did an eight-year study of sharks and rays. The study found that 41 percent of the 611 ray species are _____ . Sharks and rays are often _____ for their meat, skin and _____ . They also grow very slowly and don't have many _____ .

● Komodo dragons

Komodo dragons are the largest lizards（蜥蜴）in the world. They can grow to three meters long and as _____ as 70 kilograms! Komodo dragons live on only five islands in Indonesia, but they are now _____ extinction. They have lost a lot of their _____ because of human activities and _____ _____ .

Ⅲ. Report what you learn from the speech first to yourself, then to a partner.

围绕教材内容，通过绕口令、英文歌曲、时文等学习材料的合理开发，既补充了教材的内容、突破了教材的制约，又拓宽了农村校学生英语听说学习的渠道，增加了听说练习的输入和输出途径。

（三）课堂上：基于任务型语言教学法的课堂听说活动

任务型教学（Task-based Approach）于 20 世纪 80 年代由语言学家 N. S. Prabhu 提出，主张以意义为中心，以完成交际任务为目标，强调"从做中学"（Learn by Doing Things）（丰玉芳，唐晓岩，2004）。"任务型"教学模式由"课堂导入""参与任务""学习新知""巩固新知"和"操练运用"环节构成，由简到繁，层层深入。针对农村校学生缺乏英语口语自信和交流环境的特点，教师可以围绕阅读语篇设计听说教学活动，在主题意义的探究中，通过复述（Retell）、角色扮演（Role Play）、讨论（Discussion）、展示（Presentation）等一系列听说活动，发展学生的听说能力。

以人教版《英语》九年级 Unit 11 Sad movies make me cry. Section B 2b The Winning Team 的阅读教学为例。该文本讲述了 Peter 输球后非常沮丧，在父亲的鼓励和团队的理解下走出阴影、重树信心的故事。课文原文如下：

The Winning Team

Peter kept his eyes on the ground. He felt like there was a heavy weight on his shoulders as he walked home alone. It was the worst day of his life. His mind would not stop thinking about what happened only just an hour ago on the school soccer field. How could he have missed scoring that goal? He had let his whole team down. His stupid mistake made him angry. His team had lost the game because of him. He was really worried that his coach might kick him off the team.

As soon as he walked through the door, his father asked, "What's wrong, son?" Peter's feelings were written all over his face. "I lost the game," Peter replied. Then he went into his room without another word. Ten minutes later, Peter heard his father knocking on his bedroom door. He opened the door to let him in.

"Look, Peter. I don't know what happened. But whatever it was, don't be too hard on yourself."

"I lost the game, Dad. I failed my team. They'll probably never let me play again."

"Soccer is about team effort. You're not the only reason your team lost. If you have a good team, you should support each other. Besides, winning or losing is only half the game. The other half is learning how to communicate with your teammates and learning from your mistakes."

Peter didn't say anything, but what his father said made him think carefully.

The next day，Peter went to soccer practice with courage rather than fear in his heart.

"Hey，guys，" he said to his teammates. "I'm really sorry about yesterday. We were so close to winning that game. But I think if we continue to pull together，we're going to win the next one."

To his surprise and relief，his teammates all nodded in agreement.

"Yeah，" they said，"don't worry about it. It's never just one person's fault. We should think about how we can do better next time."

Peter smiled. It made him feel lucky to know that he was on a winning team.

教师可以在读前、读中和读后三个环节中设计以下口语活动。

1. 读前讨论：激活背景知识，预测文本内容

教师引入话题：Have you ever made a mistake？ How did it make you feel？ Talk to your partner about what happened. 学生通过谈论自己的犯错经历，激活相关表达，为后面共情 Peter 的心理做铺垫。

教师呈现文本标题 "The Winning Team" 和插图（穿着队服的球员），引导学生预测文本内容，并提问 What makes the team a winning team？

2. 读后复述：归纳故事情节，内化文本语言

教师呈现表 3.38，从故事发生的时间、地点、人物、事件入手，引导学生从文本中查找信息，理清人物关系和故事脉络。

表 3.38　人教版《英语》九年级 Unit 11 复述活动

When	Where	Who	What
An hour ago			
When Peter got home			
The next day			

在此基础上，教师鼓励学生运用课文语言，根据所填表格，复述故事情节，从而内化语言。

3. 读后角色扮演：体会人物心理、揣摩人物形象

教师引导学生关注表格第一行的内容，重读课本第 1 段，并请学生再现 Peter 输球后 "kept his eyes on the ground" "there was a heavy weight on his shoulders" 等描写的人物状态。通过形象的表演，感受语言背后传达的人物心理。

教师再引导学生关注表格第二行的内容，重读文章第 2~6 段，并请学生角色扮演 Peter 和父亲的对话，同时追问：

a）When Peter's father asked his son what was wrong, it shows that he…

b）Peter's father knocked on Peter's bedroom door, it shows that he…

c）Peter's father said "whatever it was, don't be too hard on yourself", it shows that he…

d）Peter's father said "the other half is learning how to communicate with your teammates and learning from your mistakes", he was trying to…

通过角色扮演和链式问题，学生心中逐渐呈现出一个关爱孩子、理解并尊重孩子的父亲形象。

4. 读后讨论：深化主题意义，挖掘标题内涵

教师引导学生关注表格最后一行，重读文章第 7 ~ 11 段，并给出如下问题，并请学生分组讨论：

a）Why did Peter think they were on a winning team even though they lost the game?

b）Do you think "The Winning Team" is a good title? Why or why not?

c）Now what do you think makes a team a winning team?

通过对以上开放性问题的讨论，不仅帮助学生加深了对文章主题意义的理解，同时培养了学生的批判性思维和创造性思维。

5. 读后展示：续写故事情节，展示创编能力

课后作业环节，教师设置了读后续写的活动，What will the coach say? What will Peter and his teammates do later? What will Peter say to his father? Will the team win the next game?

学生基于本节课对主题意义的探讨，课后再创造性延展语篇。次日以口头展示的形式，在全班交流。

以上教学实例基于任务型语言教学法，在主题意义的引领下，通过角色扮演、讨论、展示等一系列口语输出活动，不仅充分利用和开发了学生资源，创设了开放性的师生、生生互动的交流与分享平台，更激发了学生的已有知识、经验、想象力和创造力。在发展学生思维品质的同时，提高了英语听说能力。

（四）课堂下：基于数字学习资源的听说自主学习活动

信息技术的发展不仅为英语教学提供了丰富多样的教学资源，还创造了跨时空的语言学习和使用机会。为了引导学生从不同渠道以不同形式学习英语，教师可以从学校和家庭两个方面进行资源开发。

在学校不具备语言实验室的情况下，农村校教师可以利用活动课和学科活动为学生创造英语听说机会。如笔者所在的教师团队利用教室里的多媒体设备，面向不同程度的学生，先后开设了《看迪士尼电影学英语》《学唱英文歌》《自信英语演讲》《英语奇葩说》等极具趣味性的选修课，在激发学生英语学习兴趣的同时，培养学生的听说能力，建立学生学英语的信心。另外，利用学校的多功能厅，不同年级可以开展多样的学科活动，如初一年级英语朗读大赛、初二年级英语趣配音大赛、初三年级英语演讲大赛等。以活动为平台，以赛事为契机，鼓励学生开口说英语，在参与中展示自我、挑战自我。

教师还应引导学生建立和利用自己个性化的学习资源。例如，鼓励学生在家长的监督下，利用 E 听说、一起中学等手机软件，每天练习听说。结合单元教学内容，设计录制英语视频的周末作业。如人教版《英语》八年级上册 Unit 8 How do you make a banana milk shake？的单元作业，就可以设计为拍摄一段 1 分钟以上自己制作美食并解说步骤的视频，以实现学生口头描述食物制作过程的单元教学目标。假期时，教师还可以指导学生跟读有声读物（如《典范英语》）和观看英文电影（如哈利·波特系列），并以适当的方式进行交流和分享，培养学生自主进行课外英语视听活动的习惯，引导学生学会学习。

课堂下跨时空的听说学习资源和渠道的拓展，不仅符合了《课标（2022 年版）》要求的"课外试听活动每周不少于 30 分钟"的要求，更有助于学生养成良好的终身学习习惯，从而推动英语学科核心素养的持续发展。

结语

本研究基于农村校学生英语听说能力培养的需要，解决农村校听说课程资源利用和开发不足的问题，在语言输入和输出理论的指导下，根据《课标（2022 年版）》要求，构建基于"教材"和"课堂"的四位一体的初中英语听说资源开发和利用模型，并提出具体操作建议，以期促进农村校学生英语听说能力的提高和核心素养的发展。在实际教学中，教师还需要根据学情和学段特点因地制宜，让课程资源的开发与利用服务于有效教学。

第 4 章

走向成功——听说中考

2018 年北京中考英语满分减到了 100 分，其中笔答卷为 60 分，听力口语为 40 分。口语从不考到考的变化，显示出教育部门对初中生综合语言运用能力的重视程度。面对英语中考的口语听说考试，老师们应当如何指导考生去应对？针对这个问题，本章将以具体题型为例进行分析，提供教学备考思路。

一、课标要求

首先，教师应当指导考生了解初中英语阶段课程标准对听说的要求，明确奋斗的目标。以下是对《课标（2022 年版）》中比较重要的部分进行的摘录：

《课标（2022 年版）》对学生听的能力的要求包括：

（1）能听懂相关主题的语篇，借助关键词句、图片等复述语篇内容。

（2）能利用语篇所给提示预测内容的发展，判断说话者的身份和关系，推断说话者的情感、态度和观点。

（3）能理解多模态语篇（如广播、电视节目等）的主要内容，获取关键信息。

（4）能通过影视作品等材料获取与中外文化有关的基本信息，比较文化异同。

《课标（2022 年版）》对学生说的能力的要求包括：

（1）朗读相关主题的简短语篇时，连读、停顿自然，语音、语调基本正确。

（2）能根据口头交际的具体情境，初步运用得体的语言形式，表达自己的情感、态度和观点。

（3）能选用正确的词语、句式和时态，通过口语语篇描述、介绍人和事物，表达个人看法，表意清晰，话语基本通顺。

（4）能用所学英语，通过口语语篇简单介绍中外主要文化现象（如风景名胜、历史故事、文化传统等），语义基本连贯。

（5）能讲述具有代表性的中外杰出人物的故事，如科学家等为社会和世界作出贡献的人物，表达基本清楚。

二、考试方式

其次，教师要指导考生明确听说考试的方式。初中英语听说考试时间约为半个小时，考试形式是人机对话。考试题型分为四道大题：第一大题，听后选择；第二大题，听后回答；第三大题，听后记录和听后转述；第四大题，朗读短文。

三、备考关键

备考中考听说，关键就在于：课本是基础（课本中词汇与句型是保障，课本中的话题是考试中对话和独白的来源），听力技巧是应试的手段，两者缺一不可（图4.1）。

图4.1　听说备考策略示意图

具体可以理解为：①复习课本——词汇是基础，听说考试不是笔试，不能光"认字"，要重视单词的发音、拼读、在语意群中的含义。课本中的基础句型是关键，没有句型就无法构成对话，也就没有交流，无法沟通。②熟练掌握中考话题——英语考试不可能重复考生以往学过的对话和文段，但是话题是不变的，熟练掌握课本话题就可以发现听力材料中内容的共性，举一反三，通过已有知识去分析听到的信息。初中阶段的口语话题包括自我介绍，个人爱好，出游与度假，问询与指路，生病与建议，环境与保护，文化与风俗等，老师在复习阶段可以引导学生进行归纳整理，以话题为线索进行总结。③利用有效资源反复练习——某些手机APP，如"一起中学""E听说"等，都是考生在学校以外有效的复习手段，坚持每天听说，形成有效的语言环境，才能熟能生巧，处变不惊。④总结题型规律，掌握做题技巧——听说考试不同大题在做题技巧方面的侧重点各有不同，接下来本文将对如何应对每一道大题进行相应的解析。

四、题型解析

（一）听后选择

北京英语听说考试第一题听后选择为客观性试题，即选择题，它重点考查考生听取信息的能力，以及对所听到信息进行加工和理解的能力。第一大题包括三段对话和一段独白，其中每段对话或独白播放两遍，每段对话或独白有两道小题，从 A、B、C 三个选项中选择最佳选项，并用鼠标点击该选项提交。第一大题的考试题目数量为 8 题，每小题分数为 1.5 分，总计分数为 12 分，总计时长为 9 分钟，其中第一节对话包括第 1 至第 2 小题（3 分），第二节对话包括第 3 至第 4 小题（3 分），第三节对话包括第 5 至第 6 小题（3 分），第四节独白包括第 7 至第 8 小题（3 分）。本题中的对话和独白的难度逐渐增加。下面将以样题为例，来分析第一大题的相关考试技巧。

（1）第一节、第二节对话。

例题一：

请听一段对话，回答第 1 至第 2 小题。

1. What would the man like to eat?

A. A sandwich.

B. A hamburger.

C. French fries.

2. How much is the meal?

A. ＄8.

B. ＄9.

C. ＄10.

听力材料一：

W：Good morning. What can I do for you?

M：I'd like a large hamburger, please.

W：Beef or chicken?

M：Beef, please.

W：OK. Would you like something to drink?

M：Well, a cup of coffee.

W：Alright. Altogether that will be ＄8.

M：Here you are.

答案：B，A

例题二：

请听一段对话，回答第 3 至第 4 小题。

3. Where is Emma now?

A. At home.

B. At the theatre.

C. In the hospital.

4. When is Emma coming back to school?

A. In one week.

B. In two weeks.

C. In three weeks.

听力材料二：

M：Hi，Lucy. Can you go to see a movie with me after school?

W：I'd love to，but I can't. I am going to see Emma.

M：What's the matter with her?

W：She has a stomachache. The doctor asked her to stay in hospital.

M：Oh，I am sorry to hear that. Hope she'll be better soon.

W：She's much better，and the doctor said she could go home the day after tomorrow.

M：Well，is she coming back then?

W：Oh，no. She is coming back to school in two weeks.

M：Oh，poor Emma. That'll be boring.

W：You're right. Let's visit her and tell her what happened at school.

M：That sounds like a good idea.

答案：C，B

例题一和例题二中的 4 道小题可以归纳为事实题，它们的考查的内容是听力
文段当中的基础信息。这类题型属于简单题的范畴。通过中考真题汇总我们可以
得出结论，第一大题的第一节和第二节听力题的出题规律为：简单对话，信息获
取直接，没有干扰内容，答案按顺序出现。因此，我们在做题时应当遵循图 4.2
的原则。

具体做题的步骤可以分为如下三步：

■ Step 1 Pre-listening：read & guess

■ Step 2 Listen & Write

■ Step 3 Choose and Input

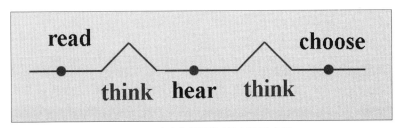

图 4.2 听选简单题解题步骤示意图

也就是说，第一步要做预听——快速阅读听力的题干及选项，从而思考猜测接下来听到的内容。第二步要听且记录——在听的过程中不能因为题目简单直白就忽略好习惯，充分利用考试所发的草稿纸进行记录。第三步要选择且输入——找到正确答案后，从容地点击正确答案并提交，一定要确定自己的输入正确，不要提交后才发现自己误输入了错误答案。

（2）第三节对话。

第一大题的前两节对话的难度与试题比较简单，但是第三段对话中如何应对干扰信息呢？以下面的样题为例。

例题三：

请听一段对话，回答第 5 至第 6 小题。

5. Where are the two speakers？

A. At home.

B. In a museum.

C. In a shop.

6. Which dress are they going to buy？

A. The red one.

B. The blue one.

C. Neither.

听力材料三：

M：Oh，look at that dress，Maria. It's perfect for you.

W：The blue one？I'm not sure.

M：No，the red one.

W：Oh，that？Hmm. Red isn't a good color for me.

M：Well，you prefer the blue one？How much is it？

W：It's ＄120！I like the blue one，but that's too expensive！I can't afford it.

M：Hey，let me get it for you. It's your birthday present.

答案：C，B

例题四：

请听一段对话，回答第 7 至第 8 小题。

7. How did the woman go to the country？

A. By boat.

B. By car.

C. On foot.

8. What did the man do last weekend？

A. He repaired his car.

B. He bought a new car.

C. He made a model car.

听力材料四：

M：So，what did you do this weekend，Kate？

W：Oh，Mike and I went for a drive in the country.

M：That sounds nice. Where did you go？

W：We walked along the path through the forest and had a picnic by the lake. How about you？ Did you do anything special？

M：Not really. I just worked on my car all day.

W：That old thing！ Why don't you just buy a new one？

M：But then what would I do every weekend？

答案：B，A

根据以上两段对话和题目可以看出，第一大题的第三节对话在内容上更加复杂，而在题目的选项上也增加了干扰选项。这就需要考生在获取信息的基础上加以分析，排除错误答案，或者对所获信息进行加工，比如：例题三中并没有提到对话者的所在位置，但是我们可以根据他们对话中的关键词"dress""expensive"等，推测出他们正在购物，因此得出结论，他们在商店；而第二题需要考生判断最终他们买了哪条裙子时，材料既提到了"red one"，又提到了"blue one"，这就需要考生来进行判断，如果根据"can't afford it"，就认为哪条都没有买的话就过于武断了，如果冷静地把文章听完，通过最后的内容"let me get it for you. It's your birthday present."，了解另一说话人当作礼物送给她后，就比较容易进行选择了，这也是考查考生分析处理所听到的信息的能力。

又比如：例题四中的第一小题，询问说话人的出行方式，这也是人教版《英语》七年级下册第三单元 Unit 3 How do you get to school？ 的相应话题，考生最熟悉的句型就是"How do you get to school？"，以及"by bus/by bike/on foot"等答案，但是在听力材料当中并没有体现课本中的基础知识，而是发生了迁移，用教材当中其他单元出现的词组"go for a drive"（开车兜风）进行代替。这就需要考生能够听懂相应信息并加以转换。而第二小题询问另一人周末的活动时，首先需要考生能够认识选项当中的重点动词过去式，"repair—repaired"（修理），"buy—bought"（购买），"make—made"（制造）。然后，还要根据听力内容进行判断，如"worked on my car all day"，以及问答"Why don't you just buy a new one?""But then what would I do every weekend?"分析得出说话人整日在自己的车上下功夫，并且以此为乐而拒绝购买新车，进而得出结论——他是在修理自己的旧车。

因此，考生在处理此类听力题时应该做到如下几点（图 4.3）：①预听——快速阅读听力的题干及选项，从而思考猜测接下来听到的内容。②听且分析记录——根据所听到的内容判断哪些是与题目有关的信息，记录并排除干扰项。干扰项的排除可以遵循"肯定否定"原则，即不管过程有多复杂，把握最终结论，抓住关键词，如"yes""I will take it."等，正确的保留，错误的放弃。③合理利用草稿纸进行记录——在一些题中经常会出现数字信息，甚至简单的计算，比如一张门票是 20 元，一家三口去需要多少钱等。这就需要考生在听的过程中记录信息并加以利用。④做出选择并输入提交。

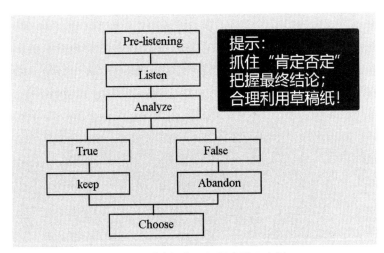

图 4.3　听选复杂题解题步骤示意图

（3）第四节独白。

前三段对话的做题方法是针对对话的，那么第一大题第四节的独白如何处理呢？以下面的样题为例。

例题五：

How many kinds of jobs are offered to the students?

A. Three.

B. Four.

C. Five.

听力材料五：

Hello, I am John Smith. As the head of School Daily, I'd like to introduce you to our newspaper. We'd like some volunteers to help us improve our paper. Experience isn't important, but writing and typing are important. We want some people to rewrite articles. We need an expert to take photos. We also need several engineers who know how to plan printing work since the paper comes out five days a week. You know, our paper is very popular among the students and many people in the city are interested in it as well. So, we also need some students to send the papers. Good marks are a must for working on the paper. There is some money for you according to how much work you do for the paper, but don't expect to get rich. This isn't something you do for the money. Mostly it's just for fun. Anyone who is interested in joining us should speak to me after this meeting. Be ready to start working right away. Thank you for listening.

答案：B

例题五是一道细节归纳题。题干要求计算工作的种类。因此在预听环节考生就可以预测这段独白的内容有可能和招聘有关，并在听前预设相关知识进行准备。本段独白中学校报社有四种工作需要学生去做。一是"rewrite articles"，二是"take photos"，三是"plan printing work"，四是"send the papers"。有些学生会误认为文章开头提到的"typing"也是一项工作，其实不然，文中说的是"Experience isn't important, writing and typing are important."会打字和能写文章是从事报社工作的人所要具备的能力，并不是报社需要一个专门的打字员。真正的工作种类是从下面的文字中开始的，而且这些工作都涉及人，因此我们能通过和人有关的名词加以判断，比如"some people""an expert""several engineers""some students"。综上所述，独白中的细节题需要考生在听独白的过程中，利用好草稿纸认真记录并加以分析整理，从而得出结论，做出正确判断。

例题六：

What is the passage mainly about?

A. The ball games for the weekend.

B. The school weekend guide.

C. How much are the tickets to the school concerts.

听力材料六：

Good morning, boys and girls. Here is your weekend guide for Riverside High School, and we are here with some suggestions for you as usual.

My first suggestion is about ball games. It is a good weekend for football. On Friday, Riverside High School will play against Lowland High School at Riverside, and then they will face Maple Road High School on Saturday at Center Park. If you want to watch the football games, you can buy tickets at the school ticket office. There are also some tickets for the Saturday night concert by the Big Apple Band. Most of the tickets are ten dollars; there are also some five-dollar seats on sale. To get the seats, call the Student Center at 646 – 578, or go to the box office. Also, the school museum will be open from 10：00 a. m. until 5：00 p. m. on Sunday, besides, the stamp show and the photo show of early people, there will be a special show of paintings. The tickets are free.

答案：B

例题六是一道主旨大意归纳题。此类题是难题，要求考生对听到的内容有一个整体的把握和全面的领会。任何一段文字都是围绕一个中心展开的，有时主旨大意较明显，有时则需要归纳、概括。因此，在认真审题（题干、选项）的基础上，考生听第一遍的过程中要理清独白的结构——是总分，分总，还是总分总。根据独白的结构，重点听开头或结尾的几句话，一般情况下，这几句话中会有主题句。本段独白的结构为总分结构，因此在文章开头的第二句话"Here is your weekend guide for Riverside High School, and we are here with some suggestions for you as usual. "中就能够概括出答案 suggestions for the weekend 或 the guide for the weekend。部分考生容易犯的错误就是被选项 A 和 C 的内容所迷惑。虽然独白中确实出现了相应的内容，但是球类比赛和音乐会的票价只是周末活动的一部分，由于考生没有掌握文章的整体内容，只听到了细节信息，才出现了以偏概全、盲人摸象的错误。

例题七：

What does the speaker expect the listeners to do?

A. To learn a lesson.

B. To know the news.

C. To offer some help.

听力材料七：

Good morning, ladies and gentlemen. Welcome to the Lincoln School Parent-Teaching Meeting. Before we begin our meeting, I'd like to talk to you for a few minutes about something very important. Well，let's take our city as an example. The population of our city is about 7.8 million. The number means not only children but also grown-ups. Now，how many grown-ups – I mean people over 16 – do you think are illiterate in our city? But first，let me tell you what "illiterate" means. It means that people who can't read road signs and maps are illiterate. They can't write letters. And they can't read bedtime stories to their children. Take a minute to think about this. How many grown-ups would you guess are illiterate in our city? You'll be surprised. In our city there are almost one million illiterate grown-ups. I think we have to know what's happening in our school. We have to make sure that every student who leaves our school isn't illiterate. It's not only our duty but also yours. I hope we can discuss the problem at this meeting.

答案：C

这是一道总结说话人发言目的、意图的题。此题需要考生根据所听到的内容对信息进行加工、整理，透过现象看本质。根据说话人的说明与举例，发现其内在的目的与意图，从而选出与说话人想法相同的一项。从本文说话人在最后的结尾处提到了"It's not only our duty but also yours. I hope we can discuss the problem at this meeting."，可以看出说话人并不是陈述事实，他在最后呼吁大家进行讨论并解决问题，希望大家伸出援助之手，共同商讨对策。以此为判断依据，就容易做出选择了。

根据以上三道例题的分析，在应对第一大题第四节独白部分的题型时，我们可以把技巧概括为：分析题型，勤记录；抓住结构，听首尾。

（二）听后回答

北京英语听说考试第二题听后回答为主观性口语试题，即口头回答问题并录音。它考查考生听取并记录信息的能力，以及考生发音的准确性、口语表达语法的正确性（图4.4）。

第二大题包括5段对话，每段对话播放两遍，每段对话后有一个问题，考生听完对话后，在10秒内口头回答问题并完成录音。第二大题题目数量为5题，每小题分值为2分，总计分值为10分，总计考试时长为5分钟。这种包含了听与说的题型除了掌握基础知识与拥有好的语音语调外，还有什么好的应对策略呢？第二大题的题目难度一般不会很高，同时评分由人工判卷完成，抓住答题时的关键信息作答并且减少语法错误就可以获得较高的分数。因此把握题型和相应的答题技巧就是重中之重。下面以样题为例。

例题八：

Who played football yesterday?

听力材料八：

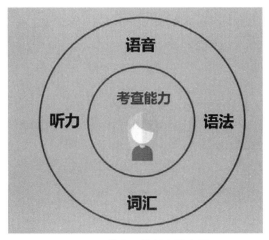

图 4.4　听后回答考查能力图

W：Hi，Frank. Did you play football yesterday?

M：Yes，I did.

W：What did you do after you played football?

M：I played chess with John.

W：Are you going to play chess again this afternoon?

M：No，we aren't. We're going to plant some flowers with David in the yard.

W：That sounds great.

答案：Frank（<u>played</u> football yesterday）.

本题题干考查的是主语，因此答案的关键词是"Frank"，答出即可满分。有些考生习惯完整作答，但是要务必注意题干中的时态为过去时，如果在口头表达时出现将"played"读作"plays"的错误，就要减去相应的分数，实在是得不偿失，画蛇添足。

例题九：

What did Sally buy for her sister?

听力材料九：

M：Hi，Sally. How was your vacation?

W：It was great! I went to Hong Kong.

M：Did you go there with your parents?

W：No. I went with my friends. Everyone had a great time.

M：Did you do anything interesting there?

W：Yes. I went to a fun park and I did some shopping. Things are expensive there but I did buy my sister a beautiful handbag.

答案：A beautiful handbag.

本题题干考查的是宾语，在对话的结尾处可以获得答案"a beautiful hand-bag"。为了避免出现语法错误，在此还是不建议考生用完整的句子回答问题。但是，容易出现的语法错误是考生口头作答时会忽略冠词"a"，只回答"beautiful handbag"，这会被扣除相应分数。所以教师在辅导学生时应当提醒考生回答简要的同时也要注意答案的完整性。

例题十：

When are they going to clean the room?

听力材料十：

W：Bill，what are you doing now?

M：I'm playing computer games.

W：Could you clean your room now?

M：Mum，I cleaned it last Friday.

W：You have to clean it again for your party.

M：OK，mom！I'll do it with dad after dinner.

答案：After dinner.

例题十一：

Where are the keys?

听力材料十一：

W：You look so worried，Andy. What's the matter?

M：I have lost my keys.

W：Oh，what a bad luck！Have you searched your desk and pocket?

M：Of course！I've looked everywhere in the room.

W：Look！What're those at the door?

M：Wow，the keys！Thank goodness，and thank you for your help.

答案：At the door.

以上两题题干考查的是时间状语和地点状语，在作答时除了注意完整的简要答案以外，务必要注意介词不能省略。

例题十二：

What can Ann's sister do for Bill?

听力材料十二：

M：Hello！This is Bill speaking. Could I speak to Ann，please?

W：Sorry，she is out at the moment. I'm Ann's sister. Can I take a message for you?

M：Yes，please.

答案：She can take a message.

本题题干考查的是谓语，与以上题目的答题技巧不同的是，回答谓语的题目不能过分省略，要注意语法的正确性，只回答动词短语而缺少主语是不完整的。因此，此类题目在回答时务必要回答整句，保证句法的正确。

例题十三：

What does the man come here for?

听力材料十三：

W：Your English is very good. Where do you come from?

M：I come from America.

W：What do you come here for?

M：I come here to meet my friend Sally. She works in the city.

W：A friend? What does she do?

M：She is a teacher.

答案：To meet his friend Sally.

本题题干考查的是目的状语，答案在文中十分明确，但是要注意答案的关键部分是动词不定式，而动词不定式要有 to，还要注意人称的变化。

例题十四：

Why does the man look so tired?

听力材料十四：

W：Hi，Tom. You look so tired. Why?

M：Hi，Mary. I didn't sleep well last night.

W：I think a little exercise would do you good.

M：Well，I also think so. But I don't have time to go to a gym.

答案：Because he didn't sleep well last night.

本题的特殊疑问词是"why"，在日常的练习中为了让考生做到答题规范，我们始终要求学生用"because"开头。虽然没有也无伤大雅，但是细节决定成败，容易做到的就不要忽略。

针对听说考试第二大题，我们可以将答题技巧归纳为如下的几句话：完整答语应简要，有些单词不能掉，发音准确语音亮，语法正确毛病少。

（三）听后记录和听后转述

北京英语听说考试第三题分为两节，第一节为听后记录，是主观性笔试题，共5小题，每题1分，共5分，时长约为5分钟，考生听完两遍录音后，通过键盘输入记录表，每空一词。此题多考查名词（单复数），动词（不同时态），形容词、副词等。第二节为听后转述，是口语试题，共5分，约为7分钟。考生听完第三遍录音后，准备2分钟，并在2分钟内完成表格的转述，一般转述的开头都会给出。

本大题的第一节考查考生中考词汇的掌握情况，要求考生在语境中根据语义听懂单词及属性（如单复数、时态变化等），能够正确拼写单词并记录。5道题的答案在听力文段中按顺序出现，考生可以按照表格内容抓住关键信息，但在听的过程中要注意说话者清辅音（如复数结尾S的发音）和吞音的变化，避免漏听和错听；并且在理解前后语境的基础上拼写符合语义的单词，避免形近字和同音字的干扰。

本大题的第二节考查考生复述的能力，是口语考试中难度较大的一题。考生在听第三遍的过程中需要将表格中省略号处的两点信息听出并记录在草稿纸上，并且在2分钟的准备时间内将全部信息转化成文段的形式口述并录音。此题的技巧可以归纳为如下几个字：不求有功，但求无过。下面我们就通过举例来具体分析。

例题十五：

第一节，听两遍短文，然后根据所听内容和提示将所缺信息填写在相应位置上（表4.1）。

表4.1　听后填表

Activities for dads and kids on Father's Day	
Make a meal.	• make 1. _____ for Dad • cook together
Play games.	• plan a game • invite his 2. _____ and your...
Read a book.	• pick a book • share a 3. _____ • take turns...
Create a 4. _____	• bring out best ideas • give Dad a kiss and a thank-you 5. _____

第二节，听第三遍短文，然后根据所听内容和提示信息转述短文。

Chris shared some ideas on Father's Day activities. We can…

听力材料十五：

Good morning. I'm Chris. We are going to talk about some activities for dads and kids to do together on Father's Day.

Make a meal. You can make breakfast for Dad on that day. It is fun to have the whole family cook together. Try to do much of the food preparation and cooking.

Play games. It's a good idea to plan a game for Dad. If he loves playing football, you can invite his friends and yours to have a game with him.

Read a book. Pick a book and spend the afternoon sharing a story with each other. And then take turns reading or acting out the story for the rest of the family.

Create a gift. Bring out your best ideas and work on them together. Remember, the most important gifts include a kiss and a thank-you card.

Hope you'll have a happy day with your dad.

答案：

第一节：1. breakfast　2. friends　3. story　4. gift　5. card

本道例题的第一节考生在准备时需要通读表格内容根据问题前后的语境加以分析，才能在听的过程中迅速找到答案。比如第 1 题考了名词 breakfast，考生可根据一级标题 make a meal 得出线索；第 2 题考查了 friend 的复数形式，考生能够在听前预测此处需要填写的是一个名词；第 3 题也考查了单词 story，但前面的提示词 share 原文给的是 sharing 形式，需要考生鉴别出来；第 4 题考查了名词 gift，这里很难猜出，但考生听到后面 the most important gifts include a kiss and a thank-you card 就能返回猜到是"创造一个礼物"（create a gift）；第 5 题考查了名词 card。由于此处听力原文和表格信息有出入，考生需要先通过 kiss 确定需要听的位置，然后听出单词。但此处很容易听错成 car，学生需要通过前面给的语境 thank-you 推测出是感谢卡。这些都是在听的过程中需要学生留意的细节。

第二节：

Chris shared some ideas on Father's Day activities. We can make a meal. We can make breakfast for our Dad on that day, and it is fun to cook with the whole family. **Next**, play games. It's a good idea to plan a game for Dad. If he loves playing football, we can invite his friends and mine to have a game with him. **What's more**, we can read a book together. Pick a book and share a story with each other. We can take turns reading or acting out the story for the family. **Finally**, create a gift. Bring out our best ideas and work on them together. We can give Dad a kiss and a thank-you card. That way, we will have a happy day with our dads.

本道例题的第二节需要考生在听第三遍的过程中进行一定的记录。第二节要求考生将表格的第一级标题和第二级标题内容全部转述，还要在此基础上补充出两处省略号部分的内容。省略的部分往往是一个从句或者并列短语的一部分。从上面的样题可以看出，表格所给信息较少，而且与听力材料的内容有一定变化，比如原文给的是"Remember, the most important gifts include a kiss and a thank-you card."，而表格中的信息是"give Dad a kiss and a thank-you…"。这种情况下，要求考生在听第一遍时，根据空格前后的提示词，基本听出所缺的5个单词。第二遍听时，考生要先核对自己所填的单词词性、词形是否正确。在有把握的情况下，听出一处省略号处的信息并做记录。第三遍听时，考生可以核对已经听出的部分，并继续听和记录另一处省略号的信息。文章还有其他信息是表格中所没有的，这里考生完全可以忽略，言简意赅地完成要求即可，这也就是前面提到的"不求有功，但求无过"原则。

在进行转述之前，考生要利用好所给的准备时间。在这段时间内，首先理清楚表格所给信息的前后逻辑。一般文章为总分结构，大多是提建议的句型。然后确定转述时的人称，比如 invite his friends and your friends 这里的 yours 是否换成 mine，要在准备时间内确定好。人称虽然不是扣分点，但考生要想拿到满分，最好保持转述中的人称一致。在听之前，考生可以在草稿纸上给出几个信息点所用的连接词，如 first, second, next, what's more, finally 等。在转述时，要注意几个扣分点：①没有将表格信息转述完全，即少要点，缺少表格内容。②转述过程中考生部分单词发音错误，影响判卷者理解及句子的语音语调不标准。③录音效果差，声音含糊不清，令判卷者无法听清转述内容。

有考生经常提出类似问题，即我在转述过程中发现自己读错单词或漏读内容应当如何处理。其实只要及时发现错误，马上重新朗读该单词或该句即可，判卷者不会因此而不近人情地减分。这种改错方法也适用听说考试的第四大题。还有考生提出，转述时是否要按照原文逐字复述。这一点考生大可不必担心，只要转述时达意即可，考生可以在充分理解原文语义的基础上，用自己的语言进行复述。

（四）短文朗读

北京英语听说考试第四题将显示一篇短文，考生有90秒钟做朗读准备，并在2分钟内完成录制。本题共8分，时长约4分钟。

考生在准备的过程中，先在心里默读，会读的词尽量清晰地表述，并且将文段中的生词找出来并判断其读音；不会读的词尽量根据所学拼读规则试读，不能跳过。另外，尽可能多地将句子中的重音、连读、吞音等的位置在心里默记。同时注意句型不同，语调的升降也不同，如：陈述句、特殊疑问句降调，一般疑问句升调等。

考生在朗读的过程中要注意时间限制，避免前松后紧，做到有条不紊，沉稳、有节奏地平顺朗读。也就是说，考生在朗读时适当停顿是有必要的，如句与句之间的停顿（注意逗号、句号的换气）；较长的句子中不同语意群间可适当停顿，如：复杂句中的主语从句、宾语从句、定语从句，时间、地点状语从句等。下面的一篇样篇就可以锻炼相应的技巧。

例题十六：

Good afternoon, boys and girls. I'm really honored to be invited here. If you ask me what the key to success is, it is a long story. But there are some keys that we can share this afternoon. （请注意第一自然段中宾语从句和定语从句的朗读技巧）

First of all, live life "on purpose". When you live your life on purpose, you will think more of what you do, so there is a chance for you to succeed. （请注意引号部分的强调和复杂长句的停顿）

The second thing is that you should write out a plan. Trying to do anything without an action plan is like driving around the world without a map. The wasted time, energy and money will cause you to give up. （请注意表语从句和长主语的停顿）

朗读的水平不是一朝一夕就能提高的。因此，在日常的复习备考过程中，考生应当时时刻刻磨炼自己。在背单词时，一定要读音与拼写一起掌握，以防在朗读短文时明明认识单词，却没有读出正确的发音，导致丢分。另外，考生平时也可以利用课本听力材料，尽量模仿朗读者的语音语调。并且利用多媒体平台，对自己的录音反复听、多次修正，通过对比的方式进一步提高。比如，"一起中学"的手机学生端就可以针对课本录音逐句跟读，并由系统打分，考生根据系统给出的改正建议进行重复朗读，直到达到自己满意的成绩。如果学生认为课本的内容不能满足需要，也可以使用"英语趣配音"这一软件来提高自己的朗读水平，通过听原版影视材料并进行模仿，使自己的语音语调逐渐接近母语朗读者的层次。而中考听说考试系统是由科大讯飞提供的，考生也可以使用配套的 APP "E 听说"进行模拟考试，不断练习。

综上所述，中考英语听说考试需要充分的准备，不仅仅是考生，也对英语老师提出了更高的要求。考生需要实践去历练，老师也需要找准试题改革的窍门。随着听说中考机制的日益成熟，命题的难度和灵活度也会有变化。老师不仅要紧跟中考改革的方向，更要注意完善教学方法，在日常的教学过程中去摸索、提高自己的教学水平，真正培养出学生的英语听说能力，让学生在三年的初中英语学习后通过听说考试作为走向成功的开始，达成自己的目标。

How We Have Changed

北京市第一零一中学　陈　爽

教材：人教版《英语》九年级全一册

课题：Unit 4 I used to be afraid of the dark.

一、单元分析（Unit Analysis）

1. 单元主题语境（Unit Content）

本单元的主题语境是"人与自我"，单元主题是"我的变化"，涉及谈论过去的性格、外貌、特点及喜好等，借此学习 used to... 这一特有的用来表述过去经历和习惯的语言结构。

2. 单元教学目标（Unit Targets）

语言目标：

1）学生能正确使用 used to 结构描述或询问过去的情况

Paula used to be really quiet.

I didn't use to be popular in school.

A：You used to be short, didn't you?　B：Yes, I did. /No, I didn't.

A：Did he use to wear glasses?　　　B：Yes, he did. /No. he didn't.

2）能够正确使用外貌、性格、爱好、习惯、学习等方面的词汇

3）能够使用常用表达：from time to time, deal with, in public, in person, take pride in...

能力目标：

1）能根据上下文语境推测生词或短语的含义

2）能根据篇章内容的前后逻辑联系判断缺失信息

3）能灵活运用不同短语表达相同含义

文化目标：

1）谈论他人相貌、性格并进行今昔对比时的语言运用自然得体

2）认识自身变化，实现自我完善

二、教学设计思路（Teaching Design）

1. 语篇分析（Discourse Analysis）

本单元话题涉及谈论过去的性格、外貌、特点及喜好，借此学习 used to…这一特有的用来表述过去的经历和习惯的语言结构。Section A 通过对人物性格特点和相貌的今昔对比让学生感知新语言内容的结构特征、体会其用法。Section B 部分在 Section A 的话题基础上进行延伸和拓展，由描述人物性格、外貌变化转向讨论人物行为习惯、爱好的改变；在语言上，该部分除了进一步巩固 Section A 所学重点语言内容外，还复习巩固了有关行为习惯及爱好的短语，同时通过语篇呈现了其他词汇；从技能上看该部分由听、说转向综合性听、读、写的训练。

Unit 4 Section A 1a – 1c 练习巩固学生已有的有关性格和相貌的词汇，另一方面通过听说活动导入 used to 这一语言结构，并借助主题图创设语境，模拟生活情境，引导学生开展初步的对话操练。

Unit 4 Section A 2a – 2d 向学生介绍更多描述性格的形容词，并通过倾听关于人们今昔变化的对话，让学生体会 used to 在真实的日常交际中的运用，进而理解其功能意义。

课标内容对标：

课程要素	内容要求
主题语境	人与自我
语篇	日常对话
语言知识	在语境中运用所学语法知识进行描述、叙述和说明。
语言技能	1）借助语境克服生词障碍，理解口语语篇的信息和意义 2）在听读看的过程中针对语篇的内容有选择地记录信息和要点 3）口头概括对话大意，转述他人的简单谈话
文化知识	1）谈论他人相貌、性格并进行今昔对比时的语言运用得体 2）自我完善

续表

课程要素	内容要求
学习策略	1）从形式、意义和使用三个角度关注和学习，善于发现语言规律，并运用规律举一反三 2）乐于参与课内外英语实践活动，积极沟通表达，不怕犯错

学业质量水平对标：

序号	质量描述
3 – 1	能够听懂相关主题语篇，借助关键词句、图片等复述语篇内容
3 – 9	能根据口头交际的具体情境，初步运用得体的语言形式，表达自己的情感、态度和观点
3 – 10	能选用正确的词语、句式和时态，通过口语描述、介绍人和事物

2. 学情分析（**Analysis on Students**）

初三阶段的学生已经学习了相关话题单元，基本掌握了人物外貌、性格特点、爱好、校园生活等话题词汇。本单元话题深入学生生活，有利于激发学生的学习兴趣和学习动力。初三 3 班学生 34 人，男生 17 人，女生 17 人，互相关爱，具有深厚的友情。学生思维活跃，具有一定英语基础，上课积极发言。学生对自身和他人身上的变化有浓厚的兴趣，但是阐述自身和过去对比发生的变化是学生应该掌握的新知内容，学生还不能准确运用。学生基本能够转述听力文本要点，但是语言完整性和逻辑性还需加强。基于英语学习活动观，创设真实情境、合理设计教学活动是学生掌握新知的重要手段。

3. 教学设计要点（**Design Essentials**）

（1）教学重难点。

重点：通过听力语篇捕捉关键信息，让学生学会用"used to"转述他人外貌和性格上的变化。

难点：通过常设真实情境，让学生用"used to"描述自身的变化。

（2）学习策略。

a. 在获取的信息与个人经历之间建立有意义的联系。

b. 根据表达意图，有意识地选择和应用语言。

c. 根据主题表达需要，合理运用语篇知识，有逻辑地组织信息结构。

（3）教学策略。

根据学生实际情况，遵循学生身心发展的普遍规律，按照学生认知水平和能力，从学生实际生活经验出发，由易到难，逐级铺设台阶，合理整合教材、安排教学内容，注重学生学习英语的过程。本课强调学以致用，通过听力活动设计，关注听力文本主题、关键信息；设置真实情境，以学生感兴趣的话题开展听说任务，在课堂上为学生"架起课堂与实际生活的桥梁"。

（4）本课时教学目标。

By the end of the class, students will be able to

a. get the information of people's changes from listening;

b. describe the changes in appearance and personality with "used to";

c. retell the changes of Paula;

d. talk about your own changes with "used to".

三、教学过程（Teaching Procedures）

学习活动 Learning activities	设计意图（Purpose）
Warm-up Show a picture of teacher's childhood and ask "In what aspects will people change"	引入话题，引导学生关注人物变化
Listening Section A 1b Pre-listening 1. Show Ss a picture and lead Ss to guess the content of the dialogues 2. While-listening 3. Play the radio twice and ask Ss to fill in the blanks Post-listening 1. Check the answers with Ss 2. Introduce "used to" and ask Ss to retell kids' changes of appearance 3. Show some pictures of the Ss and ask Ss to complete the sentences	预测听力内容，为理解内容做好准备 培养学生获取关键信息的能力，并让学生掌握"used to"的用法
Listening Section A 2a Pre-listening 1. Show a picture and a form and ask Ss to predict the content of listening 2. While-listening 3. Play the radio twice and ask Ss to fill in the blanks Post-listening 1. Explain the structure of retelling and ask Ss to retell in pairs 2. Show a sample and ask Ss to read aloud 3. Ask Ss to think about what they think of Paula's changes	让学生掌握转述的基本技巧，并注重内容的完整性和逻辑性

续表

学习活动 Learning activities	设计意图（Purpose）
Speaking 1. Ask Ss to think about their changes and fill in the form 2. Ask Ss to work in pairs and introduce their own changes and note down partner's changes 3. Ask Ss to introduce partner's changes	将所学知识与实践相结合，巩固提升"used to"的使用和转述技能

板书设计

Unit 4 I used to be afraid of the dark

	Appearance	
	Personality	
As for	Study	_____ used to have/be/do,
	Hobby	but now _____
	Habit	

Assignment

（1）Retell your partner's changes and write it down. （A 层）

（2）Retell Paula's changes and write it down（B 层）

四、教学评价（Evaluation）

Can-Do Checklist
I can describe the changes of appearance ◡ ̈   =̈   ◠ ̈
I can describe the changes of personality ◡ ̈   =̈   ◠ ̈
1 question I still have

点评：

本节课运用真实的照片做情境导入，快速激发学生对单元话题的兴趣，并收集学生自身照片用作语法练习，让课堂内容更具有代入感，让学生更有参与感。

根据学生实际情况，从学生实际生活经验出发，听力练习任务由易到难，逐级铺设台阶，注重学生学习英语的过程。本课强调学以致用，通过设置真实情境，在课堂上为学生"架起课堂与实际生活的桥梁"。

本课时涉及初一初二所学内容，学生掌握情况不同，课前需要根据情况适当增加词汇复习环节，激活学生已学内容，使学生的新旧知识更快建立联系，更好地为输出做铺垫。

How We Have Changed 学案

1b listen and fill the blanks

	In the past	Now
Mario	be _____	He is _____
	wear _____	
Amy	have _____ hair	
	be _____	She is _____ than the other kids.
Tina	have _____ hair	has _____ hair

2b listen and write

	In the past	Now
Paula	be _____ be never _____ enough to ask questions be always _____	be more _____ in _____ play _____ almost every day be on a _____ team play the _____ from time to time be _____ …
	got a better _____ in _____ be good in _____ class	
	play the _____	

Retell：

Paula has really changed a lot.

As for her personality，…

As for her study，…

As for her hobbies，…

People sure change

Write down your changes

	In the past	Now
appearance		
personality		
study		
hobby		
…		

The changes of your classmates…

听力文本

Section A，1b

Listen. Bob is seeing some friends for the first time in four years. What did his friends use to look like?

Conversation 1

Bob：Mario, is that you?

Mario：Yeah, it is. It's Bob! Hey guys, it's Bob! I haven't seen you for four years!

Bob：Yeah. I'm here with my parents. We're visiting for a couple of days. Wow, Mario, you look different! You used to be short, didn't you?

Mario：Yes, I did. Now I'm tall. And so are you!

Bob：That's true. And you used to wear glasses.

Conversation 2

Bob：Hey, Amy, it's great to see you.

Amy：Hi, Bob. How are you?

Bob：Fine. Wow, you've changed!

Amy：Really? How?

Bob：You used to have short hair.

Amy：You remember that? Yes, I did.

Bob：And you used to be really tall!

Amy：Not anymore. You're taller than me now, Bob.

Conversation 3

Tina：Hiya, Bob.

Bob：Hi, Tina. You've changed, too.

Tina：Oh, yeah?

Bob：You have blonde hair!

Tina：Yeah, it used to be red, didn't it?

Bob：And it's straight!

Tina：Yeah, it used to be curly.

Section A，2a

Paula：Hey, Steve! Over here! Don't you remember me?

Steve：Oh, wow! You're Paula, aren't you?

Paula：That's right. We were in the same science class during Grade 8.

Steve：Yes, now I remember. You used to be really quiet, didn't you? I remember you were always silent in class.

Paula：Yeah. I wasn't very outgoing. I was never brave enough to ask the teachers any questions！

Steve：Well, but you were always friendly. And you got a better grade in science than I did, haha. And I remember you were really good in music class, too. Wait a minute！Did you use to play the piano?

Paula：Yes, I did. But now I'm more interested in sports. I play soccer almost every day, and I'm on a swim team. But I still play the piano from time to time.

Steve：Wow, you're so active！People sure change.

Famous Inventions

北京市第一零一中学　陈　爽

教材：人教版《英语》九年级全一册
课题：Unit 6 When was it invented?

一、单元分析（Unit Analysis）

1. 单元主题语境（Unit Content）

本单元的主题语境是"人与社会"，单元话题为"发明"，介绍了我们日常生活中一些常见的物品的发明历史，如汽车、电脑、电视、电话、拉链、茶叶等，包括它们被发明的时间、被什么人发明以及作用或发展等内容。

2. 单元教学目标（Unit Targets）

语言目标：

1）能用被动语态过去时简要谈论发明的历史

When was. . . invented?

It was invented in. . .

Who was it invented by?

It was invented by. . .

2）能简单谈论发明的用途

What is the hot ice-cream scoop used for?

It is used for serving really cold ice-cream.

3）能正确使用发明话题的相关词汇

4）能正确使用常用表达

have a point，by accident，take place，without doubt，all of a sudden，divide…into，look up to，the Olympics

能力目标：

1）能制作思维导图，并借助思维导图记忆有关知识

2）能通过快速阅读获取文章主旨或段落大意

文化目标：

1）了解我国茶叶发明及其传播的简要历史

2）了解篮球的发明及其发明的简要历史

二、教学设计思路（Teaching Design）

1. 语篇分析（Discourse Analysis）

Section A 介绍了日常生活中一些常见物品的发明历史，如电视、电话、拉链、茶叶等，包括它们被发明的时间、被什么人发明及其作用或发展等内容；从语言结构上，需要学习被动语态的过去时。Section B 要求学生继续学习和巩固相关的内容和语言知识。听说和阅读训练分别介绍了现代生活中常见的两项发明：薯条和篮球。在语言技能方面听说读写的专项训练和综合性训练在本部分均有体现。在语言策略上，本单元明确提出了让学生学习使用"思维导图"以加深对文章的理解和对知识的记忆的学习策略。

Section A 1a－1c 是整个 Section A 的基础，活动 1a 要求学生使用 I think it was invented before/after…句型讨论图中发明的先后顺序。活动 1b 要求学生通过听力练习验证自己的预测，并将以上发明与其时间匹配。听力材料中输入了本单元重要的语言结构：When was it invented？It was invented by…What was/is it used for？It was/is used for…从活动安排和内容上，2a 要求学生听对话讨论三项小发明，并按所听顺序为其排序；2b 需要学生听懂发明的用途，补全表格。2c 要求学生结伴谈论听力发明中的用途。2d 作为示范性对话，介绍了日常生活中随处可见的小发明——拉链，它的发明者、发明时间以及被广泛运用的时期等信息。

为了使课堂教学与英语听说中考相结合，听力材料被改编为听后记录信息和听后回答，利用话题语境训练学生获取信息的能力。

课标内容对标：

课程要素	内容要求
主题语境	人与社会

续表

课程要素	内容要求
语篇	日常对话
语言知识	在语境中运用所学语法知识进行描述、叙述和说明
语言技能	借助语境克服生词障碍、理解口语语篇的信息和意义 在听读看的过程中针对语篇的内容有选择地记录信息和要点 口头概括对话大意，转述他人的简单谈话
文化知识	中外优秀科学家，其主要贡献及具有的人文精神和科学精神
学习策略	从形式、意义和使用三个角度关注和学习，善于发现语言规律，并运用规律举一反三 乐于参与课内外英语实践活动，积极沟通表达，不怕犯错

学业质量水平对标：

序号	质量描述
3－1	能够听懂相关主题语篇，借助关键词句、图片等复述语篇内容
3－9	能根据口头交际的具体情境，初步运用得体的语言形式，表达自己的情感、态度和观点
3－10	能选用正确的词语、句式和时态，通过口语描述、介绍人和事物

2. 学情分析（**Analysis on Students**）

初三 2 班学生 36 人，本班学生为年级的 A 层，思维活跃，具有一定英语基础，上课能够积极发言。学生互相关爱，具有深厚的友情。在九年级上册 Unit 5 中已经基本掌握了被动语态的句型结构，能够用 be made of 和 be made in 描述产品的材质和生产地，但是对被动语态在过去时语境中的运用不够熟练。

3. 教学设计要点（**Design Essentials**）

（1）教学重难点。

- 用 was invented in 和 was invented by 描述发明的历史
- 用 be used for 描述发明的用处
- 用目标语言描述自己的小发明

（2）学习策略。

元认知策略：

a. 搜索并利用线上线下资源丰富自己的英语学习内容。

b. 经常和同学组成小组，合作学习英语。

认知策略：

a. 在学习中激活并关联已知。

b. 从形式、意义和使用三个角度关注和学习语法，善于发现语言规律，并能运用规律举一反三。

交际策略：

在沟通与交流中，借助手势、表情等体态语表达意义。

情感管理策略：

a. 对应于学习保持主动性和积极性，激发动机，端正态度、降低焦虑，保持自信。

b. 乐于参与课内外英语实践活动，积极沟通表达，不怕犯错。

c. 根据学生实际情况，遵循学生身心发展的普遍规律，按照学生认知水平和能力，从学生实际生活经验出发，由易到难，逐级铺设台阶，合理整合教材、安排教学内容，注重学生学习英语的过程。

（3）教学策略。

本课强调学以致用，通过设置真实情境，在课堂上为学生"架起课堂与实际生活的桥梁""系起课堂与外国文化的纽带"。

（4）本课时教学目标。

By the end of the class, students will be able to

a. talk about the history of inventions with "It was/They were invented in…"

b. talk about the use of inventions with "it is/they are used for…"

c. introduce their own inventions

三、教学过程（Teaching Procedures）

学习活动 Learning activities	设计意图（Purpose）
1. Warm-up Ask Ss "What do you think is the greatest invention in the world?" Show some pictures of inventions and ask Ss to name them	引入话题并借助图片复习已知关于发明的词汇
2. Listening Section A 1b	
Pre-listening • Show Ss some pictures and ask： • *What can you see in the picture?* • *Can you guess which one of them was invented first?* • *Which of them was invented last?* • *Was the TV invented before the car or after the car?* Lead Ss to guess the content of the dialogues	让学生关注对话的主题

学习活动 Learning activities	设计意图（Purpose）
While-listening Play the recording twice and ask Ss to fill in the blanks	练习听取细节信息
Post-listening 1）Check the answers with Ss 2）Introduce "was invented in" and ask Ss to retell the history of inventions 3）Show the pictures of some other inventions and ask Ss to make new dialogues with partner with the information given	让学生关注被动语态的语言结构并在真实语境中练习使用
3. Listening Section A 2b	
Pre-listening 1）Show a picture of microwave oven and ask Ss "What is the microwave oven used for?" And show the answer 2）Ask Ss to match the use of inventions and make a sentence with "be used for" 3）Show a picture of three inventions and ask Ss to predict what they are used for	1. 让学生关注句式结构 2. 让学生练习使用目标语言造句 3. 让学生预测听力的内容，做好听力练习准备
While-listening Play the radio twice and ask Ss to fill in the blanks	让学生练习听取关键信息
Post-listening Explain the structure of retelling and ask Ss to retell in pairs	让学生练习目标语言
4. Listening Section A 2d	
Pre-listening Show a picture of zipper and ask Ss to think about the use of it	让学生为听力练习做好准备
While-listening Play the recording twice and ask Ss to answer the questions	让学生练习听取关键信息
Post-listening 1）Check the answers with students 2）Ask Ss to think about： *Why were the inventions invented?* *How were they invented?*	让学生深入思考发明出现的原因和发明的过程
Activity：Teenage inventor	

续表

学习活动 Learning activities	设计意图（Purpose）
Ask Ss to design their own inventions and introduce it with group members The following information must be included: ● What is the name of your invention? ● Why do you invent it? ● What is it used for?	让学生使用目标语言在真实语境下练习口语

板书设计

Unit 6 When was it invented?

It was/They were invented in 1876.

What is it/are they used for?

It is/They are used for cooking and heating food.

Assignment：

（1）Write a short passage to introduce your invention.

（2）Review the listening materials of Section A 1b, 2a and 2d, and make notes.

四、教学评价（Evaluation）

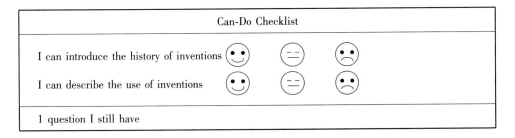

Can-Do Checklist

I can introduce the history of inventions

I can describe the use of inventions

1 question I still have

点评：

本节课话题关于发明创造，与学生生活息息相关，能引导学生关注身边的事物，关注人类历史与社会发展。本课时为本单元的第一课时，主要功能为话题导入，从听力文本着手创设真实情境，让学生联系生活实际和历史知识，在获取关键信息的过程中逐渐关注到目标语言的使用，在练习中不断巩固内化新知。依托课本听力材料中讨论的小发明的用途，引发学生思考生活中的难题和解决方法，最终让学生自己创造一个小发明，并用目标语言介绍其用途和意义，层层铺设台阶，任务由简到难。

Famous Inventions 学案

Ⅰ. Section A 1b Listen and fill in the blanks：

＿＿＿＿＿＿＿ Inventions	When was it/were they invented?
telephone	
＿＿＿＿＿	
＿＿＿＿＿	
＿＿＿＿＿＿＿	

Retell：

When Alice's grandma was a kid,

she had a…It was invented in…

But she didn't have a…it was…. She couldn't afford one…

Ⅱ. Section A 2a, 2b Listen, fill in the chart and retell：

＿＿＿＿＿＿＿ Invention	What is it/are they used for?
shoes with ＿＿＿＿＿＿＿	＿＿＿＿＿＿ in the dark
hot ＿＿＿＿＿＿ scoop	＿＿＿＿＿＿ really cold ice-cream
shoes with ＿＿＿＿＿ heels	＿＿＿＿＿＿ the style of the shoes

Retell：

These are some of the interesting inventions that Carol is writing about for her English homework. They're the…

Ⅲ. Section A 2d Listen and answer the questions：

1. What's the subject for Paul's school project?

＿＿＿＿＿＿＿＿＿＿＿＿＿＿＿＿＿＿＿＿＿＿＿＿＿＿＿＿＿＿＿＿＿＿＿＿＿

2. Why does Roy think it is a great invention?

＿＿＿＿＿＿＿＿＿＿＿＿＿＿＿＿＿＿＿＿＿＿＿＿＿＿＿＿＿＿＿＿＿＿＿＿＿

3. When was the zipper invented?

＿＿＿＿＿＿＿＿＿＿＿＿＿＿＿＿＿＿＿＿＿＿＿＿＿＿＿＿＿＿＿＿＿＿＿＿＿

4. When did the zipper become popular?

＿＿＿＿＿＿＿＿＿＿＿＿＿＿＿＿＿＿＿＿＿＿＿＿＿＿＿＿＿＿＿＿＿＿＿＿＿

Teenage Inventor Competition

Student A：What is the name of your invention?

Student B：Why do you invent it?

Student C：What is it used for?

Student D：How can it change our life?

Sample：

Student A：It's a great honor to introduce our invention here. This invention is called "Candy Pen".

Student B：We invent it because it is easy to get hungry when doing homework at night.

Student C：It is used for serving candies at the other side of the pen.

Student D：With this "Candy Pen", we can make doing homework more enjoyable. Hope you will like it.

听力文本

Section A, 1a

Alice：Was your life very difficult when you were a kid?

Grandma：Oh, not really. Why?

Alice：Well you didn't have modern inventions like a telephone, right?

Grandma：Of course we did! How old do you think I am? The telephone was invented in 1876. You need to take a history class, Alice!

Alice：Haha! How about cars? They weren't invented yet, were they?

Grandma：Yes, they were. Cars were invented in 1885. My family had a car.

Alice：Well, did you have a TV?

Grandma：No, we couldn't afford one. They were expensive those days. The TV was invented around 1927, I think.

Alice：Well, I know that you didn't have a computer, because we learned in school that personal computers were invented in 1971.

Grandma：You're right. But I have one now!

Section A, 2a

Alex：Hi, Carol. Wow, what are those?

Carol：Hello, Alex. Oh, these are some of the interesting inventions that I'm writing about for my English homework.

Alex：I see…What's that, then?

Carol：They're shoes with lights. You use them for seeing in the dark when you get up at night.

Alex：Oh，that's a cool idea！I always hit my toes against something on the way to the bathroom at night.

Carol：Next is a special ice-cream scoop this is my favorite invention. It runs on electricity and becomes hot.

Alex：I know what it's fro！It's used for serving really cold ice-cream.

Carol：Yes，that's right！The last invention I'm going to write about is shoes with special heels. You can move the heels up and down.

Alex：What are they used for？

Carol：Well，you can change the style of your shoes. You can raise the heels if you are going to a party or lower them if you are just going out for shopping.

Section A，1d

Paul：Hey Roy，the subject for my school project is "Small inventions that change the world". Can you help me think of an invention？

Roy：With pleasure！Let me think…hmm…I know！The zipper！

Paul：The zipper？Is it such a great invention？

Roy：Think about how often it is used in our daily lives. You can see zippers on dresses，trousers，shoes，bags…almost everywhere！

Paul：Well，you do seem have a point…

Roy：Of course！I thought about it because I saw a website last week. The pioneers of different inventions were listed there. For example，it mentioned that zipper was invented by Whitcomb，Judson in 1893. But at that time，it wasn't used widely.

Paul：Really？So when did it become popular？

Roy：Around 1917.

Ways of Transportation

北京市第一零一中学　王冬慧

教材：人教版《英语》七年级下册
课题：Unit 3 How do you get to school？

一、单元分析（Unit Analysis）

1. 单元主题语境（Unit Content）

本单元主题为谈论出行方式，属于人与社会主题范畴，主题群属于社会服务与人际沟通。以学生生活相关即如何来学校的话题为主线，呈现本单元重点 How do/does...？的询问以及...by/on...的回答。在充分利用书本材料进行教学与操练的基础上，学生们自然交流，培养学生快速捕捉和获取文章大意的能力，培养学生对语法及句型的掌控能力、善于表达的良好习惯。

2. 单元教学目标（Unit Targets）

本单元学习后，学生能够：

- 获取听力对话中谈论到的交通出行方式以及描述距离远近的表达；
- 通过描述自己每日上学的交通方式，关注、提取、归纳并内化出行方式以及形容出行路径的语言表达方式；
- 运用相关的语言表达，与同伴角色扮演采访出行方式调查，能够谈论合适的出行方案；
- 通过梳理阅读文本，了解山区同学的艰辛求学之路，引导学生树立环保意识以及珍惜时间的生活及学习态度。

二、教学设计思路（Teaching Design）

1. 语篇分析（Discourse Analysis）

本单元 Section A 部分是基本的语言、语法内容，包括词汇、语法、功能等，听力输入、口语输出、阅读输入为主要教学形式，是初步体验和感知语言的阶段。Section B 部分是知识的扩展和综合的语言运用，在进一步听说训练的基础上，重点发展学生的篇章阅读和写作能力。本单元话题取材于《义务教育英语课程标准》话题项目表第 17 项旅游与交通（Travel and Transport）中的第 58 条交通运输方式（Modes of Transportation）。本单元以"交通"为话题、以谈论出行方式为功能，以紧扣话题的 5 个对话和 1 个短语篇为载体，在具体语境中呈现了 How，How far，How long 引导的特殊疑问句及回答，谈论如何到达目的地、行程时间及距离多远。

Section A 部分展现了学生以不同交通方式上学的场景，自然而然地将学生带入有关彼此上学方式、出行花费的时间，以及家与学校的距离等问题的讨论中。1a－1c 呈现了各种交通工具的名称，以及表达"使用某种交通工具"的动词搭配，如：take the bus，ride a bike 等，还导入了谈论出行方式的句式。2a－2e 部分进一步深化"出行"话题，先让学生学习并掌握英语十位数和百位数的表达方式，再让学生捕捉听力对话中的数字信息，然后训练学生询问和回答两地距离和出行花费时长。

Section B 对出行交通方式这一话题进行更深入的探讨，语境更加复杂，呈现了"换乘"的概念。1a－1b 旨在扩充本单元话题词汇，教授换乘交通工具的表达方式，并在听说活动中训练学生捕捉细节信息的能力和叙述较复杂事情的能力。1c－1e 通过进一步的听力输入和口语输出帮助学生练习本单元的目标语言结构。2a－2c 为阅读教学部分，介绍了偏远乡村孩子上学的故事。这一题材展现了偏远地区孩子上学的艰苦，目的是唤起城市孩子的关注，同时让他们懂得珍惜自己的生活和学习条件，从而更努力地学习。本部分教学难点是熟练掌握本单元与交通出行相关的词汇和表达，以及描述较为复杂的"换乘"经过并实现笔头输出。

课标内容对标：

课程要素	内容要求
主题语境	人与社会
语篇	日常对话、独白
语言知识	语音方面，根据重音、意群、语调与节奏等语音方面的变化，感知和理解说话人表达的意义、意图和态度；词汇方面，在特定语境中，根据单元主题，运用词汇给事物命名，描述事物、行为、过程和特征，说明概念，表达与主题相关的主要信息和观点；语法方面，在语境中运用所学语法知识进行描述、叙述和说明
语言技能	围绕相关主题口头表达个人的观点和态度，并说明理由；在口头和书面表达中使用常见的连接词表示顺序和逻辑关系，连接信息，做到意义连贯
文化知识	不同国家青少年的学习和生活方式
学习策略	交际策略：沟通和交流遇到困难时，主动提问，请求澄清或寻求帮助

学业质量水平对标：

序号	质量描述
3－1	能听懂相关主题的语篇，借助关键词句、图片等复述语篇内容
3－9	能根据口头交际的具体语境，初步运用得体的语言形式，表达自己的情感、态度和观点
3－17	积极参与课堂活动，与同伴一起就相关主题进行讨论，合作完成学习任务

2. 学情分析（Analysis on Students）

● 自然情况：初一（6）班，班级人数 42 人，英语水平属于 B 层。经过将近一年的学习，他们逐渐形成了良好的英语学习习惯；有较好的用英语表达的欲望；喜欢课堂环节紧凑、有序；学习态度积极，喜欢小组合作。

● 已有知识和能力储备："交通"这一话题与学生日常生活紧密相连，与上一单元日常描述话题一脉相承，学生有真实的体验，以及通过课本单元词汇的预习，学生能够运用小学已有知识对交通工具进行简单的口头表达。

● 存在问题：学生虽已接触过交通方式相关话题，但学生在表达时存在句式结构混淆、不能灵活运用各种句式等问题。此外，距离表达上需要用到的数字，是学生的薄弱处。

● 解决办法：通过问题链的设置引导学生在语境中感知、体会语言的特点；教师需要搭建脚手架，为学生提供语言库。此外，教学中注重借助图片和表格等思维工具帮助其形成良好的思维品质。

3. 教学设计要点（**Design Essentials**）

（1）教学重难点。

①To talk about ways of transportation.

②To retell the listening material about the distance and the time of going to school correctly.

（2）学习策略。

在本节课的学习过程中注意渗透认知策略：运用多种方法、借助多种资源学习和记忆词语，如拼读、联想、搭配、分类，以及构词法等。

（3）教学策略。

情景教学、合作学习。

（4）本课时教学目标。

By the end of the class, students will be able to

①list out the words, phrases of the transportation.

②talk about different ways to go to school.

③talk about the distance and the time of going to school.

三、教学过程（Teaching Procedures）

Ⅰ. Lead-in

学习活动 Learning activities	设计意图（Purpose）
Ask students to look at the theme picture of unit 3 and ask a question: *What kinds of transportation can you see?*	引导学生思考上学交通方式，激发学生学习兴趣，引出单元话题——交通方式

Ⅱ. Pre-listening and Speaking

学习活动 Learning activities	设计意图（Purpose）
Ask students to look at the picture of 1a and answer：how do they get to school	引导学生猜测图片，预测听力材料内容，降低听力难度

Ⅲ. While-listening and Speaking

学习活动 Learning activities	设计意图（Purpose）
1. Listen to the conversation and fill in the chart 2. Ask Ss to check the answers in pairs	引导学生关注听力表格中的信息，同时，在全班核对答案前，进行同伴互相核对答案，关注细节

Ⅳ. Post-listening and Speaking

学习活动 Learning activities	设计意图（Purpose）
1. Ask students to talk about how the Ss in 1a get to school according to the pictures 2. Ask students to find the rules of expressing ways of going to school according to the sentences they just talked about 3. Pair work：ask Ss to practice the conversations by using target languages	引导学生在练习中巩固目标语言，学会表达自己每日上学交通方式，提高学生学习兴趣

Ⅴ. Pre-listening and Speaking

学习活动 Learning activities	设计意图（Purpose）
1. Ask students to review the numbers 2. Ask students to listen and dictate the numbers. Write down the Arabic numbers with textbook closed	引导学生复习数字表达，降低接下来听力过程中遇到的障碍

Ⅵ. Post-listening and Speaking

学习活动 Learning activities	设计意图（Purpose）
1. Listen and fill in the blanks 2. Ask Ss to check in pairs according to the instructions	引导学生在语境中感受如何表达上学交通方式以及表达距离远近的问答

Ⅶ. Post-listening and Speaking

学习活动 Learning activities	设计意图（Purpose）
Ask students to retell according to the chart	通过转述活动，给学生再次操练目标语言的机会，巩固练习

Assignment：

（1）Tell your parents how your friends get to school and write it down.

（2）Make a poster about transportation words.

一、教学评价（Evaluation）

（1）在第一项听力活动中，教师通过观察学生在听的过程中的笔记记录情况，通过能否顺利补充表格中的信息掌握学生学习情况。

（2）在听后活动中，提问学生能否顺利切换两种不同方式表达每日上学交通出行方式。

（3）教师通过学生小组合作展示对话情况，了解学生对于交通方式表达的掌握情况。

（4）学生通过小组合作的方式先在组内进行每日出行方式介绍；再由组长进行汇报，描述他人日常出行交通方式。

点评：

充分利用课本资源，在导入环节放大课本图片，通过一系列问题链，充分调动学生学习积极性，引出话题；

利用图片表格，梳理听力材料，同时，通过创设的单人、小组活动引导学生在活动中习得语言，操练语言。本节课从磨课阶段到最终的呈现，一开始活动过于冗杂拖沓，结合教学师父的建议，将迁移创新部分与第二次听力结合，大大缩短了时间，今后在活动设计上也要结合布鲁姆的目标分类法，认真分析有些活动是否为达成目标服务，从而删减相关性不大的活动，提高课堂效率。

特色学习资源分析、技术手段应用说明

前期利用"问卷星"对于班内同学日常上学交通方式进行了调查。调查结果显示如下：

每日上学交通出行方式？

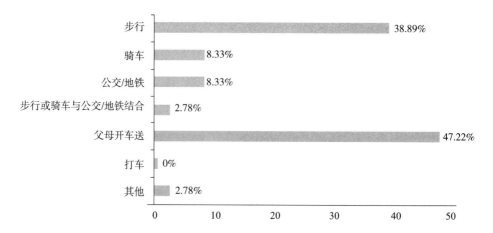

你认为你的出行方式是否环保?

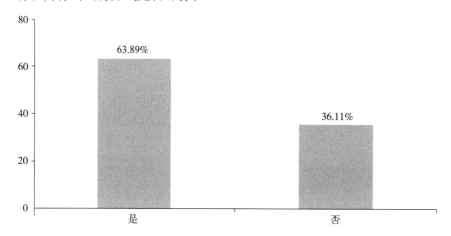

你选择此出行方式的主要原因是什么?

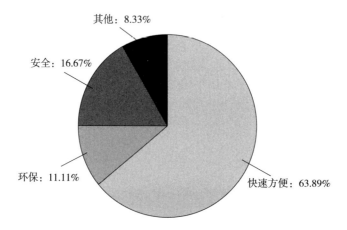

从调查结果可以看出：班里大部分同学家距离学校较近，因此，很多同学选择步行或者骑车的方式到校，其中，步行占 38.9%，骑车占 8.33%；但也有 47.22% 的同学选择父母开车送的方式。在"你的出行方式是否环保"这个问题上，63.89% 的同学认为自己的出行方式是环保的，但仍有 36.11% 的同学认为自己的出行方式不够环保。在"你选择此出行方式的主要原因"这个问题上，超过一半的同学表示快速方便；16.67% 的同学认为安全；只有 11.11% 的同学考虑环保因素为主，因此，在教学设计环节，本节课的最后笔者补充了环保的重要性，同时，为本单元 Section B 阅读部分做铺垫。

Unit 3 Ways of Transportation 学案

TASK 1

1. Listen to the conversation & fill in the chart

Name	How to get to school
Bob	takes the ____①____
Mary	takes the ____②____
John	takes the ____③____
Paul and Yang Lan	____④____
Jim	____⑤____ his ____⑥____

2. Check the answers in pairs

A：How does... get to school?

B：He/She/they... to school.

3. Practice：Listen and write down the Arabic（阿拉伯）numbers.

①_____ ②_____ ③_____

④_____ ⑤_____ ⑥_____

TASK 2

4. Listen to 2 conversations & fill in the chart

Who	How	How long	How far
Tom			
Jane			

5. Check the answers in pairs

A：How does. . . get home from school?

B：He/She. . . to his/her home.

A：How long does it take?

B：It takes him/her. . . to get home from school.

A：How far is it from his/her home to school?

B：It's about. . . from his/her home to school.

6. Report

Different students have different ways to get back home.

Tom _____

But Jane lives far. She _____

As for me, I _____

East or west, home is best. Finally, everyone can make it.

听力文本

Section A, 1a

Boy：How do Bob and Mary get to school?

Girl：Bob takes the train and Mary takes the subway.

Boy：How does John get to school?

Girl：He takes the bus.

Boy：How do Paul and Yang Lan get to school?

Girl：They walk. Look, there they are now!

Boy：Does Jim walk to school?

Girl：No, he doesn't. He rides his bike.

Section A, 2a

Mary：How do you get home from school, Tom?

Tom：I walk.

Mary：How long does it take?

Tom：It takes about 20 minutes.

Mary：Wow! That's quick! How far is it from the school to your home?

Tom：Only about two kilometers.

Clip 3

Peter：How do you get home from school, Jane?

Jane：I take the bus.

Peter：How long does it take?

Jane：Oh，about one hour and minutes.

Peter：Wow！That's a long time！

Jane：Yes，I only go home on weekends.

Peter：How far is it from your home to school？

Jane：It's about 60 kilometers.

Rules at home

北京市第一零一中学　　王冬慧

教材：人教版《英语》九年级全一册

课题：Unit 7 Teenagers should be allowed to choose their own clothes.

一、单元分析（Unit Analysis）

1. 单元主题语境（Unit Content）

主题语境是"人与社会"，语篇承载表达主题的语言知识和文化知识，为学生提供多样化的文体素材。本单元主题是规则（Rules），功能是能谈论允许或不被允许做的事情（Talk about what you are allowed to do），能表达同意或不同意（Agree and disagree）。单元主题属于人与社会范畴，单元主题群为社会服务与人际沟通；子主题内容为良好的人际关系与人际交往；通过本单元的学习，学生能够学会谈论他们允许和不被允许做的事情以及他们同意和不同意的观点。

2. 单元教学目标（Unit Targets）

本单元学习后，学生能够：

● 读懂、听取、说出青少年被/不被允许做的事情。

● 熟练运用 should（not）be allowed to do 和 agree/disagree，表达自己对不同规则的看法。

● 通过朗读 Mom Knows Best 这首诗理解并说出父母时而呵护有加、时而严格的教育方法背后的原因。

● 说出 Liu Yu 和父母产生冲突的原因和各自的观点，结合自己所学和个人认知给 Liu Yu 写一封信，表达个人的建议。

二、教学设计思路（Teaching Design）

1. 语篇分析（Discourse Analysis）

本课是人教版《Go for it!》九年级 Unit7 的听说课。本单元主题是规则（Rules），功能是能谈论允许或不被允许做的事情（Talk about what you are allowed to do)，能表达同意或不同意（Agree and disagree）。

Section A 中的话题主要围绕日常生活中的个人行为准则和人们对这些行为的看法。这部分内容的听力文本中涉及了母女、朋友、同学等不同的人物关系，能从不同的立场出发来形成对规则的观点，并论述自己的理由。Section A 的听力文本中辅以不同的插图，对这些插图的分析能够帮助学生预测文本内容，加深对不同立场观点的理解。教师可以借助这部分插图培养学生用插图进行预测的学习策略。

本单元的语言教学重点"should be allowed to"和表达同意与不同意，在这个部分中均有涉及，教师需要通过引导学生观察听力题目中的句型，来引导学生在对话中简单输出观点，表达立场。

Section A 的阅读文本是一首英文诗，这首诗以一个孩子的口吻详尽叙述自己从呱呱坠地到成年过程中妈妈的付出。所以可以尝试以时间为主线串联诗歌：每个人都会经历婴儿时期（Babyhood）、幼儿时期（Childhood）、青少年时期（Teenage Time）、成年时期（Adult Time）。每个时期都有不同的 rules，随着人生阶段的改变，对 rules 的态度也在改变，体现人在心理和生理两个方面的成长。该文本标题为"Mom knows best"，对这个句子的理解能帮助学生预测或总结主旨。同时配以视频资源，帮助学生借助音视频更好地理解、赏析诗歌。

Section B 进一步巩固和扩展了本单元的话题内容——青少年应该做什么、不应该做什么，再现了本单元的重点语法结构和词汇，同时也设置真实语境再现前面两个单元所学的一般现在时和一般过去时的被动语态用法。

听力语篇通过一段父子间有关校园学习、迟到、考试、校规等问题的对话，巩固之前所学过的被动语态的语法知识，培养学生在真实的语境中灵活运用语言的能力和意识。

课标内容对标：

课程要素	内容要求
主题语境	单元主题属于人与社会范畴，单元主题群为社会服务与人际沟通；子主题内容为良好的人际关系与人际交往
语篇	日常对话、独白
语言知识	语音方面，根据重音、意群、语调与节奏等语音方面的变化，感知和理解说话人表达的意义、意图和态度；词汇方面，在特定语境中，根据单元主题，运用词汇给事物命名，描述事物、行为、过程和特征，说明概念，表达与主题相关的主要信息和观点；语法方面，在语境中运用所学语法知识进行描述、叙述和说明

续表

课程要素	内容要求
语言技能	围绕相关主题口头表达个人的观点和态度，并说明理由；在口头和书面表达中使用常见的连接词表示顺序和逻辑关系，连接信息，做到意义连贯
文化知识	世界主要国家待人接物的基本礼仪和方式，体现文化的传承和人与人之间的相互尊重
学习策略	交际策略：沟通和交流遇到困难时，主动提问，请求澄清或寻求帮助

学业质量水平对标：

序号	质量描述
3 - 1	能听懂相关主题的语篇，借助关键词句、图片等复述语篇内容
3 - 9	能根据口头交际的具体语境，初步运用得体的语言形式，表达自己的情感、态度和观点
3 - 17	积极参与课堂活动，与同伴一起就相关主题进行讨论，合作完成学习任务

2. 学情分析（**Analysis on Students**）

● 自然情况：班级学生整体水平参差，班里小部分同学主动参与意识强，喜欢思考，上课状态活跃，喜欢小组分享与合作；但由于从小没有养成好的英语学习习惯，不少同学参与意识较弱，上课不活跃，对英语学习的主动性不够。

● 知识背景：本课话题贴近学生生活实际，学生有话可说。

● 存在问题：多数学生相关话题的词汇、句型等知识积累不足，沟通表达能力受限；逻辑及全面表述问题的能力较弱，使用批判性思维思考、分析问题的能力有待提高。

3. 教学设计要点（**Design Essentials**）

（1）教学重难点。

教学重点：学习并使用本课谈论问题的词汇、词组及句型等表达方式。

教学难点：通过思考问题发生的原因、表现和自身感受来清晰全面地表达问题。

（2）学习策略。

在本节课的学习过程中注意渗透认知策略：运用多种方法、借助多种资源学习和记忆词语，如拼读、联想、搭配、分类，以及构词法等。

（3）教学策略。

情境教学；合作学习。

（4）本课时教学目标。

By the end of the class, students will be able to

①get specific information and the main idea by listening to conversations about rules

②retell what they have learned and talk about what teenagers should and shouldn't be allowed to do and the reasons

三、教学过程（Teaching Procedures）

Ⅰ. Pre-listening and speaking

学习活动 Learning activities	设计意图（Purpose）
1. Ask students to look at the picture on page 49 and have a guess： What might be the relationship between Anna and the woman? What might they talk about? 2. Ask students to read the statements and circle A for agree or D for disagree in 1a.	引导学生关注主题内容，引出话题，充分利用教材中的插图，通过设置一系列问题链的方式，追问学生看到了图片中的哪些内容，借助图片视觉，引导学生关注本课时听力中遇到的生词短语，如：driver's license；earring；pierce；safety，从而为接下来的听力部分做铺垫

Ⅱ. While-listening and Speaking

学习活动 Learning activities	设计意图（Purpose）
Ask students to listen and fill in the chart and at the same time think about the main idea of the conversation	结合表格，挖掘文本，引导学生关注目标语言，在填写表格后，尝试写出听力文本大意，培养学生的概括能力

Ⅲ. Post-listening and Speaking

学习活动 Learning activities	设计意图（Purpose）
Let students try to retell the chart by themselves first and then ask one or two of them to share	先让学生自我复述，选取个别学生转述后，全班一起转述，给学生充分操练的机会来吸收落实语言

Ⅳ. Pre-listening and Speaking

学习活动 Learning activities	设计意图（Purpose）
Ask students to look at the picture in 2a and analyze the main idea of the conversation	听力材料中的话题与亲子关系之间产生不同观点，借助图片，自然引出同龄人之间存在不同观点的表达；引导学生关注不同行为背后有着不同的原因

V. While-listening and Speaking

学习活动 Learning activities	设计意图（Purpose）
Ask students to analyze the part of speech of the blanks in the chart and then listen and fill in the blanks Let students write down the main idea of the conversation	引导学生在听力练习之前关注表格中的词性及其不同变化形式，培养自主学习能力；再次利用表格，强化学生在归纳主旨时多关注表头信息，同时，要尝试使用名词性短语及宾语从句等描述大意

VI. Post-listening and Speaking

学习活动 Learning activities	设计意图（Purpose）
Ask students to work in pairs to make a list of things teenagers should and should not be allowed to do according to their own opinions Let students make a conversation to tell each other their opinions and reasons	迁移创新：设置情境为假设学生正在和自己的父母就家中某项家规讨论，双方持有不同观点，表达出具体使用，引导学生实际运用，同时，感悟良好的沟通是解决问题的基础，当与某项规则持有不同意见时，要仔细寻找规则背后的原因，辩证看待事物

VII. Assignment

Prepare a presentation（80 – 100 words）covering the following questions：

（1）What rules do you have to follow at home?

（2）Do you agree with them? Why or why not?

四、教学评价（Evaluation）

Can-Do Checklist
I can pronounce the words correctly. ☺ ☹ ☹
I can retell the chart fluently. ☺ ☹ ☹
I can describe the distance logically. ☺ ☹ ☹
1 question I still have... _____

点评：

本课结合主题内容，运用家规制定情境设计了整节课的大情境，充分挖掘教材上的图片，无痕导入亲子之间讨论家规话题，让学生在情境中体悟语言、运用语言，让学生形成态度体验，从而帮助他们更好地理解文本、掌握知识内容、发展语言能力。

本节课围绕英语学习活动观三个层次设计活动，从学习理解到应用实践再到迁移创新，层层递进，符合学生认知发展规律，紧扣主题意义探究，凸显建构生成，重视内化与迁移创新。这样设计的活动与主题紧密关联，具有非常强的实践性。

由于听力文本难度偏大，篇幅相对较长，本节课设计时给学生搭建了脚手架，例如表格填充的运用，让学生能够进入情境、自主探究、合作交流，最终顺利完成所有的学习目标，发展学生的自身语言与思维能力，提升学生的英语学科核心素养。

Unit 7 Rules at home 学案

1 – 1b Listen, fill in the blanks and then retell.

Anna is asking her mom _____.

Anna's desires	Her mom's opinion
go to the _____ with John	shouldn't be allowed to _____ not _____ enough worried about her _____

续表

Anna's desires	Her mom's opinion
_____ Gaby get her ears pierced	shouldn't be _____ to get their ears pierced too _____
buy a new _____	shouldn't be allowed to _____ their own clothes

Retell the information in the table in your own words.

Anna is asking her mom _____.

First, _____

2 – 2a, 2b Listen and complete the missing information, and then retell the content.

The speakers are talking about _____

Information about Larry	Kathy's/Molly's Opinions or advice
He is working _____.	shouldn't be allowed to _____ at night
His hair is too _____	_____ his hair
wear an _____.	stop wearing that _____ one
not seem to have many _____.	not work on _____ _____ time with them

Retell the information in the table in your own words.

The speakers are talking about _____.

First, _____

3 – 2c. Match the statements with the reasons.

( ) Sixteen-year-olds should not be allowed to work at night.

( ) Larry shouldn't work every night.

( ) He should cut his hair.

a. It doesn't look clean.

b. Young people need to sleep.

c. He needs time to do home work.

4 – 2d. Make a list of things teenagers should and should not be allowed to do according to your own opinions. Discuss your list with your partner.

Teenagers should be allowed to	Teenagers should not be allowed to
Choose their own clothes	

Imagine you are talking with your parents about rules. Make a conversation to tell each other your opinions and reasons.

Topic：Should teenagers be allowed to _____？

I：Do you think _____？

My mom/dad：_____ because _____

I：I disagree. I think _____ because _____

My mom/dad：_____

...

Homework：

Prepare a presentation （80 – 100 words） covering the following questions：

What rules do you have to follow at home？

Do you agree with them？ Why or why not？

_____

_____

_____

_____

_____

_____

听力文本

Section A 1b

Anna：Mom, can I go to the shopping center with John？ He just got his driver's license.

Mom：No way！ I don't think sixteen-year-olds should be allowed to drive. They aren't serious enough. I'm worried about your safety.

Anna：But Gaby's getting her ears pierced at the shopping center and I want to watch.

Mom：Sixteen-year-olds shouldn't be allowed to get their ears pieced either. They're too young.

Anna：I agree，but it's fun to watch. Can I take the bus then？

Mom：Well，OK.

Anna：Great！I want to buy a new skirt，too.

Mom：What kind of skirt？Maybe I should go with you.

Anna：Aww，Mom. I'm not a child. I think teenagers should be allowed to choose their own clothes.

Mom：Well，I just want to make sure you get something nice.

Section A 2a

Kathy：Hi，Molly. Where's your brother Larry？I thought he was joining us.

Molly：Hi，Kathy. I'm sorry. Larry can't join us after all. He is working late to-night.

Kathy：Oh，Larry's working late again？

Molly：Yeah，he is.

Kathy：I see... I really don't think sixteen-year-olds should be allowed to work at night. Young people need to sleep.

Molly：Oh，I disagree with you. Teenage boys never get tired.

Kathy：Well，maybe. But Larry shouldn't work every night.

Molly：That's true. He needs time to do homework.

Kathy：And you know，Molly... he should really cut his hair.

Molly：Oh，I don't know. Do you think it's too long？

Kathy：Yes，I do. It doesn't look clean. And I think he should stop wearing that silly earring.

Molly：Hmm... I disagree. I kind of like it. It looks cool！

Kathy：You know another thing that worries me？Larry doesn't seem to have many friends.

Molly：Yeah，I know. I think he shouldn't work on weekends.

Kathy：That's right. He needs to spend time with friends.

My Favorite Animal
张家口未来学校　杨芳

教材：人教版《英语》七年级下册

课题：Unit 5 Why do you like pandas？

一、单元分析（Unit Analysis）

1. 单元主题语境（Unit Content）

本单元为人教版英语义务教育教科书《Go For it》七年级下册的第五单元，话题是谈论动物园里的动物，属于人与自然主题语境，与学生的日常生活紧密相关。学生有话可说，学习兴趣浓厚。本单元主要是要教会学生描述各种常见动物以及能表达自己对动物的喜好，读懂关于动物的文章，并能正确使用表示性质和品质的形容词进行口头展示。

2. 单元教学目标（Unit Targets）

（1）习得与动物有关的词语，能够简单表达对动物的喜好。
（2）在语篇中恰当地理解和使用表示性质和品质的形容词进行口头展示。
（3）能根据话题、语境和场合等各种因素，描述自己喜好的动物。

二、教学设计思路（Teaching Design）

1. 语篇分析（Discourse Analysis）

本节课的授课内容为"Why do you like pandas?"。音频主要通过对话形式，归纳总结可以从哪方面描述自己喜欢的动物。Unit 5 Section A 1a – 1c 练习巩固学生已有的有关于动物的词汇，模拟生活情境，引导学生开展初步的对话练习。Unit 5 Section A 2a – 2d 引出描述动物性质和品质的形容词和能力的短语，让学生在真实的日常交际中，学会描述各种常见动物以及能表达自己对动物的喜好。所选内容丰富，难度适中，较为容易激发学生的学习兴趣。

课标内容对标：

课程要素	内容要求
主题语境	人与自我
语篇	日常简短对话
语言知识	1. 根据话题、语境、场合和人际关系等各种因素，选择适当的词语进行比较流利的交流或表达 2. 围绕相关主题，在语境中运用所学语法知识描述人和物，进行简单的交流
语言技能	1. 在听、读、看的过程中有目的地提取、梳理所需信息 2. 以口头形式传递信息，发表观点，表达情感 3. 简单介绍自己喜欢的动物，如外形特征和生活环境等

续表

课程要素	内容要求
文化知识	在交际过程中初步体现交际的集体性和有效性
学习策略	1. 在获得的信息与个人经历之间建立有意义的联系 2. 根据主题表达需要，合理运用语篇知识，有逻辑地组织信息结构 3. 敢于开口，表达中不怕出错

学业质量水平对标：

序号	质量描述
3 – 1	能听懂相关主题的语篇，借助关键词句、图片等复述语篇内容
3 – 9	能根据口头交际的具体情境，初步运用得体的语言形式，表达自己的情感、态度和观点
3 – 10	能选用正确的词语、句式和时态，通过口语或书面语篇描述、介绍人和事物，表达个人看法，话语基本通顺

2. 学情分析（**Analysis on Students**）

本节课授课对象是初一年级学生。学生英语基础薄弱，处于中等偏下水平，词汇量很小，但是该班学生整体外向、开朗、思维活跃，愿意配合老师的教学活动，有用英语进行表达的欲望。在之前的学习中，学生已经积累了相关的词语表达。在本节课中，学生将继续深入学习各种常见动物的相关描述以及能表达自己对动物的喜好，读懂关于动物的文章，并能正确使用表示性质和品质的形容词介绍自己喜欢的动物。

3. 教学设计要点（**Design Essentials**）

（1）教学重难点。

教学重点：能够识别动物和描述动物的特点。

教学难点：能够运用形容词并结合程度副词对动物进行描述。

（2）学习策略。

①在获得的信息与个人的经历之间建立有意义的联系。

②根据表达意图和受众特点，有意识地选择和应用语言，运用内部语言在大脑中重现学习材料或刺激，以便将注意力维持在学习材料上的方法。

③根据主题表达需要，合理运用语篇知识，有逻辑地组织信息结构，将新学材料与头脑中已有知识联系起来从而增加新信息的意义的深层加工策略。

（3）教学策略。

①通过听力活动的设计，关注听力文本的主题、关键信息，以及情感态度。

②设置真实情境，以学生感兴趣的话题开展听说练习，引导学生一步步提炼生词短语，整理，比较，分析，并最终形成自己的观点。

（4）本课时教学目标。

By the end of the class, students will be able to

①recognize the animals from different countries in the world

②describe animals by using description words

③introduce Chinese symbolic animals

三、教学过程（Teaching Procedures）

Ⅰ. Pre-listening

学习活动 Learning activities	设计意图（Purpose）
T plays a guessing game with students.	引入话题，引导学生复习相关词汇

Ⅱ. While-listening and Speaking

学习活动 Learning activities	设计意图（Purpose）
Ss listen for the first time and get the main idea of these three conversations	培养学生获取段落大意的能力
T advises Ss to listen these three conversations for the second time and ask them to fill in the blanks	锻炼学生的听力技巧，培养学生获取信息的能力
Ss need to check it with their partner, and they need to check it in a different way in class	
T leads Ss to use "Why" question to give some reasons about their expressions	
Ss listen to another conversations and ask them to fill in the blanks	
Ss suppose they are Julie or John to introduce their favorite animals	让学生掌握转述的基本技巧，并且注重内容完整性和逻辑性
T asks Ss some questions about their pets in their family	锻炼学生的听力技巧，培养学生获取信息的能力
Ss listen to another conversations and ask them to answer four questions	
Ss check their answers with their partners	

Ⅲ. Post-listening and Speaking

学习活动 Learning activities	设计意图（Purpose）
Ss watch a video about koalas，and know the koalas' information	将所学知识与实践相结合，巩固所学知识
Ss read a short passage about koalas and analyze it	
Ss watch a video about pandas，and know the pandas' information	

Ⅳ. Assignment

（1）Retell that short passage about Koalas.（A 层）

（2）Take a picture with your favorite animals and introduce it.（B 层）

四、教学评价（Evaluation）

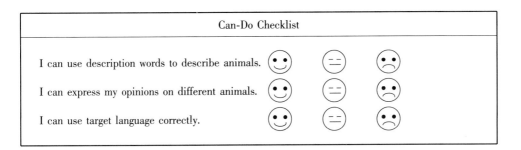

点评：

本节听说素材内容与单元主题融为一体，教师希望学生能够在课堂中体验真实语境下叙述自己喜欢的动物。

1. 特色学习资源分析、技术手段应用说明

本节课使用猜词游戏导入作为学生词汇复习的方法，有具体、情境化的特点，容易调动学生视和说双重感官，有利于课堂学习的推进。

2. 以学生为本，从学生已有认知出发进行授课

从学生已有认知出发，学生在日常生活中积累了许多关于动物的知识点，形成了对动物本身的感性认知，凸显学生主体地位。

My Favorite Animal 学案

Task 1：

1b. Listen and fill in the blanks.

It talks about		
Girl		
Boy		
Girl		

Task 2:

2a. Listen and Write down the animals, description words and the countries they are from.

Name	Animals	Description words	Countries
Julie	1. _____	_____	China
John	2. _____	cute	_____
Julie	3. lions	really _____	_____

Task 3:

2d. Listen and answer the questions

1. What does the girl think of Peter's pet?

_____

2. What does Peter think of his pet?

_____

3. What can Dingding do?

_____

4. Why is the cat called Lazy?

_____

Task 4:

Please introduce your favorite animal to your partner.

<h3 style="text-align:center">听力文本</h3>

Section A, 2a

Julie: Let's see the pandas, John.

John: Why do you like them, Julie?

Julie: Because they're kind of interesting.

John: Where are they from?

Julie：They're from China.

John：Well，I like koalas.

Julie：Why do you like them?

John：Because they're very cute and they are from Australia.

Julie：Well，I don't like lions.

John：Why don't you like them?

Julie：Because they're really scary.

John：Where are they from?

Julie：Most of them are from South Africa.

Section A，2d

Jenny：Your dog is really cute，Peter!

Peter：He's my new pet，Dingding. He's very smart.

Jenny：Really? What can he do?

Peter：He can walk on two legs. He can dance，too.

Jenny：Wow!

Peter：Does your family have a pet?

Jenny：My mom has a big cat，but I don't like her.

Peter：Why don't you like the cat?

Jenny：Well，because she's kind of boring. She sleeps all day，and her name is Lazy.

Peter：Haha，then that's a good name for her!

Section B，1b

Tony：Where do you want to go now?

Mary：Let's see the elephants.

Tony：The elephants? Why do you like elephants?

Mary：Oh，they're interesting. And they're really smart.

Tony：Yes，but they're lazy，too.

Mary：Oh，Tony! So，where do you want to go?

Tony：Let's see the pandas. They're kind of cute.

Mary：Oh，yeah. I love pandas. They're beautiful. But they're also kind of shy. Where are they?

Tony：They're over there，not far from the koalas.

附　录

附录1：英语听说学习基本情况调查问卷

亲爱的同学，下面是一份关于你英语学习，尤其是英语听说学习的调查，调查结果是完全保密的，请你根据自己的实际情况和真实感受填写。每个题目只能选择一个选项，谢谢！

1. 你父母的最高学历是：（　　　）

A. 初中以下　　　　　B. 初中　　　　　　　C. 高中或中专　　　D. 大专

E. 本科及以上

2. 你父母对你现在的英语学习能给予一些知识上的指导：（　　　）

A. 完全同意　　　B. 基本同意　　　　C. 不确定　　　　　D. 不同意

E. 完全不同意

3. 你对自己目前的英语综合水平评价是：（　　　）

A. 优秀　　　　　B. 良好　　　　　　C. 中等　　　　　　D. 较差

E. 非常差

4. 在进行英语学习时，你最大的动力是：（　　　）

A. 老师的要求　　　　　　　　　　B. 获得好成绩

C. 提升英语交际能力　　　　　　　D. 学习的乐趣

5. 在学习英语时，以下最符合你实际情况的是：（　　　）

A. 对于学好英语缺乏信心　　　　　B. 对于学好英语比较缺乏信心

C. 对于学好英语比较有信心　　　　D. 对于学好英语很有信心

6. 目前你在练习英语听说时做以下事情的频率是怎样的？

内容	A. 从不	B. 有时	C. 经常	D. 总是
1）听前根据问题预测所听内容				
2）听中根据关键信息进行简单推断				
3）听后围绕核心内容或观点练习转述				
4）敢于开口，不怕出现错误				
5）修正自己表达不准确的部分				
6）注意到中外交际习俗的文化差异				

1. 开学以来，你的老师在英语教学的过程中做以下事情的频率是怎样的？

内容	A. 从不	B. 有时	C. 经常	D. 总是
1）引导我们建立所学内容与生活的联系				
2）采用除课本以外的音频、视频教学				
3）引导我们了解中西文化异同				
4）引导我们朗读时关注整个句子的含义				
5）让我们模仿听读材料的语音语调				
6）与我们进行互动和交流				
7）给我们留出充分的时间进行思考练习				
8）给我们提供表达或展示的机会				
9）对我的听说能力给予针对性指导				

2. 当你用英语与别人交流时，你最大的障碍是：（　　　）

A. 语音语调差　　　　B. 词汇量少　　　　C. 语法错误多

D. 听不懂对方的意思　　　　　　E. 害怕别人笑话，缺乏自信

F. 其他（请写出来）＿＿＿＿＿＿＿＿＿＿＿＿＿＿＿＿

3. 你每周在课外收听英语音频、观看英语视频的时间大约为：（　　　）

A. 小于 10 分钟　　　　　　　B. 10—30 分钟

C. 30 分钟—1 小时　　　　　　D. 大于 1 小时

附录 2：初一音标练习校本教材

Exercise 1

一、英语音标学习——前元音

/i：/	eat	bee	feel	he	feet	me	pea	sea	heat
/ɪ/	it	big	listen	fit	hill	sit	hit		
/e/	bed	bread	pen	beg	get	wet	tell	bet	lesson
/æ/	match	and	cap	black	bad	cat	hat	bag	catch

二、朗读下面的绕口令

1. A cheap sheep is cheaper than a cheap ship.

一只便宜的绵羊比一艘便宜的船更便宜。

2. Bill was beating a big beast with his big fist, and his big fist was badly bitten by the big beast.

比尔正用他的大拳头打一头大野兽，但他的大拳头被这只大野兽狠狠地咬了一口。

3. Ted sent Fred ten hens yesterday so Fred's fresh bread is ready already.

特德昨天给弗莱德送去了十只母鸡，所以弗莱德的新鲜面包已经准备好了。

4. Whether the weather be fine or whether the weather be not.

Whether the weather be cold or whether the weather be hot.

We'll weather the weather whether we like it or not.

无论晴天或阴天，无论是冷或是暖，不管喜欢与否，我们都要经受风霜雨露。

5. A fat fat cat catches a fat fat rat.

一只大肥猫抓住了一只大肥老鼠。

6. Can you can a can as a canner can can a can?

你能够像罐头工人一样装罐头吗?

Exercise 2

一、英语音标学习——中元音

/ɜ：/	dirty	term	girl	bird	learn	work	firm	nurse
/ə/	famous	panda	above	ago	around			
/ʌ/	duck	but	fun	cup	fund	us	bus	luck

二、朗读下面的绕口令和弱读形式

1. I learn that learned earnest men earn much by learning.

我得知有学问而认真的人靠学问挣很多钱。

2. Sir, your bird stirred the girl's birthday party.

先生，你的鸟儿搅了女孩的生日派对。

3. Elizabeth has eleven elves in her elm tree.

伊丽莎白的榆树上住着十一个小精灵。

4. I can try to do it. 我可以试试。

/aɪ kən traɪ tə duː ət/（元音弱读）

5. Father and son have fun playing in the sun.

爸爸和儿子在太阳下愉快玩耍。

6. Double bubble gum bubbles double.

双重的泡泡糖能吹双重的泡泡。

Exercise 3

一、英语音标学习——后元音

/uː/	food	fool	cool	pool
/ʊ/	foot	cook	good	took	book	should
/ɔː/	horse	born	warm	sort	north	law	ball	talk
/ɒ/	hot	cock	not	block	dog
/ɑː/	harm	farm	car	art	garden	bar	hard	dark	star

二、朗读下面的绕口令

1. He foolishly took the school cooling pool for a swimming pool.

他愚蠢地把学校的冷却池当成了游泳池。

2. A good cook could cook as much cookies as a good cook who could cook cookies.

一个好的厨师能做出和其他好厨师一样多的小甜饼。

3. Paul called from the hall that he couldn't get to the door.

保罗在大厅里喊他够不着门。

4. Tom has got a lot of dots on his pocket, and he will use a pot of hot water to wash off the dots.

汤姆的口袋上有很多斑点印迹，他要用一盆热水把这些斑点印迹洗掉。

5. Can you drive the large car to that far bar?

你能把这辆大车开到那个离得很远的酒吧吗？

Exercise 4

一、英语音标学习——双元音

/eɪ/	date	bay	gate	fate	hate	late	lake	tale	face
	wait	bake

/aɪ/ high	sky	fight	my	light	like pie	rice
/aʊ/ house	now	sound	cloud	out	town	
/ɔɪ/ boy	soil	noise	oil	toy		
/əʊ/ boat	coat	low	coke	know	rope	hole
/ɪə/ beer	dear	ear	fear	here	near	
/eə/ air	bear	dare	hare	there	chair	
/ʊə/ sure	tour					

二、朗读下面的绕口令和谚语

1. Haste makes waste. 欲速则不达。

2. I like to ride my light white bike. 我喜欢骑我白色轻便的自行车。

3. The mouse and the cow sounded a rousing song. 老鼠和奶牛发出的声音像一首欢快的歌曲。

4. That noisy boy has a voice that's most annoying. 那个吵闹的男孩的声音真是让人讨厌。

5. He rowed the boat over the ocean and wrote home hoping for a loan.

他划船穿过大海并且写信回家希望能得到借款。

6. Next year the bear will bear a dear baby in the rear.

明年熊将在后方生下一头可爱的小崽。

7. I met a fairly unfair affair upstairs. 我在楼上遇到一件颇不公平的事。

8. I assure the jury that a sure insurance is ensured.

我向陪审团保证一笔有把握的保险已被担保。

Exercise 5

一、英语音标学习——辅音 1

/p/ pea	peach	peak	pie	pig	speak		
/b/ bee	back	beach	bad	bill	book	big	bye
/t/ bet	boat	fate	tip	tent	to	tea	
/d/ bed	dad	deer	dig	window	do	duck	need
/k/ cow	back	kill	come	cap	kick	kite	card
/g/ bag	gap	gum	girl	big	glass		

二、朗读下面的绕口令

1. A pleasant peasant keeps a pleasant pheasant and both the peasant and the pheasant are having a pleasant time together.

一位和气的农民养了一只伶俐的野鸡，而且这位和气的农民和这只伶俐的野鸡在一起度过了一段很美好的时光。

2. A big black bug bit a big black bear, made the big black bear bleed blood. 大黑虫咬大黑熊，使得大黑熊流血了！

3. A tidy tiger tied a tie tighter to tidy her tiny tail. 一只老虎将领带系紧，清洁它的尾巴。

4. The man beyond the bond is fond of the second wonderful diamond.

那位不受约束的人喜欢第二颗奇异的钻石。

5. A bloke's back bike brake block broke. 一个家伙的脚踏车后制动器坏了。

6. The eagle is eager to anger the tiger in danger. 那只老鹰渴望激怒处在危险中的老虎。

Exercise 6

一、英语音标学习——辅音 2

/tʃ/	chain	catch	cheap	check	chair	watch	
/dʒ/	jeep	gym	joke	Jane	orange		
/f/	fail	fat	fall	phone	leaf	fine	life
/v/	leave	very	violin	vote	vase	live	
/θ/	bath	faith	both	mouth	teeth	thank	birthday
/ð/	breathe	clothes	they	that			

二、朗读下面的绕口令

1. The teacher changed the question in the challenge. The challengers changed the answers for the question.

老师在挑战中改变了问题，挑战者改变了这个问题的答案。

2. How much dew would a dewdrop drop if a dewdrop could drop dew?

如果一颗露珠会掉下露水，那么一颗露珠会掉下多少露水呢？

3. Fifty-five firefighters fried fifty-five French fries.

五十五名消防人员炸出五十五根薯条。

4. The beloved novelist put her lovely gloves above the stove.

受人爱戴的小说家把她美丽的手套放在火炉上方。

5. I thought a thought. But the thought I thought wasn't the thought I thought I thought.

我思考一个问题。可是，我所思考的问题并不是我认为自己正在思考的问题。

6. Their other older brothers wear leather. That makes their mother bothered.

他们的其他哥哥穿皮革，这使他们的母亲烦恼。

Exercise 7

一、英语音标学习——辅音 3

/s/ice	face	sake	same	price	sea	sing	race
/z/eyes	knees	prize	raise	zoo			
/ʃ/shake	shame	she	wash	rush	machine	shell	
/ʒ/garage	pleasure	usual					
/h/hair	harm	high	hate	hat	high		

二、朗读下面的绕口令

1. She sells seashells by the sea shore. The shells she sells are surely seashells. So if she sells shells on the seashore, I'm sure she sells seashore shells.

她在海岸卖贝壳，她卖的贝壳是真正的贝壳。因此，若她在海岸上卖贝壳，我肯定她卖的是海岸贝壳。

2. The crazy jazzman gazed at the blaze on the razor with amazement.

疯狂的爵士音乐演奏者惊愕地盯着剃刀上的光辉。

3. "Shall we show you the shop for shoes and shirts?" Shirley said to Shelley.

"我带你去看卖鞋子和衬衣的商店好吗，"雪莉对谢利说。

4. George placed his broken television in the garage. In his garage there have been three broken televisions.

乔治把他坏了的电视放到了车库，在他的车库里已经有三台坏电视了。

5. A hard-hearted hunter hunted a hard-hunted hare.

一位硬心肠的猎人猎杀了一只难以猎杀的野兔。

Exercise 8

一、英语音标学习——辅音 4

/m/come	game	gum	some				
/n/ run	thin	son	gun	nine	nice	night	
/ŋ/ king	sing	song	English	thing			
/l/ lead	late	life	play	light	lie	fly	tall	ball
/r/ free	race	red	rest	pray	rain	rate	

二、朗读下面的绕口令和谚语

1. The manly Roman woman manager by the banner had man's manner.

军旗旁那位有男子气概的罗马女经理具有男子风度。

2. If you notice this notice, you will notice that this notice is not worth noticing.

若你看到这张告示，你会发现这张告示是不值得留意的。

3. The spring brings many charming things.

春天带来了很多迷人的东西。

4. He who laughs last laughs best.

谁能笑到最后就是真正的赢家。

5. A little pill may well cure a great ill.

一粒小药丸可能治愈大疾病。

6. Roger threw round rocks on our red roof. The round rocks rolled from the roof onto the red floor.

罗杰在我们红屋顶上扔石头。圆石从屋顶滚到红地板上。

Exercise 9

一、英语音标学习——辅音 5

/ts/	goats	gates		
/dz/	beds	birds		
/tr/	street	tree	try	treat
/dr/	dress	driver	dry	drink
/w/	white	why	where	wheat
/j/	year	you	yes	young yet

二、朗读下面的绕口令

1. The cats and rats sitting in the room，all they do is sits and shifts，all they do is sits and shifts.

猫和老鼠坐在客厅里，它们所做的就只是坐着、动着、坐着、动着。

2. Afterwards, I went towards the yards and looked upwards, downwards, inwards, outwards, forwards and backwards.

后来我走向院子，向上下内外前后看了看。

3. Never trouble about trouble until trouble troubles you!

不要自找麻烦！

4. The driver was drunk and drove the doctor's car directly into the river.

这个司机喝醉了，他把医生的车开进了河里。

5. While we were walking, we were watching window washers wash Washington's windows with warm washing water.

当我们走路时，我们看着清洁窗户的人用温水清洗华盛顿的窗户。

6. The yellow bird has yelled for many years in the yard of Yale.

那只黄色的鸟儿在耶鲁大学的校园里歌唱好多年了。

附：48 个英语音标表（DJ 音标 IPA88 新版）

元音	单元音	前元音	[i ː]	[ɪ]	[e]	[æ]	
		中元音	[ʌ]	[ɜ ː]	[ə]	
		后元音	[u ː]	[ʊ]	[ɔ ː]	[ɒ]	[ɑ ː]
	双元音	开合双元音	[eɪ]	[aɪ]	[ɔɪ]	[əʊ]	[aʊ]
		集中双元音	[ɪə]	[eə]	[ʊə]	
辅音	爆破音	清辅音	[p]	[t]	[k]	
		浊辅音	[b]	[d]	[g]	
	摩擦音	清辅音	[f]	[s]	[ʃ]	[θ]	[h]
		浊辅音	[v]	[z]	[ʒ]	[ð]	
	破擦音	清辅音	[tʃ]	[tr]	[ts]	
		浊辅音	[dʒ]	[dr]	[dz]	
	鼻音	（浊辅音）	[m]	[n]	[ŋ]	
	舌则音	（浊辅音）	[l]	[r]	
	半元音	（浊辅音）	[w]	[j]	

参考文献

［1］ 鲍勤．支架式教学模式对英语写作教学的启示［J］．云南电大学报，2007
（1）：53–55．

［2］ 陈烨君．模拟联合国活动培养英语学科核心素养［J］．中小学班主任，2019
（8）：30–33．

［3］ 程晓堂．基于主题意义探究的英语教学理念与实践［J］．中小学外语教学
（中学篇），2018，41（10）：1–7．

［4］ 崔允漷．追问"学生学会了什么"——兼论三维目标［J］．教育研究，
2013，34（7）：98–104．

［5］ 董晓燕．教育生态学视角下的高中英语课堂生态研究［D］．山西师范大
学，2015．

［6］ 范文芳，庞建荣．英语听说教学论［M］．南宁：广西教育出版社．2018．

［7］ 高航．从构式语法视角看语块在二语习得中的作用［J］．解放军外国语学院
学报，2017，40（2）：86–94．

［8］ 何锋，章玉芳．夯实语音基础 优化初中英语听说教学——从江苏省中考听
力口语考试反馈说起［J］．中小学外语教学（中学篇），2012，35（12）：
42–46．

［9］ 黄远振．论多元智能理论与英语教学的整合［J］．课程．教材．教法，2003
（11）：39–42．DOI：10.19877/j．cnki．kcjcjf．2003.11.010．

［10］ 黄正翠，彭德河．基于主题意义探究的高中英语听力教学设计改进［J］．
中小学外语教学（中学篇），2019，42（6）：8–12．

［11］ 蒋京丽．以评促教促学，落实英语教、学、评一体化的五点实施建议［J］．
英语学习，2021（9）：4–9．

［12］．九年义务教育全日制初级中学语文教学大纲（试用修订版）——中华人民

共和国教育部制订［J］. 语文知识, 2000（7）: 68 – 73.

［13］李赟. 语言输入理论与英语教学［J］. 教育教学论坛, 2011（6）: 83 + 75.

［14］李炯英. 从建构主义理论谈二语习得中的语言输入［J］. 中国外语, 2005（3）: 38 – 40.

［15］李顺英. 大学英语课堂生态环境的现状、问题与对策研究［J］. 西南交通大学学报（社会科学版）, 2007（6）: 16 – 20 + 113.

［16］林崇德. 中国学生发展核心素养: 深入回答"立什么德、树什么人"［J］. 人民教育, 2016（19）: 14 – 16.

［17］刘东楼, 周海平. 沉默期理论及其对外语教学的启示［J］. 外语学刊, 2013（3）: 114 – 118. DOI: 10.16263/j. cnki. 23 – 1071/h. 2013. 03. 026.

［18］吕国征. 发展学生高阶思维能力的阅读教学策略研究［J］. 中小学外语教学（中学篇）, 2020, 43（9）: 39 – 44.

［19］孟碧君. 基于主题意义探究的初中英语听说教学实践［J］. 中小学外语教学（中学篇）, 2022, 45（4）: 13 – 18.

［20］钱乃荣. 论语言的多样性和"规范化"［J］. 语言教学与研究, 2005（2）: 1 – 13.

［21］钱萌. 支架理论在《牛津高中英语》Project 教学中的运用［J］. 中小学外语教学（中学篇）, 2016, 39（12）: 44 – 48.

［22］田延明, 王淑杰. 心理认知理论与外语教学研究［M］. 北京: 清华大学出版社, 2010.

［23］仝亚军. "经典英文演讲欣赏"校本课程的行动研究［J］. 基础外语教育, 2015, 17（6）: 47 – 54.

［24］王栋, 盛佳飞. 英语课堂教学中教师纠错反馈的策略及其运用［J］. 中小学外语教学（中学篇）, 2021, 44（7）: 24 – 27.

［25］王蔷. 促进英语教学方式转变的三个关键词: "情境""问题"与"活动"［J］. 基础教育课程, 2016（5）: 45 – 50.

［26］王蔷. 全面和准确把握英语课程内容是落实课程目标的前提［J］. 英语学习, 2022（4）: 18 – 33.

［27］王蔷, 钱小芳, 桂洲, 张力青. 以戏剧教学促进小学生英语学科能力的发展——北京市芳草地国际学校英语戏剧课探索［J］. 课程. 教材. 教法, 2016, 36（2）: 93 – 99. DOI: 10.19877/j. cnki. kcjcjf. 2016. 02. 014.

［28］王毅敏. 从建构主义学习理论看英语情境教学［J］. 外语教学, 2003（2）: 85 – 87. DOI: 10.16362/j. cnki. cn61 – 1023/h. 2003. 02. 023.

［29］么海燕. 基于建构主义的思维导图在高中英语写作教学中的应用［J］. 中

国教育学刊，2019（S2）：78 – 79 + 84.

［30］叶蜚声，徐通锵. 语言学纲要［M］. 北京：北京大学出版社，2010：22.

［31］尹青梅. "支架" 理论在 CAI 英语写作教学中的应用［J］. 外语电化教学，2007（1）：28 – 31.

［32］张国荣. "支架" 理论在英语写作教学中的应用［J］. 外语与外语教学，2004（9）：37 – 39.

［33］张献臣. 人教版初中英语教材中示范对话的功能与教学［J］. 中小学外语教学（中学篇），2014，37（11）：18 – 22.

［34］中华人民共和国教育部. 义务教育英语课程标准（2022 年版）［M］. 北京：北京师范大学出版社，2022.

［35］周培蓓. LIFEBOAT 评价策略在小学英语课前演讲中的运用［J］. 中小学英语教学与研究，2021（10）：6 – 9.

［36］BROWN H D. Teaching by principles：an interactive approach to language pedagogy［M］. 北京：外语教学与研究出版社，2001：256 – 257.

［37］Donate R. Collective Scaffolding in Second Language Learning［A］. In Vygotsky Approach to Second Language Research［C］. Ed. Lantolf J. et al. New York：Adlex Publisher，1994.

［38］Gardner，H. Multiple Intelligences：The Theory in Practice［M］. New York：Basic Books，1983.

［39］Krashen，Stephen D. Language Acquisition and Language Education：Extensions and Applications［M］. London：Prentice Hall International，1989.

［40］Morley，J. Academic listening comprehension instruction：Models，principles，and practice. In D. Mendelsonand，& J. Rubin（Eds）. A guide for the teaching of second language listening［M］. San Diego：Dominie Press，1995.

［41］Murcia. Tracing the history：Listening and language learning. In M. Celce，& Murcia（Eds）. Teaching elt. ccsenet. org English Language Teaching Vol. 10，No. 6；2017 27 English as a Second or Foreign Language.（p. 70）. US：Thomson Learning Press，2001.

［42］Vygotsky，L. Mind in Society：The Development of Higher Psychological Processes［M］. Cambridge：Harvard University Press，1978.

［43］Wilkins，D. A. Linguistics in language Teaching［M］. London：Edward Arnold Ltd. 1978.